AS I PLEASE

AS I PLEASE

by

Jimmy Reid

MAINSTREAM
PUBLISHING·EDINBURGH

First published in 1984 by
MAINSTREAM PUBLISHING
7 Albany Street
Edinburgh

ISBN 0 906391 58 X

Typeset by Hewer Text Composition Services, Edinburgh
Printed and bound by Clark Constable (1982) Ltd., Edinburgh

Contents

CONTENTS

Introduction

TEMPTATION abounds. It's everywhere and takes many forms. Anything meticulous and well ordered screams out for an upset. In a highly serious atmosphere an innocuous, tentatively humorous remark can set off waves of hysterical laughter that smacks of reprisal. Idolatry invites iconoclasm and there's nothing like purity for stimulating the impure.

Like most I'm a sucker for temptation. It's kinda irresistible and no more so than when you're given a chance to do some retrospective correction. You can get hooked on hindsight. When people are asked—"Given your life to live over again, would you change anything?" and reply, "No. I'd do the same again."—I think, Ah, there goes an arrogant, insufferable, smug son-of-a-bitch or a liar.

In this collection of articles, I had to resist the great temptation to do a re-write, here and there, in the light of subsequent experience. Alas! "The moving finger writes and having writ, moves on, nor all thy piety, nor wit shall lure it back to cancel half a line nor all thy tears wash out one word of it", and all that jazz decrees that I shouldn't try even a wee re-write. Also there is always the danger that someone might have to hand the original article and shout, "Cheat". Now cheating is bad. It's a darn sight worse when you're found out. Cheating if it has to be done must be seen not to be done. So making a virtue out of fear, not to say necessity, this book represents my views and is a cross-section of my writings over the past six years, unexpurgated and warts an' all.

A few I acknowledge to be wrong which seems an insufficient reason for exclusion. Most I will stick by.

This should not be seen as indicating certitude. Marx was right when he asserted that the only thing that's constant is change. It's amazing how many Marxists believe this applies to everything except their own minds. Doubt, I'm convinced, is a supreme intellectual quality and the right to doubt a fundamentally essential freedom.

To question prevailing orthodoxies, to probe your own conclusions, are a form of preventative medicine and help preserve public and personal mental health. Those whose minds are closed to the possibility of being wrong are mentally if not clinically dead. Zombies trying to suffocate living ideas with the dead hand of dogma. Some even pine for that absolute certitude which renders redundant any need to think for themselves. They yearn for a penitentiary of the mind that will cocoon their thoughts from the challenges of life. The real problem is how to constantly doubt without being permanently indecisive. The trick, I think, is to settle for an approximation to the truth as the only possible guide to action and to see this as the best to which we can aspire. Indeed it's the most. So remember, when reading these pages that even at my most emphatic I'm seared with doubt and proud of it. In today's world, this is the only credible attitude for a democratic socialist. He must doubt, be a dissident and yet, at the same time be a realist. Society isn't changed by conformists or ditherers.

It's a false choice to pose absolute certainty against total uncertainty. This would mean that only fanatics could be men of action and the rest condemned to inaction, as we watch the zealots fight each other. If we waited until we were certain about everything, we would never do anything. Rational doubt and reasonable decisiveness go hand in hand. A combination which triggers off the mechanism of progressive social change.

In the twentieth century, at least in the developed countries, we also need a commitment to democracy. Maybe this is necessary in underdeveloped countries as well. There is, however, at the back of my mind the nagging thought that democracy might only be possible in the modern world at a certain level of economic and social development such as reached in Western Europe, North America and a few countries elsewhere.

This is not to imply that democracy automatically flows from such circumstances. We've already seen this century democracy extinguished in Nazi Germany and under serious threat in America during the height of the Cold War. Yet when you look at the map of the world, you can't help notice an apparent relationship between advanced economies and modern democracy. If you are starving, as millions are in the Third World, your priorities might understandably lie elsewhere.

To a European socialist, the principles and spirit of democracy are integral to his whole philosophy. My perception of the progression to socialism in Britain is of a process towards a fuller democracy where government of the people, by the people, for the people applies in the economic as in the political sphere. It's ridiculous when economic decisions affecting entire communities, or the nation, can be taken in a democracy and not be subject to any form of democratic control or accountability. Yet it happens.

The argument for Socialism in Britain is essentially democratic and implicitly recognises that social change in this country can only be validated by the democratically expressed assent of the people. Only the nut-case-left challenge this premise with their fanciful notion that people who will not vote for socialism at the polls will still be prepared to die for it on the barricades. This doesn't merit serious attention.

Modern communism, which in reality is Leninism, a theory of revolution based exclusively on experiences in Tsarist Russia, is also incompatible with democratic socialism. This theory is concerned with seizing rather than winning power. The ideas are elitist. A self-appointed vanguard (i.e. the Communist Party) will lead the masses to socialism. The right to do so is claimed through a form of mysticism dressed up as materialism. It goes something like this. . . .

12

Marxism has the answer to all the problems of humanity (a claim which incidentally Marx would have repudiated). The Leninist Parties are the custodians of this philosophy. This enables them to understand the laws and secrets of historical change and this in turn qualifies them and them alone for leadership. All others, whether they like it or not, whether they know it or not, are destined to be led and shepherded into the future by the chosen few, chosen that is by themselves. Such arrogant elitism is presented in the rhetoric of collectivism.

Actually it's the product, not of a Labour Movement as we know it, but of a tradition sustained over the years by Russian intellectuals ranging from Tolstoy to Solzhenitsyn with their pronounced messianic tendencies. Lenin, and for that matter, Trotsky, were in that tradition. As I argue in an article on the ultra left their experiences were exclusively those of the radical intelligentsia in an autocratic society, with a backward working class and an even more backward peasantry. Infertile soil for the seeds of democratic ideals. Hardly surprising if they saw as the only way for Russia, a revolutionary coup in which an enlightened few would seize power and exercise this on behalf of the downtrodden un-enlightened masses. This whole concept relegates the role of the people to that of spectators whose liberation is secured for them by others. Such outrageous paternalism inevitably bred the all powerful Father figure which is the very essence of Stalinism. The theory, the strategy and tactics this spawns has no relevance to the life and struggles of people in Britain or any other country where democratic norms have been established.

Integral to a democratic outlook is tolerance. To tolerate only those opinions with which one agrees puts you in the same category as Attila the Hun, Hitler and Stalin. It also pre-supposes that you have nothing to learn from those who hold views contrary to yours—and that can be a dangerous folly. I've learned to differentiate between the person and his or her politics. Sometimes where the politics and the person are so indistinguishable, as in the case of Mrs Thatcher, then this is difficult and maybe impossible. This, however, is the exception.

Let me put it this way. There are some socialists whose whole outlook and demeanour appears to be based on bile. To spend a social evening with them is an experience to be enjoyed only by those with masochistic tendencies. On the other hand, there are a few Tories I know who are delightful company. I think their political views are wrong. To be wrong isn't necessarily to be evil. Anyway, let he who is without wrong cast the first stone. There must be about twelve million people in this country who are members, supporters or voters for the Conservative Party. To consider them personally and collectively as the enemy, a homogenous reactionary force, is intolerant and self-defeating. I had never personally met a Tory until going to London for a meeting in my teens. They weren't exactly ten-a-penny in my Glasgow. I've studied them ever since. They are human. Well, "Wets" are. If there is to be an irreversible shift towards the left in British politics, millions of Tories have to be persuaded that socialist policies are good for this country. You can't persuade people if you won't talk to them.

You see, tolerance isn't a liberal luxury, but the very heartbeat of democracy. Doubt and tolerance are lovely bed fellows. They produce good offspring, particularly humour. The brethren of the closed mind are invariably without humour. Hitler was hardly Mr Laugh-a-minute, nor was Stalin. When tyrants tell you, "I'll slay you with this one", it's more likely to be a gun than a joke.

Apart from anything else, often the most effective way of illustrating a point, is by humour. To laugh at life's absurdities and follies, including your own, is good for you, and helps to preserve sanity in a mad world. I want to help change that world for the better. Now nowhere is it specified that only those who are grimly serious, qualify for such a task. In fact, we are more effective than zealots at influencing people who understandably distrust their joylessness. In my experience, politicians who read nothing except political text books and articles are a dead loss. It is those with a broadly based culture who are most effective. The Bevans, Churchills and Lloyd Georges. One brilliantly perceptive creative writer can teach us more about life, society and ourselves, than all the political pundits put together.

Life is beautiful and such a conviction fuels a desire to make it more so. No experience is really wasted providing you retain a curiosity, a wonder about the world. Music, sport, the company of friends, discussions, arguments, to eat and drink with your pals, to joke and have a good laugh, to marvel at nature and the universe, to love and be loved, that's what it's all about.

Yet, sadness can never be far away. Sadness at the cruelties endured by so many fellow human beings. Sadness at the plight of millions starving in Africa, Asia and Latin America, while obesity becomes a serious medical problem in the affluent West. Sadness, that the nuclear arms race endangers life on this beautiful planet. Sadness can, however, be self indulgent, unless it becomes an anger that resolves to end these obscenities.

So, in this book, you will find me meandering up many alleyways of life and a few cul-de-sacs. The latter like everything else, can be useful. When you've been up some dead ends, you appreciate more the highways of discovery which lead to new ideas.

A great sense of comfort to me in the past decade has been the writings of George Orwell. His essays, overshadowed by *Animal Farm* and *1984*, have been an inspiration. I admire his objectivity, the highest form of honesty, and his courage. When the history of this century is written, his place will be secure. He has helped me and countless others rationalise developing attitudes, wrung, often laboriously, from life and study. His socialism embraced the liberal values which have evolved as a civilising influence over the centuries as it reached out to engage the challenges and the problems of social change in the second half of the twentieth century. Some of Orwell's best essays and articles were in a series called *As I Please*. I've borrowed the title for this collection of articles as a token of respect.

As I please, so I'm pleased. But if my views don't please, then it's too bad. I can't change them to please, I can only hope that they will.

Jimmy Reid
January, 1984

14

On Politics and Pundits

WHY EXPERTS ALWAYS GET IT WRONG

A FEW months ago in the early days of speculation about the Hillhead by-election I got involved with some colleagues in a discussion as to the likely outcome.

The consensus was categorical. In fact the consensus was unanimous except for me if you see what I mean. It was a certainty for Roy Jenkins: in fact, it was all over bar the shouting.

It was a waste of time and money even to have an election. Roy should just have been installed.

This was understandable. In the immediate aftermath of Crosby, where Shirley Williams had toppled what had hitherto looked an unassailable Tory stronghold, the SDP bandwagon was viewed as being virtually unstoppable.

However, your intrepid columnist, in a minority of one, ventured to express some serious doubts about this prognostication. The hoots of derision when I suggested that Labour or Conservative might win are easily and immediately recallable. The opinion polls show that such an outlandish prospect is now possible or indeed probable.

However this is not an "I told you so" piece, which invariably sounds churlish even when it's me that's doing the telling you so. This is something else. It's an attempt to find an explanation as to why and how political commentators are always wrong, and have an unerring talent for error surpassed only by economists. Their consistency in arriving at the wrong conclusions or in developing an irrelevant hypothesis is positively breathtaking.

When, for example, Jim Sillars launched the Scottish Labour Party, it was doomed, right from the start. Political media pundits flocked to join and thus sealed its fate. No political party can withstand the devastating consequences of their unbridled approval. Their actual membership in any new party is virtually the kiss of death.

That is why I knew for certain that the SDP were slithering towards the slippery slope. It was inevitable when the media pundits started to enlist. Roy Jenkins, if he has any sense, will expel them all pronto. Bill Rodgers would be easily persuaded to transfer the lot to the Liberals.

15

What really intrigues me is from where or what do they derive this almost mystical sixth sense. This infallible technique which enables them albeit non-consciously to detect and embrace decline and political disintegration long before it becomes discernible to ordinary mortals. Their benediction of any political cause is usually the prelude to the funeral march.

Maybe the gipsies of Transylvania, experts on werewolves and how a full moon could stimulate hair growth, might understand, for who knows what we are dealing with here. It could be sinister black forces from the nether regions of the mind or Hell or even that well-known Fleet Street hostelry, El Vino's.

As you can see, this whole area of speculation tends to impinge on the metaphysical and as there weren't many practising metaphysicians in Govan, I am not too familiar or even happy in this particular terrain. So let me advance a theory steeped in what used to be called Wilsonian pragmatism. Wilsonian as in Harold and not the geriatric athlete of the *Wizard*, the well-known comic book for boys.

The political pundits generally incline towards the personalisation of politics. After all, this makes better copy. They might for all we know even start to believe that politicians actually shape the destiny of nations. A patently absurd and laughable proposition. We even read and hear from them of the plots and the counterplots at the Palace of Westminster as if they really mattered. As everyone knows Sir Arnold Weinstock of GEC and Arthur Scargill of the NUM have more real power than all the backbenchers in Westminster put together. It's all a delusion or even an illusion of power. Just like Biggles flying over the cuckoo's nest. And sometimes the commentators get sucked into the vortex of this madness.

It's a kind of incipient megalomania. A virus probably picked up in the corridors of powerlessness adjacent to the bars at Westminster.

This is rather a shame for I happen to be one of those for whom the Parliamentary system is important. It has, however, to be acknowledged that in Britain its powers have been eroded over the years so that today the House of Commons has probably less control over the executive arm of government than any other legislative assembly in the democratic world.

MPs who adopt pompous airs, create the impression of having to discharge momentous duties and responsibly exercise non-existent power, are not only fools but dangerous fools who conceal the loss of real authority by the democratically elected Parliament of the country.

Far better if they openly acknowledged their lack of real authority and enlisted the support of constituents in demanding that power be once again restored to the floor of the House of Commons and thus, through the democratic process, to the people.

Apart from anything else this might help those media men who actually mistake their empty pomposity as the stamp of real authority and therefore tend to conceive of politics in terms reminiscent of Walter Mitty. From such an absurd standpoint they sometimes ride forth directly into politics with disastrous results for all concerned and bringing no credit to the media.

Some time ago I let you into the secret special Reid method of research into the ramifications of by-elections and the fluctuations, if any, in the fortunes of the various candidates. It's dead simple. You simply eavesdrop on pub conversations.

This method, I contend, is more scientifically sound and more accurate than the technique of those ultra expensive organisations who conduct these sample polls. For example, the Systems Three people at present working on behalf of the *Glasgow Herald* will be relieved to know that my findings in no serious way invalidate their most recent report.

Succinctly put, my research reveals the following: if Mr Jenkins doesn't win then the victor will most likely be Mr Malone, the Conservative, or Mr Wiseman, the Labour candidate. Failing this then Mr Leslie of the SNP will, I can reliably indicate, almost certainly have pulled off a surprise victory.

I am further prepared to put my method and its hard-earned reputation right on the line and predict that the other candidates, including Pastor Jack Glass, he of the Anti-Pope Crusade, are almost certain to be defeated.

The Primate of Rome will no doubt be relieved to hear this from such a reliable and scientifically-tested method of research. Mind you, the Conservationist, not to be confused with the Conservative, must be making some impact. I swear to have heard a drunk in Partick singing "I think that I shall never see a Pontiff lovelier than a tree".

Glasgow Herald 15 March 1982

DESTINY AND A TOUCH OF THE EXTRAPOLATIONS

THE best comedy show in town last week was the response of the media men to the reaction of the politicians to the result of the Hillhead by-election. After the polls closed I eagerly waited to see on the telly the opening shots in what is sure to be a long saga lasting at least till the General Election. We were not to be disappointed.

To start with the pundits had a minor disagreement. Was Hillhead the most important by-election in the last 50 years or in the past century? The arguments flowed and surged amid the canapes in the late-night sessions in the hotels within the constituency that enjoyed a boom reminiscent of the watering places in Chicago during the roaring 'twenties. The footsoldiers of punditry grew more confidently profound with each gin and tonic. Faces that launched a thousand by-elections dropped cliches in world-weary voices and peered bibulously across the crowded gloom. It was just a pity that it couldn't be in a more convenient place like Hampstead or even Hemel Hempstead.

But never mind the inconvenience, or the mad illusions of the local yokels who actually thought they were sophisticated because they lived in some hole called Kelvinside; Hillhead was, after all, a rendezvous with destiny. Mould shattering experiences, it should be noted, are not exactly ten a penny.

And wasn't it fortunate that the honour had fallen to a place bursting at the seams with "A" levels and university graduates? It could just as easily have been somewhere like Blanefield, full of money and dunces. To those of you who claim to know too many bampots with academic qualifications ever to be fooled by the proposition that education and intelligence are synonymous then all we can say is—sour grapes. Anyway, you probably failed your qually.

The trouble really started just after 11 p.m. when the engagingly frank young Conservative candidate conceded victory almost before the count had started. This enraged Sir Robin Day, whose task of maintaining tension for the next two hours had just been rendered impossible. That was out of order.

The law should be amended to ensure that the democratic process is never allowed to interfere with Sir Robin's programmes. I mean people should get their priorities right.

Then the analysis started. Question: when is a victor not a victor? Answer: when he has just won a by-election. The television geezers were adamant that every one and every party had been clobbered. The politicians after an exhaustive examination of the figures that must have lasted for all of two minutes were quite categorical and equally insistent that each of their parties had won.

For the SDP the result was the bees knees. Their spokesperson, who shall remain anonymous, was so overcome that she threw away her crutches. For instant remedial therapy Lourdes has now a rival in Roy Jenkins. For an encore he should turn water into claret. It would save him a few bob. I must however warn him that any laying on of hands in Byres Road is likely to be misunderstood.

The Tories had just lost a seat held by them for donkeys years, if they will forgive the term. Any fewer votes and you get the feeling they would have claimed victory.

Labour's vote fell and was greeted as the best thing since sliced bread. At one time a lap of honour by the Labour candidate and his seconds seemed a possibility.

The Nationalists who lost their deposit reckoned the result could well be the rebirth of the SNP as an electoral force.

Anyway our media men, who know a lot about politicians, and little about politics, are now experts on psephological extrapolation. Now I know it's a mouthful but you will have to get used to it. Our pundits will never look a gift gadget in the mouth.

In the months ahead they will be extrapolating all over the place. On Thursday night and Friday morning they were doing it all over my living room. It can get kind of messy though nothing that a good opinion poll will not clear.

According to the dictionary, extrapolation means to compile against the future, probable vital statistics based on a known series of numbers relating to past years. Fiddlesticks. In the hands of Sir Robin and his cohorts it becomes pure magic. Peter Snow has nabbed the gadgets and nobody else gets playing with them. He presses buttons and on the screen are projected piles of what look like 50 pence pieces. The size of the piles and how they behave means something to Peter like a gypsy reading the tea leaves in the bottom of a cup. It's better than space invaders.

With this paraphernalia and a touch of the extrapolations, Peter can prove anything. He simply needs a percentage, any percentage, and he could show for example that Mick Jagger's uncle was a hippo or for that matter the King of Siam.

The politicians are getting in on the game and beginning to extrapolate like mad. With precisely the same figures they could show that every party was simultaneously on the crest of a wave that would sweep them to power at the next General Election. I reckon that with a good extrapolator Pastor Jack Glass could prove that he was the real winner.

His vote of 388 was more than a 100% up on his previous vote. Projected into the year 2004 this trend could mean a vote of 10 billion and in time he could become the sole and sovereign ruler of the world. Celtic would be bang in trouble.

There were other intriguing aspects of this election. What did "P" stand for in P? Gerald Malone? It's like talking of E. George Robinson instead of Edward G. Or say F. Delano Roosevelt. And the same to you with knobs on, would have been the likely reply of Franklin. We could even have P. Jack Glass. I couldn't stand it any longer and nobbled a Tory friend and put it to him straight. "What did the 'P' stand for?" He looked over his shoulders to the left and then the right and whispered from behind his hands: "Peter". So there you are, the secret is out.

Maybe Pete Malone was considered too downmarket for a Scion of the Glasgow Bar and a rising young star of Glasgow Conservatism. That would be a piece of nonsense. A guy called Willie Whitelaw happens to be the Tory Home Secretary and that sounds like the name of a small-time steeplechase trainer from Penrith.

David Wiseman, the Labour candidate, like many big people is a genial and gentle man. The media wanted to harpoon him with an earring that once he wore but had now rather unsportingly abandoned. "Where's your earring?" he was asked in the tones of grave displeasure. He also wouldn't admit to being a Bennite which further enraged some people.

Well it's understandable. People in by-elections should conform to the stereotype predetermined for them by the media. It makes it easier all round.

George Leslie, for my money the best candidate available in the SNP, also didn't play the game. Where was the kilt and the haggis and the rolling rrrrs, to match Roy's wobbling wwwwwws?

If there wasn't the kilt of the personality there was certainly the cult of the individual. Right from the outset Mr Jenkins was cast as the star and from last Thursday night the fat cats of London have welcomed him back to the fold. *The Times* in an editorial last Saturday commented: "So Roy Jenkins is back where he belongs." It's the new divine right of ROYalty.

They should make him a life member of the finest club in the world, and exclude him from the tiresome process of elections. The "great" man himself told the world: "There were times during the campaign when I admired my own courage." He is also acquiring a residence in the constituency. The least the District Council can do is to provide a flagpole on which he could fly his standard to let us know he is in residence.

Some cold winter's night when Roy retires to the box-bed in the room and kitchen up a wally close Jennifer, already esconced there, might well exclaim: "My God, your feet are cold" to which he will reply: "Now, now dear, there is no need to be formal in bed, just call me Woy."

P.S. to all my friends in Blanefield. Honest, I am only kidding. J.R.

Glasgow Herald 28 March 1982

THE COMEDY DOUBLE ACT THAT WINS MY VOTE

THE BBC have done it again. The Corporation's genius for devising new and totally original comedy programmes seems limitless.

They have now come up with something entirely different, a new comedy format, a worthy successor to Hancock, Steptoe, Alf Garnett and Monty Python.

It's called "By-Election Special The Day and Dimbleby Laugh-in".

The resident comedian is Sir Robin Day, who presides at one end of the studio over a motley shower of knockabout politicians.

At the other end, playing the straight man, young David Dimbleby. I know he is not so young, but compared with Sir Robin, George Burns seems young.

Inside the hall where the count takes place is the unflappable Vincent Hannan who, no matter the confusion, will fluster not.

Last Thursday night and Friday morning, the Beeb produced a classic programme which could easily win some international award for television comedy. It was the "Bermondsey By-Election Special".

Mind you, they had a vast willing cast of politicians/comedians only too anxious to perform for nothing.

The casual way that David and Vincent handled these amateur exhibitionists was superbly professional.

During the early hours, David would say: "And now we will return to the

20

count where an announcement is imminent." It became immediately obvious that no announcement was imminent.

Vincent would then nobble anyone within lapel-clutching reach and ask profound questions about the parlous state of politics in our country.

As some of those milling around had obviously been celebrating or drowning their sorrows and were in an advanced stage of alcohol poisoning, this turned out to be quite hilarious.

As dawn approached, David was getting a bit cheesed off by imminent announcements that never materialised and told Vince: "We are relying on you to get it right next time."

Meanwhile, back in the studio the director—the real boss behind the scenes—had brought into play the greatest comic discovery so far this decade . . . Peter Snow and an electronic contraption that wouldn't look out of place on the space ship Enterprise.

In laymen's terms it could be called a swingometer. You see it in by-election specials.

It don't mean a thing if it ain't got that swing, and Peter is the guru who measures swings.

At the other end of the studio Sir Robin gets the performing politicians to perform. We had Peter Walker for the Conservatives.

Peter used to be part of a double act known as Slater and Walker that performed regularly in the City of London. The Stock Exchange and other institutions thought the act was a bit naughty.

They put the boot into his partner Jim Slater and put him out of the game for a long time.

The Liberal was a young man called something like Heligon or Hexagon or maybe even Pentagon, in fact he both sounded and looked like a seven or eight-sided square, if you will excuse the contradiction.

Labour's spokesman was Gerald Kaufman who tried desperately to be impressively statesmanlike. His joyless eyes, grey face and personality generated as much warmth as an iceberg.

He could be the Peter Lorre of British Politics, only more ridiculously comic.

As the world now knows, the Liberals won out the park. Peter Tatchell, the Labour candidate, argued that his defeat had nothing to do with him, the local party or his allies in the London Labour Party. Nor with their inadequacies as perceived by the electorate.

Well, it must be comforting to be the candidate in the biggest defeat for the Labour Party in a by-election this century and yet feel absolutely no responsibility for that defeat. Comforting, but stupidly self indulgent.

Mr Tatchell argued that his defeat could be explained by the unprecedented campaign waged against him as an individual.

As one who believed that he would have been beaten anyway, let me also add that his comments about the smears are justified: the anti-Tatchell campaign was grossly vulgar.

21

John O'Grady, the Bermondsey Real Labour candidate, led the pack with his song about Tatchell being a popper and wearing his trousers back to front and not knowing his this from that.

Gay Liberals came into the constituency with badges that read "I haven't kissed Peter Tatchell" and some which read "I have kissed Peter Tatchell". The Liberal candidate told us that he had nothing to do with these smears.

This would have sounded better if during the election, the Liberal Party had denounced these vilifications. The Liberals it seemed, were happy to reap the benefits without incurring the odium.

The Liberal Party could be quite vulnerable on this issue. After all, it was David Steel who piloted a bill through Parliament legalising homosexuality.

The Tories could also be in trouble if Bermondsey legitimised the hounding of politicians because of their alleged "queerness".

There is the story of the Tory Minister who, during the progress of Boy David's Bill through Parliament, was asked by his Parliamentary Secretary: "Sir, what are we going to do about the Homosexual Bill?"

"Pay it," he replied.

Daily Record 28 February 1983

SORDID AND ABSURD ... BUT THAT'S POLITICS

WHEN does one plus one equal three or maybe even one-and-half? In a General Election.

What does unemployment cost the country in strict cash terms?

Only the cost of paying unemployment benefit Mrs Thatcher told Sir Robin Day on *Panorama* last week.

Now let's assume you have a job and earn £120 a week. You pay income tax, and national insurance.

You are made redundant and no longer pay tax or insurance.

There is also then the cost of determining and paying out your dole money and any other social security entitlements.

All these factors constitute what your unemployment is costing the nation. Instead of explaining to the woman that her argument was blatantly untrue, Sir Robin apologised.

So at a stroke the "cost" of unemployment has dropped. It hasn't really, but who cares? It's General Election time and all good men—and women—must come to the aid of the party.

It's been that kind of election. Superficial, sometimes sordid and full of absurd contradictions.

For example we are told that people support the Tories because they "want the smack of firm government".

22

At the same time we are also told that Mrs Thatcher's main aim is to remove government from the everyday lives of people.

How can you have "the smack of firm government" from what is called a non-interventionary government?

Anyway, all this talk smacks of public schools.

The pupils at these dreadful institutions get smacked by masters and older pupils.

Some grow to like it and in later years it can become for them a way of life.

This probably explains why so many ex-public schoolboys, including Anthony Blunt and others became fans of Hitler and Stalin, whose smack of firm government was most resounding.

In the last week showbiz personalities have been shunted on to the campaign stage.

John Cleese, whose main contribution to British humour has been to show the comic potential of having legs that stretch all the way up to your oxters, emerged as a political sage.

Based on his experience in Monty Python's Flying Circus no doubt, he advised us to vote Alliance.

Sir Richard "goosey goosey" Attenborough must have a personal hot line to the other world, for he tells us that Mahatma Gandhi is supporting the SDP.

That settles it. Gie's muhatma coat, ah'm gaun tae vote for "Jenkie".

Melvyn Bragg of the South Bank Show also popped up to punt for Labour and told us the arts were "a complete vindication of socialism because they are fundamentally funded by the state".

You don't say, Melvyn. Gee whizz, that inspiring thought might just swing the election.

Pete Murray, that towering intellect from BBC-2's gaggle of disc jockeys, emerged as a Maggie fan.

The media, of course, has now taken over elections.

At public meetings and rallies the party faithful are herded in as extras to form a human backcloth for the leader who then speaks to and for the cameras.

With few honourable exceptions the media has grovelled to Mrs Thatcher.

She bullies and blusters and is commended for being decisive.

Any Labour leader trying the same would simply be accused of bullying and blustering.

A Tory candidate is discovered to have lied about his membership of the Fascist National Front.

Thatcher defends him and the matter is quickly dropped, while Michael Foot is assailed about Militant Labour candidates.

At the same time it has to be admitted that Labour has handled its campaign with the subtlety and sure-handedness of a tone-deaf drunk wearing boxing gloves while trying to play the violin.

It could be summed up as runaway incompetence.

Apart from David Steel, who in media terms is unquestionably the country's most effective politician, the Alliance campaigners have also been a dead loss.

David Owen has come over as a moderate bursting with extremism whose lips are inclined to curl into a snarl as he seeks to put the boot into his former colleagues.

A Norman Tebbit with hair and without Norman's charm.

Roy Jenkins has ambled through the campaign like a benign, pin-striped animated garden gnome whose only hope of success is to hold on to Boy David's coat tails and hope for the best.

Meanwhile, Bill Rodgers exudes a prissiness that makes Liberace look like Desperate Dan.

Thatcher, of course, has totally dominated the Tory campaign.

Mind you, my old pal Norman has contributed something.

Even on News at Ten he still seemed a refugee from a Don't Watch Alone horror film.

He was shown, refusing to kiss a baby.

Any candidate who won't kiss a baby can't be all bad.

My overriding impression of this campaign is of its unfairness.

Right from the start the dice were loaded against Labour.

The Press overwhelmingly has been viciously anti-Labour and pro-Tory.

The massive funds of the Conservative Party has also given this campaign a professionalism which makes the others look amateurish.

Their advertising has been the best because they could afford to buy the best.

Money was no object.

This unfairness tarnishes the whole spirit of our democracy.

We have laws in this country limiting expenditure in an election within each constituency, yet nationally there is no limit to what a political party can spend for general propaganda.

It can buy all the advertising and all the advertising agencies it can afford.

Look at what is happening.

The British people are being given not the real Mrs Thatcher or the real Mr Foot but a packaged Maggie, which advertising experts reckon is more palatable to the electorate, and an equally fictional Foot made to look too dithery for words, let alone public office.

It's the Madison Avenue approach to electioneering which "sold" Nixon and Reagan to the American electorate.

On Thursday I'll be voting Labour for a whole number of reasons.

You see, I object to people packaging our democracy and selling it by the same techniques they use to sell a cheap deodorant.

Daily Record 6 June 1983

On Mrs T. and Tories

TRUTH THAT LIES BEHIND NEW FOUR-LETTER WORD

IF only Galtieri had invaded Govan, if only Argentina had laid claim to the infinitely richer soil of Elder Park instead of the boglands of Goose Green then the "keelies" instead of the "kelpies" of the Falklands would be the recipients of considerable amounts of public money.

People can die in Britain because the country, we are told, cannot afford any more kidney machines. Scanners for the detection of brain tumours or cancer lie unused because the country, we are again told, cannot afford the money needed to use them.

According to some of our Governors, public expenditure is a new four-letter word, probably shortened for statistical reasons to Puex. When is public expenditure not public expenditure? When it has something to do with armaments or a military adventure.

Confronted with a device for saving human life we get from Whitehall lectures about the need for economies and good housekeeping and how we really can't afford this luxury, just at the moment. But how about a new missile that can slaughter millions at the press of a button? That's something different, money is then no object.

To call this sort of reasoning perverse is to misuse the English language. It borders on the obscene.

The Serpell report on the financing of railways raised as an option that we should butcher the rails network in this country, which would devastate entire communities. This would be justified, goes the argument, because the lines were unprofitable.

I daresay the provision of electricity and gas to some communities is more costly than to others. The same probably applies to sewage. Shall we cut off electricity, gas, sewage and other services to small towns and rural communities because the cost of providing such services does not tally with the cost effective criteria of some monetarist acolyte in the Treasury or in Downing Street?

After a while the combination of market forces and public service economies

25

might deem that all our population should reside in the south-east of England thereby making everything much more cost effective. With any luck the island might then capsize.

In a modern, civilised country important sectors of society and the economy should be run as a public service. I am happy to pay my whack so that everyone who is ill will receive the best possible medical treatment without charge. So that every young person should be given an education that seeks to develop their potential. I would like to see every old age pensioner except those living with younger relatives having installed in their homes free of charge a telephone. And that's only for starters.

The real quality of life is determined more by social provisions than by personal acquisitions.

You can build yourself a castle and then walk out on to streets in a society being throttled to death by the withdrawal of social services that we all have taken for granted for so many years.

It is what Galbraith called "private affluence and public squalor". In the United States this led to the urban breakdown and city riots of the 'sixties. Nobody and nobody's children were fireproof as the case of Patty Hearst showed.

In recent years we have been brainwashed into believing that social spending for the social good is bad and that an industrial or commercial subsidy is akin to some form of economic pornography. If the retention of a proper steel industry for Britain at a time of world recession requires a subsidy then it is both morally right and socially efficient that we should provide such a subsidy. The same applies to other strategically important areas of the economy.

Can we afford to do these things, is the cry that goes up. Polemically I could ask can we afford not to? The real answer is that we do have the money. At present it is being spent keeping 3,500,000 human beings on the Labour Exchange.

Even more to the point, we are spending more per head of the population on armaments than any other member of Nato including the United States.

It would be unfair to attribute all of this to the present Government alone. Successive British Governments have refused to tell the British people a simple truth. We are no longer a global power and my response is to thank God for that. Yet there are those with illusions of imperial grandeur who saddle us with such stupid commitments.

In the House of Commons last week Mrs Thatcher spoke of the "Fortress Falklands". We are to spend more than £400m each year on some marshy islands in the South Atlantic with a population of 1800. It is a ludicrous and an impossible long-term prospect both economically and logistically.

To underline this the Premier recently visited the Falklands and her plane had to be refuelled in mid-air. A difficult and risky business. In the same week that the Kilmacolm railway line was being closed as being too costly to maintain, the British Government were considering the multi-million pound cost of extending the runway at Port Stanley Airport.

The very idea that Westminster could in the 1980s conceivably govern a few islands 7000 miles away is a piece of dangerous nonsense. Lord Palmerston and the Empire are dead. Let us act accordingly.

Let me confide to you my own credo. The greatness of the British Isles and their people are not to be found in the dubious exploits of Cecil Rhodes and Clive of India but in the genius of Shakespeare and Chaucer, or Burns and Dunbar, in the teeming talents of our engineers and industrial innovators including a workforce which acquired skills with uncanny speed.

It lay in the remarkable men of medicine who pioneered so many techniques for the saving of life.

When the names of all the geriatric generals who led our young men to senseless slaughter between 1914 and 1918 are long forgotten, the name and poems of Wilfred Owen, the name of Fleming and penicillin will be remembered and respected.

When some political leader tells our people the truth about our position in the world, of what is truly significant in our heritage, then maybe, just maybe, we could be on the way to a new and better Britain.

Glasgow Herald 24 January 1983

MERCHANTS OF MENACE

WAR is terrible. Even when justified, it should never be glorified. Given modern weaponry, it must come close to the ultimate obscenity.

Yet there are politicans who seem to lust for war. Who seem to be gripped by a passion for that organised legalised violence which kills and maims young men.

Of course, such delight in military mayhem cannot openly be admitted. So it is covered up by talk of what Samuel Johnson once called the last refuge of scoundrels . . . patriotism.

Let the trumpets blow, bang the drums—and maybe people won't notice the mothers and young wives who weep or the children who will never know again their father.

Now, nobody doubts the bravery of the British servicemen in the Falklands— yet isn't it strange that so many medals were struck for this particular war?

More, it would appear, than for all those other localised wars that the British have fought since 1945 . . . Korea, Suez, Kenya, Aden, not forgetting Northern Ireland.

Were the Falklands troops so much braver or was a war for those remote islands much more important than other wars?

People are also troubled by the theatrical exploitation of the Falklands war fever.

In London and the South East of England, it has reached a pitch never seen, at least in my lifetime.

Just think how the live heroes were brought home to ports adjacent to large population centres, the ships planned to arrive in nice time to catch maximum television and radio coverage.

Contrast this with the reception accorded to the returning dead heroes.

The sad, pine boxes were dumped ashore in isolated ports. No bands played, hardly even a lament.

It was as if the coffins were an embarrassment.

Politicians, you see, want the plaudits for military victories. The price is paid by others and preferably outwith the public gaze.

Yet now we hear British engineers are installing British engines in German-built warships destined for the Argentinian Navy.

And the British Government has now also endorsed a British bank loan of £700 million to the Argentinian military regime.

This could be used to replace with more modern and therefore deadly weapons the military equipment lost in the Falklands war.

No wonder those merchants of death, the international arms dealers, are rubbing their hands.

For every life lost on both sides, someone somewhere will make a million.

As I said, war is terrible. It's also terribly profitable.

Daily Record 14 February 1983

DON'T BOTHER TO LOOK FOR SYMPATHY FROM MRS T.

IF someone took you to one of those corrupt Latin American republics and showed you magnificent houses in beautifully manicured gardens—would you conclude that these were good civilised countries?

I wouldn't. I would want to see how the poor lived.

In Brazil, Bolivia, Argentina, El Salvador or any of the others, then just down the road you would come to the shanty towns.

The corrugated hovels, often without a proper sewage system, where the great mass of the city's "have nots" live.

The children will be barefoot, and the very young could be naked.

They will also be hungry, very hungry. For many of the better-looking young girls, prostitution will be the only temporary escape.

To my mind these regimes are evil and indefensible. It is a sick joke to describe them as part of the "free world" as does that celluloid cowboy Ronald Reagan.

28

Freedom is meaningless unless it means that people are free to live with decency and dignity.

A child that dies from a preventable disease in a rat-infested slum has been denied the most fundamental of all human rights—the right to live and a right to a chance in life.

You can really only judge a society by how it provides and cares for the underprivileged.

This is why I recoil in horror from the philosophy of Mrs Margaret Thatcher.

You will search in vain through all her speeches and public statements to find one word of genuine sympathy for the have-nots, for those who are down and almost out.

Her every utterance is a hymn of praise, for the well-heeled, those whom she calls "successful".

Thatcher wants the rich to be richer and her policies have made them so. Meanwhile, the rest are getting poorer.

Since her rise to power unemployment has trebled. Thousands of youngsters now in their late teens have been without a job since leaving school.

No doubt they will one day be branded as Social Security scroungers by Mrs Thatcher's more fortunate young hatchet men.

She also wants to dismantle the Welfare State, which was created to provide a safety net to ensure that no one could fall into what sociologists now call the poverty trap.

It was by no means perfect, yet it brought a security unknown to previous generations of working men and women.

Britain's finest social achievement, the National Health Service, is now also under attack.

Some would discuss the NHS exclusively in terms of cash. If your loved one is dying through the lack of a kidney machine, what price a kidney machine?

The Health Service is about giving everyone the best medical treatment available in their time of need—irrespective of money.

To argue otherwise is to be beast-like.

My fear for my country is that it is being governed by a woman who seems utterly devoid of compassion.

Thatcher is dangerous because she is absolutely certain she is right about absolutely everything.

Her mind appears closed to the slightest possibility that she might ever be wrong.

Another five years of Thatcherism could be a disaster and could destroy all the social achievements of a century of struggle by decent men and women.

Daily Record 14 March 1983

BANG GOES MAGGIE'S IMAGE FOR A KICK–OFF

WHICH party leader would be first to tremble on the slippery skins strewn so liberally—if Mr Steel will excuse the phrase—on their electoral pathways?

Who would fall victim to what has been termed the "banana factor" by many "experts"?

Michael Foot was the hot favourite. He was accident-prone, or so they said. He didn't know his etiquette from his elbow, a donkey-jacket from a tuxedo.

Yet Footie strolled through the week and didn't put a stick out of place.

Mrs Thatcher, on the other hand, had been groomed to perfection—by the best public relations that money could buy—for her role as a mixture of Boadicea, the warrior queen, Linda Carter as Wonderwoman, and Vera Lynn as the Forces' sweetheart.

At the first press conference, however, Maggie blew it.

She pole-axed poor Francis Pym as if he were the Russian Foreign Minister and not ours.

Pym . . . sounds like the name of a bland, slightly fruity-tasting beverage.

Something not exactly unlike our Francis, who is also a Tory "Wet" to boot—which Mrs Thatcher did, and in public, too.

She did it again the following day. Poor Pym had expressed mild personal disapproval of landslide electoral victories.

Maggie chastised him once more, saying darkly that he was an "ex-Chief Whip". Freud would have been interested.

It was very bad for her image. Saatchi and Saatchi must both have been upset.

You could almost hear punters muttering: "Nae wonder auld Denis takes a drink." Or: "Ah widnae fancy takin' a short pay hame to her on a Friday night."

To make matters worse for Saatchi and Saatchi, Mr Norman Tebbit was also sighted on the telly and, ominously, he was smiling.

Now a flash of Norman's smile and you start worrying about how he manages to get home before sunrise.

Anyway, I'm right chuffed about the whole thing.

There is something fundamentally wrong when a political cause is packaged and promoted like a deodorant.

That way, we can end up getting the best politicians that money can buy.

I want the best politicians that money CAN'T buy.

Daily Record 23 May 1983

WE'VE GOT TO CURE A SICK SOCIETY

THE most heartrending thing I saw on TV recently was the report of the young handicapped lad in Aberdeen.

It was on the main news so millions must have seen it.

And it made this viewer furious.

The boy is severely handicapped and relies on special grants to help him in his studies to get a Master of Sciences degree.

But the grants have run out and in order to raise cash he was, with obvious difficulty, doing a sponsored swim over a mile.

Our society is indeed all wrong if this is considered a legitimate way by which a disabled person might secure an academic qualification.

What happens to those with no arms and legs but great intellectual potential?

A sponsored roll down Ben Lomond to raise funds for their education? That seems to be where we're heading.

Our country is now beginning to face the real consequences of monetarist policies which put social and human needs well down the scale.

Tax and public expenditure are two of the mechanisms that sustain the welfare state and the social services.

Massive cuts in public expenditure must mean the erosion and eventual collapse of the social services.

Some might think that's OK. We've got a few quid. Me and mine will be all right.

It's a stupid, ignorant attitude.

The great irony is that Britain after the last war tried with some success to find a new way.

We were pioneers. Our aim was a Britain that would integrate humanity and compassion into the social fabric of life. It was called the Welfare State.

The sick, rich or poor, known or unknown, would be treated as equals and tended by the best medical science available. All of this was a right and not a charity.

There were to be equal educational opportunities for all. Everyone was important. To give of your best was the best anyone could give.

Full employment was considered a responsibility of Government, a basic part of the nation's economic strategy and planning.

All politicians knew from their experience of the Thirties that unemployment was a cancer that could eat away the heart and soul of an individual and of a nation.

We never achieved all these glorious aims, yet we built a Britain immeasurably superior, more civilised and decent and loving and caring than anything that had gone before.

Alas, in recent years we've betrayed our noblest achievement. The new creed is called "Self Help".

Which really means helping yourself to as much as you can.

The strong will always be pretty good at helping themselves. The strong who are decent might help themselves to just enough.

The greedy strong will help themselves to as much as they can grab, leaving others without.

The whole philosophy is brutal, callous and ultimately calamitous. We are now beginning to see its effects.

Doctors in the Health Service tell us patients are dying due to Government cuts in public expenditure.

I feel strongly about this, and also have a sense of grief, sorrow, and even guilt for what is happening to our young people.

The present conditions in this country are creating a sense of hopelessness among millions. This is fraught with danger.

Once hope is gone then society has no moral claim on the allegiance of its citizens.

For many young people I fear we are dangerously near that stage.

Daily Record 29 August 1983

THE BRITISH HAVE A PASSION FOR SCANDAL

THE British are at their worst when they have a juicy sex scandal to chew on.

The scandal must always involve a public figure, though sometimes they are prepared to get excited over a schoolteacher or even a clergyman.

Sad though it seems, nobody appears interested in the love life of Joe McGlumphy, except Joe, or maybe, and only maybe, Joe's wife. I tell you, the McGlumphys of this world get away with murder.

Only politicians, however, are faced with seriously diminished career prospects as a consequence of being found indulging in a bit of hanky-panky.

Some have actually been driven from public office for having what is popularly known as "a bit on the side". They can swindle on the side, drive cars while drunk on the side, and all will be forgiven.

On the political front, they can virtually kill off old-age pensioners by paying them pensions so inadequate that they can't keep warm in the winter.

They can do a lot of other diabolical things, and will be forgiven—but anything encompassed by that word SEX is obviously so un-natural as to be beyond forgiveness.

In Britain, hypocrisy can become a way of life.

Let's put it this way. If every businessman, politician, and trade union boss who has ever had an affair were forced into retirement tomorrow then business would grind to a halt.

There would then be the frantic recruitment of thousands of new executives, presumably from among the ranks of those who inhabit monasteries and such-like places.

As you will no doubt know, I'm not exactly a fan of the Tory party and, particularly of this Tory Government.

I don't know Mr Cecil Parkinson and don't consider that I should. His private life belongs to him and those he cares to share it with.

32

Like every politician, he should be judged by the effect his policies have on fellow human beings.

On this basis, I condemn Parkinson and his colleagues in government for the miseries they have inflicted on the millions of unemployed—for the anxieties about the future they have imposed on parents and children, on young and old alike.

I could catalogue a whole number of perfectly sound reasons why Cecil Parkinson could and should be pilloried for his politics, without any need to pry into his personal life.

To put it bluntly: The one time that politicians don't worry me is when they're in bed. It's when they get out of bed that I start to worry.

That's when they do the real damage, the real dirty stuff, like dismantling the Welfare State and crippling the Health Service.

For example, in the great nuclear debate there is a profound moral dimension.

Can there be any circumstances that would morally justify pushing that button and destroying the world? I think not.

Yet those who deny there is a moral question to be answered relative to nuclear weapons can get all steamed up about Cecil Parkinson having an affair with his secretary. This compounds hypocrisy with ignorance.

My sympathies lie with Mrs Ann Parkinson and the children, and with Miss Sara Keays.

Both women are being publicly sacrificed at the altar of British hypocrisy, and for the titillation of those apparently fascinated by the sex life of others, which must be some sort of clue as to that of their own.

As a matter of principle, Parkinson should never have issued a public statement about his private life. By doing so he has opened it up for comment and discussion by others.

My own feelings are best summed up by the words of Robert Burns.

> Then gently scan your brother man,
> Still gentler sister woman,
> Tho' they may gang a kennin wrang,
> To step aside is human.

Daily Record 10 October 1983

33

On Labour and its Leaders

THE BRITISH ROAD TO SOCIALISM

I am a socialist and have been so since my early teens. My conviction, strengthened over the years, is that there can be no fundamental solution to the malaise of British society except by the process of a socialist transformation of our country. The main issue for myself and many others is the means and the best vehicle for achieving this objective.

It is my conclusion that the Communist Party in Britain is not the vehicle. This belief was arrived at over the years, slowly and reluctantly. To listen to some people, you would think it is simple to separate the subjective from the objective. In life it is not so. Maybe it is, in absolute terms, even impossible.

Intellectually, you can become convinced of an objective necessity. You push it to the back of your mind, delay its expression. Subjectively you know that it will hurt friends. The tension arising from this conflict can be considerable. For two months now I have been postponing and delaying the writing of this article. In all conscience I can delay it no longer.

The leadership of the British Communist Party has issued a new draft of the party's programme, *The British Road to Socialism.* This will be discussed within the Communist Party and will be the main item for consideration at the congress of the party in November this year. People on the Left have been invited to comment on this draft.

As someone who was involved in the commission that formulated the 1967 version of *The British Road to Socialism* and made the speech introducing it to the 30th Congress of the party in November of that year, it may be appropriate for me to record my views on the new draft and on the position of the CP and its role in British politics.

The current draft of *The British Road to Socialism* differs insignificantly from the 1968 edition. Apart from a dissertation on the changes in the structure and composition of the working class (a fact widely acknowledged in the Labour movement for years) and an interesting formulation on the national question asserting the right of self-determination, including separation while stressing the need for voluntary unity between the nations of Britain, the differences are mainly a matter of semantics.

My opinion is that, in the absence of any fundamental new development of the programme, the ensuing discussion is both unnecessary and unhelpful for the Communist Party.

The reasons for arriving at this conclusion are manifold. It is a diversion from the real problems and the long overdue analysis which is confronting the party. These problems are not programmatic. In fact they spring from the failure of the leadership over decades to translate the democratic content of the programme into practice and win conviction for it even within the party.

The ensuing pre-congress discussions will starkly reveal this weakness. The draft will be challenged, in the main, from those who reject the pluralist society, who interpret even a muted criticism of the Soviet Union as a heresy. I cannot blame such people. They are not a cause but an effect which should surprise no one.

The concept of the democratic advance to socialism in the context of the specific conditions of Britain represented a revolutionary change in the strategy of the Communist Party. It was introduced in 1951. The logic demanded a follow-through, an ideological campaign to win understanding and conviction among communists. It also required the organisational restructuring of the party from top to bottom, and a new style and spirit of work, open and honest.

Twenty-six years later it is difficult to define any important change in the life-style of the Communist Party as an entity (I can say this as someone who was in the Communist Party in 1950). This, on the face of it, appears incomprehensible, yet the explanation is simple.

The concept of *The British Road to Socialism* has never really been fought for by the leadership. In much the same way as Clause Four of the Labour Party constitution, it has become an icon. The leadership occasionally genuflects in its direction and, in practice, ignores its existence.

This view which I express is shared by some members of the Communist Party. They have told me so. Yet there is little chance of their making any impact. The pattern will be as follows: the sectarian elements will frame their amendments, and the debate will largely focus on defeating their position.

This will also be a feature of the pre-congress period. The sectarian bogeymen will be invoked as a reason for closing ranks around the leadership. Strenuous efforts will be made to mobilise members to attend the branch meetings which elect delegates so as to reduce the number of "sectarians" who will attend the congress. In other words, administrative measures will be taken to deal with what is basically an ideological matter. If that sounds familiar, it is no wonder, for these are the words used by the British party in criticism of the Soviet treatment of dissidents.

The outcome is predictable. Almost inevitably the leadership will emerge unscathed and the party unchanged. Constructive criticism will be swamped by an overwhelming insistence on the need to beat the Left "sectarians".

This has been the pattern for some years. A few districts, small in membership terms, have maintained a constant critique. Their position can be gauged from the fact that they portray the Warsaw Pact invasion of Czechoslovakia as an act of "Proletarian internationalism". As a congress approached, the leadership became apparently obsessed with ensuring their defeat.

It was easy, too easy, to get caught up in this atmosphere. The consequences were disastrous. The real problem and issues for the party were not touched. An air of unreality descended on congress.

I cannot say that this was deliberate or conscious, but I can recall saying to my closest friends in the party, "If the leadership did not have a Sid French (secretary of the Surrey party) they would have to invent one".

Facts and figures had to be presented in the report to congress in a way that played down the party's weaknesses or decline and so as not to provide ammunition for the "critics". Every Left advance in the trade unions, among students and the broader Labour movement, it was argued, stemmed, in the main, from the Communist Party. Thus the party was "relevant".

Although exaggerated, there is some truth in this assertion. From a Left standpoint, many communists play an outstandingly positive role in the trade unions. But to over-emphasise this point provides an escape hatch from evaluating the party's relevance in political terms as a political entity.

I go further and contend that some communists whose activity is exclusively in the industrial and trade union sphere have subconsciously sought refuge from the frustration of working in the direct political sphere on behalf of the party.

The consequence of all this is that the political party which speaks more than any other of "criticism" and "self-criticism" is remarkably un-self-critical.

This is illustrated in the draft of *The British Road to Socialism* by the virtual absence of any self-critical evaluation of the functioning and performance of the Communist Party.

The Labour Party does not escape so lightly, and here I quote: "The strategy we have outlined will, in the first place, help Labour to win the political majority inherent in Britain's social structure, with its huge working class—something that Labour's old strategy has signally failed to do. As far back as 1935, Labour had already won 38 per cent of the vote in a general election. In 1945 it got 48 per cent and in 1951 registered its high-water mark of 49 per cent. But in 1974, after 40 years of political experience, it was back to 39 per cent or roughly the 1935 level—a striking indication of the failure of the old strategy. Achieving a decisive advance in the Labour vote is bound up with the need for a new strategy."

Nowhere in the draft is there any reference to the communist vote. What were the votes for communist candidates in 1935, when Willie Gallagher won West Fife? How does it compare with the votes for communist candidates in 1974?

36

The answers to these questions are ascertainable facts. They show a massive, if not catastrophic decline:

1924—	55,000	(8 candidates);
1929—	50,000	(25 candidates);
1931—	74,000	(26 candidates);
1935—	27,000	(2 candidates);
1945—	102,000	(21 candidates);
1950—	91,000	(100 candidates);
1951—	21,000	(10 candidates);
1955—	33,000	(17 candidates);
1959—	30,000	(18 candidates);
1964—	45,000	(36 candidates);
1966—	62,000	(57 candidates);
1970—	37,000	(58 candidates);
1974 (February)—	32,000	(44 candidates)
1974 (October)—	17,000	(44 candidates).

Altruism in the Labour movement is something to be welcomed. It is, however, carrying it too far when you hand out gratuitously a strategy that is certain to win a political majority to another party while denying yourself the benefit of your own wisdom! "Physician heal thyself", is not, on the face of it, an inappropriate response.

An indication of the delusion that permeates the present attitude was shown by a cartoon in the *Morning Star* on March 23. It pictured James Callaghan, Denis Healey and Michael Foot sitting round a table just prior to the "no confidence" motion in the House of Commons. The latter has a paper in his hands on which Liberals, SNP and Ulster Unionists are listed, accompanied by question marks.

A secretary with a telephone in hand interrupts and says: "It's for you, PM. Says he's French and his name is Mitterrand." The inference is inescapable. Francois Mitterrand is presumably expected to say: "Form an alliance with the Communist Party. That's how we are making advances."

The unreality is breathtaking. Recently, during a visit which Mitterand paid to Scotland, I was invited to dinner to meet him. There was no opportunity for a serious political discussion, but one thing was abundantly clear. He is no fool. He is bound to know Callaghan, or have his political measure. He also knows the strength of the British Communist Party.

The simple truth is that the Communist Parties in Italy and France have won mass popular political support for well over 30 years. There cannot be a Left of Centre, let alone socialist, government in these countries without the communists. It is not a question of subjective desires, but of objective political realities.

The reality of Britain is somewhat different. The Communist Party has no mass popular political support. I will be told that this is a static view, that *The British Road to Socialism* envisages the growth of such support. So did every draft of the programme since 1951.

Indeed, every congress since 1945 has called for and predicted the development of objective political circumstances that would make possible the growth of the party with a wider base of popular support. Yet the party has declined. The real question is "Why?"

One thing is sure: the answer will not be found in a marginal revision of the party programme (a programme which should be read by all on the Left since it contains many important concepts that would be acceptable to any genuine socialist). It lies much deeper and is, by its very nature, ideological. By ideological I do not mean in the field of abstract or refined theories but something embedded in the minds of people.

The biggest obstacle is the simple fact that the British people do not trust the British Communist Party. Some years ago, in a Parliamentary by-election in Scotland, the Communist Party had a splendid candidate. One day he and I were doing street meetings in the constituency. We were both getting a bit hoarse and stopped for a quick pint in a local pub. An old local "worthy" recognised us and came over to express his admiration for the candidate. Then he told us: "I won't be voting for you." His reasons? "Well, ye see, if we put you in, will we be able to get ye oot?"

Some of the communists who are currently arguing for the dictatorship of the proletariat and for the idea that a socialist government should ban the Tory Party would snort with contempt at that old man's "political ignorance". Yet I know, as does anyone who mixes with people and, more importantly, listens to them, that this old man's attitude to the Communist Party is shared by the great majority of the British people. To be contemptuous of people's opinions is elitist, therefore justifying totally their distrust.

The avowed "sectarians" inside the CP, living in a world of pseudo-Marxist cliches, are of no real consequence. They will, I think, be defeated at the congress. If not, the party can really close up shop. But, putting aside the sectarian Aunt Sallies, how does the party leadership explain this distrust by the British people? In my experience it is ascribed by the leadership to historical reasons peculiar to Britain; to the venom of the monopoly press and media; to the deep ideological roots of social democracy; to the subtlety and intelligence of the oldest ruling class in the world.

There are some elements of truth in these reasons (although the few members of the ruling class I have met have been neither subtle nor intelligent).

But the important thing to note about this reasoning is that there is no element of self-criticism within it. The failure of the party to break through is due to "objective factors". The party, and particularly the leadership, is blameless. Well, if nothing else, that is a comforting thought!

So let's re-phrase it. It is like saying: "If only state monopoly capitalism would play the game and be fair, then our policies which would end the rule and power of the monopolists would win the day." The ruling class are to connive, so to say, in their own downfall. They may not be brilliantly intellectual. They are also not daft. Before you can change reality you must start from the present reality.

Let's put the question another way. Apart from factors outside the control of the party, is there any basis for the people's distrust? The only honest answer to this is yes. To have faced up to this fact squarely, openly and courageously could have placed the British Communist Party in a vastly different position.

This failure has also been a negative factor so far as the broader Left is concerned. The stigma of distrust has overlapped in certain areas and instances on to the shoulders of the Labour Left.

In examining the history and role of the party over its 50-plus years of existence, I have searched for that period where circumstances and leadership were combining which, if pursued, could have meant a decisive point in the process towards a mass party of the British people. There is no doubt in my mind that the thirties, leading up to and including the last war, was such a period.

Having escaped from the sectarian shackles of the late twenties and early thirties, the Communist Party had emerged by 1935 as the champion of the unemployed and as a strong anti-fascist force in British politics. It opposed the appeasement of Hitler and Mussolini and the betrayal of Czechoslovakia at Munich.

Its line was for a broad, mass popular front to halt fascism. In embryo, this movement had the ingredients of a popular patriotic alliance that could have changed the face of British politics.

The Communist Party was at the heart of this movement. It was reaching out to the organised working class, to the unemployed and to many of the young intellectuals. Harry Pollitt, the party's general secretary, was in his element. In pursuit of unity he could not be sidetracked. His inspirational leadership moved millions. Willie Gallagher's speech at the time of Munich will remain one of the most outstanding and courageous in Parliament's history.

Here is Harry Pollitt in July 1939 (and please note this date), dealing with the military menace of Nazi Germany: "Never, never will we bow the knee to fascism. Never will the cry of surrender be heard from the lips of our people, whether the foes are in Britain or Berlin. For our defence is strengthened by the memories of our past struggles. It is enriched by the collective experiences we have assimilated from the titanic struggles of those who, hundreds of years ago, saw the gleam of socialism and followed it in fair day and foul.

"We are the inheritors of their fighting traditions and sacrifices, defeats and victories. We will never besmirch their proud record. We will never let them down or sully the flags of liberty they held so proudly aloft. Our country and our people will never fall victims to fascism. The people of Britain will fight if necessary better than any other people in the world." His last sentence reads: "We have been too long kneeling. It is time to rise."

Two months later, Britain declared war against Germany. The logic of the party's policy was unassailable. Within days the Communist Party of Great Britain issued a statement of all-out support for the war, calling for the removal from the Government of those who had appeased the expansionist aims of Nazi Germany. This was a very strong position and, if maintained would have left the party poised to play a significant role during the war and, more particularly, after the Allied victory in 1945.

Then came the self-inflicted wound that was to raise serious doubts about the Communist Party's credibility as a British party. Eleven days previously, Stalin had signed the Soviet-German non-aggression pact. It had been argued that the Soviet Union was buying time to prepare for the inevitable showdown with Hitler. This was a matter of judgment for the Soviet Government, the Soviet Communist Party and the Soviet people.

But Britain was in a "state of war" with Germany in 1939. A judgment on the justice of this war was a matter for British political parties, including the Communist Party, and the British people. In the last week of September 1939, a meeting of what was then called the Central Committee of the Communist Party of Great Britain was held. In attendance was a member of the leadership of the Communist Party of the Soviet Union.

The meeting decided that the war was imperialist and was not to be supported, thus reversing the party's previous stand. Harry Pollitt and J. R. Campbell stuck to their guns and opposed this about-turn in policy. Pollitt was removed from his position as general secretary and R. Palme Dutt took his place. Two years later, in 1941, Germany invaded the Soviet Union. The party's line changed to support for a now patriotic, anti-fascist war and Pollitt was restored to his former post.

One can only now speculate as to what might have been. If the party leadership had stood firm in line with Pollitt, maybe they would have incurred the public wrath of Stalin. But much more importantly, they would have established in the minds of the British people that the party was not an adjunct of the Soviet party.

Because one step leads to another in a dialectical interaction and inter-relationship, you then wonder how the British party would have reacted to Yugoslavia's excommunication from the international communist movement in 1948. Instead of rushing into print accusing Tito of being everything from a Trotskyist to an agent of American imperialism, we might have been given a more balanced, objective view arising from our own experience.

What I believe is certain is that the party would have come through the trauma of the 20th Congress of the Soviet Party—with its revelations about Stalin—intact and with a certain sense of justification. If communist leaders are able to use "historical reasons" peculiar to Britain by way of explanation, then they cannot be selective.

The events of 1939 to 1941 raised doubts and distrust of the Communist Party. Only this week a younger colleague told me that during the Upper Clyde Shipbuilders campaign he had expressed to an older colleague how much he respected the communists, only to be told to watch the CP—and to be regaled with its attitude to the war after the Nazi-Soviet pact.

I am not raking up the past just for the hell of it. Most of the people who are in the party today were either very young or were not born in 1939. They cannot be held responsible personally. Yet a political party has a corporate being. You can handle the present only to the extent that you come to terms with the past.

The open approach would have been to admit publicly that a grave error had been made and that this occurred, at least in part, due to foreign intervention in the affairs of the British party. Such honesty would have been the best guarantee to the British people that under no circumstances would it ever be allowed to occur again. Quite the opposite happened. Let me illustrate this.

In 1964, R. Palme Dutt published a book to commemorate the founding of the First International in 1864. Prior to its publication the political committee of the party considered the final draft. I had not read the manuscript and wasn't quite sure why it was on the agenda. But the main area of concern was quickly evident: it was precisely those events of 1939–41.

Dutt was instructed to delete all references to Harry Pollitt from this part of the book. The worry was that it might raise afresh embarrassing questions from party members about what actually happened and this was to be avoided at all costs.

It is interesting to read the chapter in the published version of the book. It is like Hamlet without the Prince. Incredibly, if looked at in the light of the actual events and not the discussion in the political committee, there is not one reference to Pollitt nor his removal from the general secretaryship!

That event took place in Britain in the sixties! *The British Road to Socialism* was proclaiming the need for the free availability of information based on the democratic control of the media.

Some months ago, Stan Thorne, the widely-respected Tribune Group Labour MP, phoned to tell me how much he had enjoyed reading my then recently published book. He was also very critical of Bert Ramelson's review of it in the *Morning Star*. Stan said that he was going to write a letter to the paper expressing his criticism. I told him that they wouldn't print it. So far as I could gather, he didn't believe me. Well they didn't print it and, as I now know, Stan's wasn't the only one.

To return to the issue of trust. Can the Communist Party honestly reply to the question, "Can we get you out?", by saying, "Yes, it says so here in our programme."? You win trust not by what you put in the programme (although that can help) but by what you do in life, in the past and here and now.

Hitherto, based on hard facts, there has been some justification for doubts and suspicions. They cannot be brushed aside, nor will a revamped *British Road to Socialism* resolve them.

The problem goes deeper still. It involves the nature and specific form of the socialism which you envisage as being appropriate to your own country. That there could be a model applicable to all countries is a concept that we can safely leave to idiots. They must have some slogans to play with.

The concept in the British case must surely be a process towards socialism by the assent of the great mass of the people. Such a process will leave an indelible stamp on the character and form of the revolution. You will change and ultimately end the class nature of society and the state. Simultaneously and through every stage, the process will draw its strength and authority from the increasing participation of the people throughout the entire field of decision-making.

For us, socialism and democracy must be indivisible. This will be a revolutionary process, inconceivable without struggle, not least in the sphere of ideas, to open the minds of people to the intrinsic merit and superior ethic of our democratic and socialist goal.

Such a concept or strategic aim must determine the character, method and style of leadership. It must also determine the organisational structure of the political parties striving to achieve this objective. In other words, if you want an open, democratic, socialist society, you must have open, democratic parties. In the words of the popular song of my youth, "You can't have one without the other".

Lenin evolved his theory of the "party of a new type" largely based on the experience and needs of a party fighting for socialism in the context of Tsarist Russia. It cannot be seriously argued that this theory must be mechanically applied in all countries. Yet it was attempted. If there is no universal model of a socialist society, it would seem a logical corollary that there can be no universal method of achievement.

I think that if Lenin had lived longer he might well have modified his position on this matter. He was clearly worried about the use or abuse of power by leaders of so centralised a party after his death. Hence his testament warning of the dangers of electing Stalin as general secretary of the party. (Incidentally I had been told that this testament was a Trotskyist fabrication and only found out that it was true in the aftermath of the 20th Congress of the CPSU).

In his last years, Lenin was relentlessly warning of the dangers of bureaucracy. Speaking to trade unionists, he appealed to them to fight "bureaucratic distortions of the Soviet apparatus". He said: "Our worst internal enemy is the bureaucrat—the Communist who occupies a responsible (or not responsible) Soviet post and enjoys universal respect as a conscientious man." Note—the "worst internal enemy" is the communist bureaucrat.

Lenin always stressed that the best way to combat bureaucracy and elitism was through the masses with the people playing their historic role of initiating change. He obviously feared the recurrence of bureaucracy, so ingrained under Tsarism, in a new form within the Soviet party and state. The grey mediocrities thriving while the dedicated and creative representatives of the masses went to the wall.

The least one can say is that his fears were justified. I refuse to accept that Stalinism can be explained or defined on the basis of one individual's personal defects. For a start, it has survived Stalin's death as the Czechs will testify. Any analysis must involve an examination of the defects in the system and structure of the Soviet state and the Communist Party.

This in no way detracts from the historic importance of the October Revolution, nor from the construction of a socialist economic base that, in large measure, coupled with the heroism of the Soviet people, contributed to the defeat of fascism. It goes without saying that many peoples fighting colonialism were, and are, thankful that the Soviet Union exists.

This contribution was in spite of Stalinism. Any socialist government will make mistakes. This, in the nature of things, is inevitable. But words lose all meaning if mistakes are used to describe the deformation of socialist democracy that brought death, frame-ups, torture, disillusionments and despair to countless numbers in the Soviet Union and Eastern Europe.

It isn't the bourgeois press which provided this information. It was Nikita Khrushchev on behalf of the Central Committee of the Soviet party at the 20th Congress who revealed it. Those apologists loudly proclaiming their "love" for the Soviet people should understand that it is the Soviet people who had to pay the price of what they euphemistically call "mistakes".

Stalinism originated in the Soviet Union but it wasn't and isn't confined to that country. Stalin's speeches, articles, pamphlets and booklets became "holy grail" for communists in other countries, including Britain.

Indeed the textbooks for communist education most frequently used in this country for a whole generation of communists were Stalin's *Origins of Leninism* and the *Foundation of Leninism*. They were held in reverence; viewed catechismically. To re-read them is horrifying. Here, codified and canonised are the most vulgar distortions of socialist theory.

Read this from a speech to the Central Committee in April 1929: "We must take appropriate measures so that the press organs, both party and Soviet, newspapers as well as periodicals, should fully conform to the line of the party and the decisions of its leading bodies."

Or from *Problems of Leninism* where Stalin prescribes the role of the organisations of the people and the organs of the state and relates all of them to the Communist party, concluding: "The party, as the main directing force in the system of the dictatorship of the proletariat, whose mission is to lead all these mass organisations—such in general, is the picture of the mechanism of the dictatorship, the picture of the 'system of the dictatorship of the proletariat'."

It is interesting that everything, every organisation of the people is relegated to the role of a "transmission belt" for the leadership of the party.

Such a hierarchical structure required two additional factors to sustain it: a near-military type discipline and a rationale to justify the existence of a ruling elitist clique. They were amply provided.

Stalin spelled it out in a lecture delivered at Sverdlov University: "But iron discipline in the party is inconceivable without unity of will, without complete and absolute unity of action on the part of all members of the party . . . for only conscious discipline can be truly iron discipline." Not just ordinary human self-discipline but "iron discipline", no less.

Then there is Stalin's statement, "Communists are people of a special mould." It was almost a mania to quote this with approval in the Communist Party of Great Britain. But think of this statement and its implications. It certainly has nothing to do with the philosophy of Marx. It isn't even a political statement. If scientists will please forgive me, it could, by the wildest stretch of the imagination, be construed as a statement of belief in the field of genetics. It is on the same intellectual level, for example, as those people who believe that non-whites are people of a special mould—an inferior mould.

If it means anything at all it is that "communists" are born and not the products of human society. In fact, it is a most outrageous, arrogant proclamation of elitism. Follow the logic through. If communists are special, then some communists are more special than others—that is, the leaders.

The conclusion I draw from this is as follows. The programmatic objectives of the CPSU hadn't changed since the first heady days of the revolution. Among other things, the aims to be achieved were the electrification and industrialisation of the country. The collectivisation of agriculture. The education of the masses. All within the framework of a socialist state. In general the objectives were attained. But how were they attained? The means didn't justify but distorted the end. Take the collectivisation of agriculture. Most socialists would agree that, in a country with a large peasantry, by modern standards almost certainly inefficient, some form of co-operative farming should be sought.

In the Soviet Union in the late twenties, Stalin and the party leadership embarked on a campaign to impose collectivisation on the peasants. This was in conflict with everything Marx and Engels had warned against in the last century. There was virtually no attempt to initiate changes from—to use an appropriate term—the grass roots. Instead there was the imposition of a decree from the top.

Coercion replaced the principled task of winning conviction that such changes were necessary and desirable. The inevitable resistance of the peasants followed with bloody pitched battles and eventual enforcement, and the consequential slaughter by the peasants of their livestock. Therein even to this day, lies the probable cause of the relative backwardness of Soviet agriculture.

Collectivisation was achieved but at what a price—both economically and morally. Elitism is pernicious. If institutionalised it creates a ruling bureaucracy utterly certain that they are right and that all forms of dissidence or disagreement are a manifestation of treachery or a mental disorder. They place themselves above the accepted norms of human behaviour.

Ironically it was the way in which Beria met his death that spotlights for me the basic absurdity of a centralised bureaucratic state or party. This man was in charge of state security and the secret police under Stalin. By all accounts, Beria was a beast, responsible for the deaths of many thousands of innocent men and women, most of them communists.

After Stalin's death, he constituted a threat to the others in the top leadership. Apparently they couldn't risk bringing him to trial, so he was enticed to a specially arranged function in the Kremlin without his bodyguards. The other members of the Political Bureau were assembled. The building was heavily guarded by specially selected officers and soldiers they could trust. Beria entered the room, out came the revolvers, and they shot him—collectively.

This has nothing to do with socialism. It has more in common with a Hollywood "B" movie about the Mafia. You can't explain these things by talking about the first socialist country, surrounded by a hostile capitalist world, the objective difficulties, and so on.

I think that the worst excesses of the Stalin era will not be repeated. I further believe that Nikita Khrushchev, and presumably his comrades, wanted to break with the past. If nothing else, self-interest dictated that no person should be allowed to concentrate and control such power ever again. Yet it looks, even in retrospect, that the intention was to go further. It stopped. It is possible that the limits to the development of democracy in the Soviet Union are set not by the system of government but by the structure of the Soviet Communist Party. Maybe an open democratic Soviet Union is impossible without an open democratic Soviet Communist Party.

Stalin never seemed terribly concerned about the nuances or niceties of policy. His concern was for power: the exercise of power. Organisation, discipline, methods and style of party work were what concerned him. On reflection, his quarrel with Tito was not really about policy or ideology. It was over Tito's refusal to accept the hegemony of the Soviet Union.

I know for a fact that Stalin saw and endorsed the first draft of *The British Road to Socialism*. If my memory is correct, he publicly praised it as a creative application of Marxism, or words to that effect.

To recollect Stalin's initial blessing helped me to resolve a contradiction. *The British Road to Socialism*'s orientation towards mass struggle, the rejection of sectarianism and dogma, the concepts of democratic advance, were all things to which I could relate and identify with. But the party campaign to launch it into the Labour movement and among the people never got off the ground. That was over 20 years ago and it is still earthbound. Periodic attempts at relaunching new, more up-to-date models met with a similar fate.

It has made hardly any public impact. How could it when it never even dented the party? Like many apparently complex things in life, the explanation is quite simple. The programme had changed but the party hadn't. The character and attitude of the leadership, the method and style of work, the organisational structures, do not correspond to the concept of the democratic advance to a democratic socialist society. It's like trying to fly Concorde with old propeller engines. It won't work.

At a Communist Party congress, it is well nigh impossible to win any change of policy if it is opposed by the leadership. For the changes I am talking about that would just be impossible.

My brief conclusion is that the Labour Left should be aware of the responsibility that circumstances and history have thrust on its shoulders. The dialogue for a coherent alternative strategy to the policies of the Labour Government is urgent. Stronger links between the Left in the Labour Party and the trade unions must be forged. *Tribune*, as the forum of the broad Left, has a vital role to play. The whole question of socialist theory and perspective has been neglected. In this context, a read of *The British Road to Socialism* is well worthwhile.

Tribune 22 April 1977

HUGH SCANLON: THE TRADE UNION PEER WRITTEN OUT OF HISTORY

WHEN the dust has finally settled on the industrial battles of the 1970s and an objective evaluation becomes possible then Hugh Scanlon will emerge as one of the most significant men of the decade.

In this period he and Jack Jones dominated the TUC. They led the two biggest unions in the country which hitherto had been bastions of the Right wing and had now moved to the Left. This had shifted the fulcrum of political alignment within the British Labour Movement.

The full significance of this hasn't yet been realised by our political pundits. It meant that the old political equilibrium had gone forever.

A new one was necessary or else the Labour Movement would flounder all over the place. Equilibrium as everyone knows is about balance, achieving and keeping it. A new balance in line with new circumstances was needed.

From the Right those who refused to accept any change, and from the Left those who refused to accept any limit to change, tugged and pushed and made difficult all attempts to strike a proper balance. This is the cause of Labour's traumas in recent years.

In retrospect, people should have listened more attentively to Hugh Scanlon. He rarely went onto a political platform, and yet of all the trade union leaders of that era he had probably the best grasp of politics and political reality. He was never on the hard Left, if by that term you mean the infantilism advanced in recent years as a so-called serious contribution to political theory by some inside the Labour Party.

He was never on the Right although accused of "selling out" by would-be Lefts. I went to see him recently and we went over old times and old battles. He is retired now and lives happily with his lovely wife Nora in a house he built in Broadstairs, not far from his old adversary Ted Heath. He is a keen golfer, fancies himself as a gardener, and enjoys the role of grandpa.

In the early 'seventies he fought against the tide of Right-wing opinion in the country at large and didn't flinch when villified.

A few years later his support for the social contract brought him into dispute with his colleagues in the trade unions including myself. Some were loud in denunciation and personal abuse. Although hurt he didn't vacillate.

Hughie is happy, but not I think contented; he sees the tragedies of the 'seventies being re-enacted like a bad dream and from the background of his own involvement wants to warn people of the dangers.

He was president of the AUEW when that union was held to be in contempt by the Industrial Relations Court set up by the Heath Government.

However, events took a turn that had not been envisaged. The assumption was that as president of the union he would be imprisoned until the contempt had been purged by the payment of a fine. As the union policy was not to recognise the court and thus not pay the fine his sojourn in prison could have been lengthy. No public mention was made of this expectation and there were no heroics, but he confesses to feeling "Bloody scared stiff".

Instead, £250,000 of the union funds were sequestrated from which would be paid the fines that were to be imposed on the union. Scanlon and his executive called 1,500,000 members out on strike on a principle that concerned the entire trade union movement. The response was overwhelming.

The solidity of the strike shook many who considered union bashing a popular bandwagon. "Some missionaries", as Scanlon quaintly phrases it, approached him and asked that if the fine was paid would he call off the strike. The answer, of course, was yes. By this time Labour had won the General Election on a policy which included revoking the Industrial Relations Act.

To him it is ludicrous that a Government should be "doing the same thing all over again. The employers do not want such legislation and neither does any-one who knows anything about industry. Courts cannot create good industrial relations."

This was the crucial issue of politics in the early 'seventies and Scanlon and his union played a unique part. Yet as he says, "Somehow in some way it hardly gets mentioned." This is true. In Labour folklore this episode has completely disappeared. Scanlon has been written out of "history". I had to point out that Trotsky had even been erased from photographs, so why should he be so lucky.

A little later he was involved in the controversy surrounding the Social

47

Contract. He became convinced that the country was in "a terrible morass" and a compact between Government and the unions was an important element for recovery.

The Government promised among other things to alter the "Finance Bill" to stop increases in council house rents, the abolition of the Industrial Relations Act, a price commission, equal pay and equal rights legislation and the Safety at Work Act.

In return for this there would be wage restraint. This package was taken into the General Council, debated and agreed. The issue for most was whether the unions could deliver. Scanlon has no doubts. The unions, he argued, met their commitments, to the full. The Government, while carrying through its legislative programme, had been less successful in restraining prices.

This contract, in the absence of strict price controls, could not be held indefinitely. His analysis is very interesting. The Government were, he says, "meticulous in controlling prices at the manufacturing end, but had no control over the prices which hit the housewife. The legislation on prices didn't include the retail trade. The cost of administration, we were told, would be greater than the savings."

He nonetheless defends the social contract. It did bring down inflation and the workers had honoured their pledge to a Labour Government and then, in his words, "came the greatest stupidity of all, in which the Government said it was going for a fourth period of wage restraint and this led to the winter of discontent. They did it with Callaghan present at the TUC where he was warned publicly and privately that this was to court disaster."

Scanlon blames a number of Ministers, particularly Denis Healey, for the fiasco that ensued.

At the same time he reckons that some trade union leaders, knowing a General Election was imminent, should have been more restrained.

He argues that the lower paid actually benefited from the "contract". In the year when the agreed increase was an across-the-board £6, shop assistants, who were then at the bottom of the wages ladder with £18 a week, received a 33% increase, their biggest ever.

Hugh also believes that criticisms by the "Communist and sectarian" Left were far too sweeping. Differences were seized on and magnified and this was far more destructive than anything the Conservative opposition ever did.

I suggested to him that maybe in this period he and other union leaders were getting too embroiled in the machinery of Government? He chewed this over and then observed: "I don't know which is worse; too often at Chequers or not at all."

The biggest disappointment in Scanlon's life was the failure to get a proper amalgamation of unions in the engineering industry. The main reason for this, he believes is clear. The moment he said "the electoral system for deciding officials was not for sale" then they weren't really interested in proceeding.

In the arguments about amalgamation he was in conflict with those on the Left whom he thought were more interested in preserving a power bloc for their sect than serving the interest of workers. In the stormy debates on the social contract he was aghast at the venom displayed to him by former colleagues on the Left.

He differentiates between those, such as myself, who disagreed with him on some issues but respected his motives, and those who impugned his integrity.

He considers he was treated shamefully.

"I can't get it out of my head that perhaps if I had been accepted more, as someone at least trying to do his best, instead of someone who had sold out, it may have strengthened me not to do what I did."

What "he did" was to accept a peerage. He is now Lord Scanlon, and also argues that the Second Chamber gives him a platform which he uses to oppose the Government legislation on industrial relations and to speak on the issues close to his heart.

Well, for me Hugh Scanlon, like all others, should be judged on his life; not a bit here or a bit there, but his life in its entirety. When this is done he will undoubtedly be recognised as a giant of the modern trade union movement. And what of his critics? Who were they, history will ask?

Glasgow Herald 7 October 1982

SCARGILL'S VISION OF VICTORY FOR THE LEFT WITH BREAKAWAY TUC

HE wears dark blue, single-breasted suits, lightish coloured shirts with modestly contrasting ties. His hair is always combed and some suggest carefully coiffed, whatever that means. He is unfailingly tidy.

A well groomed and kempt man gently nudging the foothills of middle age. He works hard, drinks little, is a devoted family man, breeds Airedale dogs, supports his local football team and county cricket club, was a judo enthusiast but can no longer find time to train, listens to brass band music, likes traditional jazz, abhors violence and can be funny in private conversation.

He can also be a trifle straight-laced and sometimes downright puritanical. Nonetheless he tolerates sinners and might even befriend them—we've been friends for 25 years.

This apparent paragon of bourgeois respectability is Arthur Scargill, leader of the British miners. The bogeyman of places like Bletchley. If no man is an island then few are stereotypes. Scargill is certainly no stereotype. He is much more complex than people imagine, but then, aren't we all? It is impossible to place him in the contemporary categories of the Left. He doesn't fit.

He isn't a communist and despite what he claims is not a Marxist. Nor is he a Trotskyist or a Tribunite. There is no group or tendency within the Labour Party today that reflects or can cater for his views. This explains his false reputation as a maverick. I have always sensed a consistency about everything he does. The underlying theme that could reveal the pattern of interlocking thought and behaviour was either obscured or so unfamiliar as to escape recognition.

A few weeks ago we were chatting in Brighton at the TUC when I suddenly realised what really does make him different. Arthur Scargill is held in sway by ideas which raged during the formative years of the British Labour Movement at the turn of the century. He is a throwback, and that is not intended as a put down. Once you realise this, things begin to fall into place. He is so obviously a syndicalist that you wonder why you never noticed this before.

Syndicalism was a movement that was fairly strong in the United States and Europe about 70 years ago. It aimed to change society through a federation of trade unions which by industrial action would transfer the control of production to the workers. Industrial unionism on its own it argued, could bring about the socialist millennium. As you would expect with such concepts the movement was anti-parliamentarian.

Arthur Scargill tells how he left the Communist Party because he refused to sell the *Daily Worker* and wanted only to concentrate on building up his trade union branch which in his view was much more important. Now there are many compelling reasons for leaving the Communist Party but only a budding syndicalist could have thought of that one.

Then there is his oft told story of why he repeatedly turns down the chance of becoming a Labour MP. "As a trade union leader I can pick up a phone and get things done. An MP can't do that." To Arthur such reasoning seems irrefutable. The contempt is for Parliament as well as parliamentarians.

He would love to see in his country an energy union embracing miners and workers in gas, oil, electrical supply and power stations. He points out that he already negotiates for tradesmen other than miners in the coal industry. His eyes light up at the industrial clout such an amalgamation would have, particularly if he were at the helm.

The triple alliance, a somewhat loose arrangement between the miners, railwaymen and steelworkers should, he thinks, be firmed up into some kind of confederation.

The TUC, Arthur reckons, is in grave danger of being dominated by middle class white collar unions lacking in the traditional commitment to socialism that he considers sacrosanct. Some are not even affiliated to the Labour Party. This he contends could start the "rot".

He believes that it might be necessary to form a breakaway TUC. A new trade union centre in Britain that could "revolutionise politics". All member unions would be affiliates of the Labour Party with an initial aggregate membership of about 4,000,000. This coalition of Left trade unions would, he believes, ultimately guarantee the victory of the Left in the Labour Party.

However, Arthur Scargill's beliefs are not as rigid or as fully defined as people think. Apart from his homespun brand of syndicalism he is a rather old-fashioned type of fundamental socialist. To Arthur the revolution is just round the corner, has been there for years if only people, particularly Labour leaders, would open their eyes and look. This fervour inclines him towards exaggeration. What Marx described as "mistaking the second month of pregnancy for the ninth". Such a miscalculation could of course, excite measures to induce a birth so premature as to cause a miscarriage. This is the perennial danger of born again socialists. They can actually abort that process of change they so fervently desire.

Some years ago I sat with Arthur as he sipped a beer and played tapes of a radio documentary about Arthur Scargill. His wife Anne, superbly unimpressed by her husband's notoriety, fussed around the sitting room of their modest bungalow home a few miles outside Barnsley. His home environment is very important to him. He has a genuine disdain for the fleshpot of London and believes, with some justification, that it has corrupted some national trade union leaders. They talk like the cast in "Yes Minister" he complains. Under his leadership the head office of the miners is moving to Sheffield.

This feeling for his roots is quite genuine. Later that night, after the tapes were exhausted, we went on what could only be described as a club crawl. Don't get the wrong idea. This was no drunken odyssey. It couldn't be with Scargill. We went from miners' club to miners' club. Arthur breezed round talking to miners and their wives, remembering all the names. He was actually electioneering but there was no election. This is an important part of his personality. In a certain sense he is always electioneering. Constantly seeking reassurance and the approval of those he is desperate to serve, the miners, and in a wider idealised sense the working class.

He is much less certain about things than his public image conveys. He claims that his platform persona, confident and sometimes arrogant, is really a cover up for his innate nervousness and even shyness.

One thing of which I am certain, he is no dogmatist, belongs to no hard nosed Left sect and is his own man.

The scale of his victory in the election for president puts him in a very strong position within the union. Ironically, he owes some of this to his predecessor, Joe Gormley. If he had retired when expected the communists would have ensured that Mick McGahey was the candidate for the Left. Arthur who believed that he was the only Left who could win would have stood anyway. This would have created divisions in the camp. However, Gormley deferred his retirement until McGahey was too old to stand. The Left then had to unite around Scargill's candidature. It was the Right who were split with no fewer than three candidates. Actually Gormley or "Wily Joe" as he was called by the press was in my opinion a disaster for the 'moderates' in the NUM.

I believe Arthur Scargill will grow with this job. He is a natural mass leader. He talks but he also listens to the miners. You cannot be a mass working class leader without the capacity to feel and sense reactions, to comprehend the attitudes of others and where necessary to adjust to them. This is why dogmatists are seldom mass leaders. There is another factor. The responsibility of this office will not permit abstract sloganising. Arthur will have to think out and clarify his political attitudes. My hope is that in this inevitable re-evaluation he does not go too far. The baby must not be thrown out with the bath water.

Glasgow Herald 5 October 1982

HOW COULD THIS RIDICULOUS SECT WIN POWER?

THE Labour Party is suffering from a bad dose of the "Trots". This sounds like a bug usually picked up abroad which sends people scurrying to the toilet. A nuisance rather than a serious illness. However, if an organism is weak or in a badly degenerative condition then it might succumb and the otherwise merely bothersome bug can become potentially fatal. This might be an apt analogy.

Trotskyism is something I haven't taken seriously since leaving the Communist Party which used to expel Trotskyists with monotonous regularity. A fact which should be borne in mind by those Communist trade union leaders who would deny the right to the Labour Party.

Trotskyism could be defined as a retarded branch of Leninism and similarly based on the theories of Russian intellectuals that were in effect a response to the tyranny of the Tsarist empire. Men who by class and upbringing were elitist with touches of the messianic complex so prevalent among the Russian intelligentsia of those times. Not surprisingly they became elitist revolutionaries.

Political conspirators through necessity in a society where democracy had never existed. Living in a country with a tiny backward working class and a massive even more backward peasantry. As to be expected their concept of political change was based on seizing and not winning power. Theirs was a strategy of the coup d'etat.

That the tortuous organisational methods and political structures emanating from such circumstances should be advanced as a model for the Labour Movement of Britain or any other democratic and developed nation is, on the face of it, absolutely absurd.

Trotskyism, despite its rhetoric about working-class power, is essentially an ideology of the alienated middle-class. This explains why there are likely to be more Trotskyists in the cast of a single West End stage play than among the entire membership of the boilermakers' union.

Yet these people we are told now threaten to take over the Labour Party. This of course is a piece of nonsense. What they have done is to take control of certain constituency Labour Parties. This apart from anything else has become a political embarrassment, damaging to Labour's electoral prospects.

The question to be answered is this—how could such a ridiculous and tiny sect actually win control of these constituency parties? The main responsibility lies with those Labour MPs and councillors who deliberately enclosed the party in their wards and constituencies to a small rump of supporters that would guarantee their continued domination of the local political machine.

Jobs were then shared out among the clique. The party became defunct in all but name except at election time. These were Labour's "rotten boroughs" prevalent in the London area and a few places farther north.

They were easy prey for any little group of conspirators. Members of the National Front could have moved in, taken over and then pled for acceptance on the grounds that the Labour Party is after all a "Broad Kirk". Instead it was the Trots.

Today at Labour's annual conference, delegates will debate and decide on whether to set up a register of groups within the party. In any other context this proposal would appear innocuous. A legitimate precaution by a political party against any organised conspiracy to usurp its public role and internal democracy.

However, the Militant Tendency, an off-shoot of a Trotskyist party, would not get on the register which would then mean expulsion at least for the known leaders. This explains the brouhaha. The Trotskyists who belong to a movement steeped in heresy hunts against all who would deviate by a hairsbreadth from the gospel according to whatever guru heads their particular sect are crying "witch hunt".

The irony is that the history of Trotskyism has been one long saga of expulsions and witch hunts conducted in an atmosphere of malignity where tolerance is deemed a bourgeois weakness that has no place in the mind or heart of any self respecting "revolutionary".

The vote this afternoon will endorse the register. Ideological difficulties cannot however be resolved by administrative measures alone. Anyway the major problem lies elsewhere.

The Labour Party has plenty of policies, too many, and no coherent philosophy. The failure to develop its philosophy based on the realities of contemporary life and not slogans has meant that at a time of profound crisis and slump the British Labour Movement resounds to the battle cries of the last century.

The Left, unwittingly one hopes, are raising arguments and adopting attitudes that were shown to be erroneous in the debates that raged within the European Labour Movements of the 1890s.

At each successive Labour Party conference it seems to judge advance in how it can push policy further and further to the Left. What Labour voters or potential voters may thinks is dismissed almost as an irrelevancy.

This sectarian attitude can only detach one from life. If reality doesn't match your theory then reality is wrong. Socialist doctrines then assume a pristine purity which must be guarded at all costs against the intrusions of the real world. Inner party debate becomes the be all and end all of life.

Criticism is its very life blood. In such an atmosphere the smallest differences can inflame the wildest passions. At last year's conference the Left were snarling at each other and Neil Kinnock was booed at the Tribune rally and called a Judas for failing to cast his vote in the election for deputy leader.

Meanwhile over 3,000,000 people are unemployed. The Welfare State and the National Health are under attack. The achievements of struggle and self sacrifice over decades to build a decent life for everyone are now endangered. Millions of ordinary men and women are in despair, worried sick about the future.

It is a devastating criticism of the Labour Party that in the past three years of internal bickering it has failed to bring a ray of hope to our people that things might or could be different. This is the first essential of an Opposition. That scandal must be ended this week in Blackpool. Michael Foot should take this conference by the scruff of the neck and force it to face up to its responsibilities to the people of this country.

Glasgow Herald 27 September 1982

A GREAT DAY OUT FOR THE WORKERS

THE 100th Durham Miners Gala—or "gayla" as it's pronounced in the North-east—was held at the weekend.

A few years ago, I was honoured to be elected as the guest speaker to this event, unique in the calendar of the British Labour movement.

My wife and I were driving down and will never forget our first sight of Durham town.

I stopped the car so that we could savour the view. The sun was shining, the river glistened, the picturesque narrow streets were clean.

The scene was dominated by the magnificent cathedral, surely one of the finest structures in the world.

It was utterly beautiful.

On the Saturday morning the guests had breakfast and then went on to the balcony of the Royal County Hotel.

People had come from all over the coalfield.

Nothing seemed to be planned, yet all the bands and the glorious banners and the dance groups converged on the centre as if meticulously planned by a brilliant director.

All stopped outside the hotel to play or sing to the guests on the balcony. Then everyone assembled in the adjacent park to hear the speeches.

Afterwards came music, song and dance. It was, and is, the cultural event that comes from, and belongs to, working people.

It struck me then how the British Labour movement and much of its rallies and events lack such unashamed joyousness.

54

Too many spokesmen for Labour lack humour, lack the light and the human touch.

Their Socialism seems to spring from bile and not a love of life.

Now, I think it's possible and, indeed desirable, that those who want to change the world for the better should understand that there is no law that says they can't enjoy themselves in the process.

In fact, I would go further—beware of those, no matter their avowed creed, who are without humour.

Those who cannot laugh about the joys of life invariably cannot weep for its tragedies.

Daily Record 18 July 1983

The Global Dimension

REAGAN IN THE WHITE HOUSE

Al Just Kills Me

GENERAL Alexander Haig seems to think a nuclear missile is like a vacuum cleaner. He is prepared to lay on a demonstration for the Russians. Might we ask where, or in whose parlour? Is the device real or are the effects to be simulated—in other words is it to be a dud-squib demonstration?

If so it isn't really a demonstration. However, if it is to be the real thing, how are the Russians to tell the difference between his demonstration big bang and a proper big bang?

And then, what if the Russians plan a counter demonstration of their own big bangs? Listen, Al, I am getting worried. How do you tell the difference between a demonstration nuclear war and a straightforward nuclear war?

Al, it would be comforting for us Europeans to know as we're being blown sky-high that it is only a demonstration. Al, will you let us know?

Glasgow Herald 7 November 1981

A Show Not To Be Taken Seriously

PRESIDENT Reagan's idea for a television spectacular on Poland grinds on its grisly way. His friend, a Californian millionaire called Charles Z. Wick, seems to be in charge of the project. Mr Wick made his name as an impresario of culture as the producer of a memorable movie called "Snow White and the Three Stooges". He has responded to world-wide criticisms of the project by declaring in imperishable words: "It is a very serious articulation of the background of freedom. To remain passive is a bummer."

Mr Charlton Heston has agreed to abandon his peenie and chariot and to be the MC (Master of Costumes?). Bob Hope, well known supporter of pacifist causes like the Vietnam war and with a record of service to the cause of civil rights as long as the first joint of Ronnie Corbett's left pinkie, has also volunteered his services. Mind you, as Larry Adler once commented: "Given any chance of self-promotion then Hope springs eternal."

56

ITV has decided not to handle this programme. The BBC has yet to make up its mind.

Mr Orson Welles is going to read from the works of Tom Paine, the eighteenth century revolutionary and Mrs Thatcher, the leaderene, is putting in an appearance.

Surely Mr Al Haig, the President's sidekick, who talks and behaves like Doc Halliday on his way to the shoot-out at the OK Corral, can be given a part? He could have a contest with Kirk Douglas to find out who really is the fastest gun in the West.

At first I thought that this whole vulgar set-up might tend to trivialise the profound issues involved in the Polish crisis and might damage the cause of democracy in that unfortunate country. It will clearly now not do so. The vulgarity has got so out of hand that nobody will treat it seriously. Only one remaining thing troubles me, how did Glenda Jackson get involved with this mob?

Glasgow Herald 1 February 1982

A Gee-gee Called Alamein

PRESIDENT Reagan was presented with a white Arab stallion, a horse I hasten to add, by President Portillo of Mexico. The gee-gee called Alamein was a bit of a handful. Frisky and spirited, he was deemed a possible danger to Ronnie, the erstwhile cowboy hero of Hollywood "B" movies.

The animal was gelded. Now that the "bottle" of Alamein has apparently been lost, he is placid, and docile and obeys the commands of the President.

It doesn't half make you think. You know Al Haig was dead lucky to get out in one piece.

Glasgow Herald 30 August 1982

The Daftest Gun In The West

RONALD REAGAN, born again cowboy, is off on an new adventure. He intends to ride that vast range in the sky called outer space.

There, the fastest—or daftest—gun in the West will set about them with his laser six-shooter.

And baddie missiles that might threaten poor homesteaders—such as General Motors or the Chase Manhattan Bank—will be shot down.

Afterwards, Ronnie will meander home to his little ol' log cabin—built to MGM specifications—within the White House underground shelter, and into the arms of his ever-faithful gal, Nancy.

If Butch Cassidy and the Sundance Kid led the Hole in the Wall gang, then Reagan could be called the leader of the Hole in the Ground Gang.

Yep, pardners—our geriatric, Grecian-2000 cowpoke is at it again. The arms race is to become extra-terrestrial. Bomb-along Reagan has got to do what he thinks a man's got to do.

Space satellites are to be used to provide a shield against nuclear weapons. At least that's how it's put.

Even if this Buck Rogers fantasy was practicable, just think of the consequences.

The first of the two great nuclear powers to perfect this technology, and thus render itself impregnable, would be under colossal pressure.

The mad military men will want to launch a nuclear attack on the other before it, too, developed this technology.

You see, I have absolutely no faith in the integrity or humanity of the "hawks" in the Pentagon with their blood-thirsty record in Central and Latin America, in Vietnam and South East Asia.

Nor in the "hawks" in the Kremlin who invaded Hungary, Czechoslovakia and, more recently, Afghanistan.

Because the same technology that can shoot down missiles from outer space can obviously launch its own missiles.

Look . . . we have already polluted our own beautiful planet and threatened to turn it into a smouldering, lifeless mass of inorganic matter.

That's bad enough. So let's leave outer space free from our contaminations and try to do something positive about cleaning up our own backyard.

Which, in this sense, is our Mother Earth.

Daily Record 28 March 1983

The Sad Victims Of Power Politics

ANY day now, Nicaragua will be invaded. Blood will flow, and if the invasion succeeds, a military junta will run the country.

Thousands will be killed without even the vestige of a trumped-up trial. Thousands more will be jailed and tortured.

All opposition will be crushed. All newspapers, except those supporting the junta, will be banned.

Television and radio will come under the absolute control of the military.

All of this will have been organised and orchestrated by Ronald Reagan and the American State Department.

Nicaragua, they will then tell us, is now once again part of the "free world".

The scenario is familiar. The United States have already done this in Guatemala, the Dominican Republic and Chile.

The strategy is always the same.

The Nicaraguan economy in recent months has been deliberately undermined by the Government of the United States. It is called a process of destabilisation.

Two weeks ago, the CIA organised a raid that destroyed the bulk of the country's fuel stocks.

The CIA-trained army of the late General Somoza waits in neighbouring Honduras for their marching orders from their American masters.

The American Fleet is in position to back up the rape of a small country's independence and freedom.

The British Government will retain an absolutely contemptible deafening silence . . . and I will feel a searing shame that my country did and said nothing to try to stop this monstrous crime.

The poor people of Nicaragua will have been sacrificed for the sake of big-power politics, just like their fellow human-beings in Eastern Europe and Latin America.

The Americans and the Russians assert their right to control the destinies of millions unfortunate enough to live in those areas . . . areas that both the USA and USSR arrogantly and arbitrarily claim as their spheres.

They have no such rights, neither moral nor legal. All they have on their side is brute force.

I have complete contempt for those hypocrites who condemn the Russians for what they do in Afghanistan but turn a blind eye to America's crimes in Central and Latin America.

I view with disgust those so-called Socialists in the British Labour movement who are quick to indict American aggressions against other nations while acting as mealy-mouthed apologists for Soviet repression against the peoples of Poland and Czechoslovakia.

Let's make a concerted effort to get our MPs, councillors, trade unions, churches and any other body or organisation you can think of to get in touch with the American Embassy.

Let's tell it to convey to the White House our horror at what they are planning to do in Nicaragua.

It will probably—and I have to concede this—make no difference, for the American plans, openly admitted by the White House, are so far advanced.

But at least we will have tried.

To have tried to preserve some vestiges of freedom for fellow humans and to have failed, is better than not to have tried at all.

One is an admission of weakness, the other is an acknowledgment of complicity and guilt.

Daily Record 24 October 1983

There's No Fool Like This Old Fool

WELL, Ron's done it again. He might not frighten the Russians, but he sure as hell acts as a pretty strong laxative to anyone in the West with sense enough to fear global war.

This ageing celluloid cowboy seems to think he's a combination of Jesse James, Billy the Kid and Davy Crockett.

I don't mind the old fool having his fantasies, but when he tries to live them out as president of the most powerful country in the world, then that's something else.

Think of the events of last week.

A religious fanatic drives a truck-load of explosive into the headquarters of the US Marines in the Lebanon. Tragically, 200 young Americans are killed.

Meanwhile, back at the ranch, or to be more precise, the Augusta National Golf Club in Georgia, rootin'-tootin' Reagan, who sent the young Marines to Lebanon, is fast asleep in his cabin.

Dreaming, no doubt, of how he can outdraw and outgun Yuri "The Fink" Andropov or any two-bit sonovabitch from South of the Border, down Mexico way.

His foreman, a tough guy by the name of Schultz, and otherwise known as the Secretary of State, bursts in to tell the boss about the Beirut tragedy.

From then on, it's tragedy and farce.

Ron hasn't a clue what to do about the Lebanon. But he is having none of it, so he invades Grenada.

I tell you, it's put me off buying a house in Rothesay. Ronnie seems to have a thing about islands.

Now I know all this sounds screwy, but reports from the United States confirm that this is the real reason why Reagan sent in the eighth cavalry—or their modern equivalent—to Grenada.

It's Looney Tunes stuff. Like getting mugged in the street and rushing home in a rage to beat up a neighbour you don't particularly fancy.

Sure, the US military had plans to invade Grenada, just as they have plans to overthrow the Nicaraguan government, but the timing was pure petted-lip petulance.

What it amounts to is this—if some mutt anywhere in the world has a go at an American embassy or a group of American soldiers, then Reagan will blooter somebody or anybody.

Just to show that he is still the macho, virile man that will do what a man's gotta do.

His sidekick over the water, "Calamity Jane", the fastest gun in the Falklands, was decidedly peeved and made this clear to her Downing Street gang.

She thought that she and Ron had something strong going. A kinda special relationship she loved boasting about to "Sundance" Heseltine and "Butch" Tebbit and anyone else prepared to listen.

By all accounts, she was doing her nut.

Ronnie then indulged in what is known as retrospective justification. He invaded, he said, merely to ensure the safety of American citizens on the island.

Makes you think—we have quite a few in this country. Then he told the world that he simply responded to a request by some other Caribbean countries to be their guests on Grenada.

Now he tells us that it was to avert "a Cuban takeover".

He also makes a speech blaming the Russians for the situation in the Lebanon which somehow or other called for prompt action by him in Grenada.

The last explanation is so ludicrous that it surely must win some kind of prize.

All of this raises one fundamental question about relations between states.

We can disapprove of regimes. We have the right and sometimes the duty to condemn those that are cruel and despotic.

But—and this is a big but—no country, neither the Americans nor the Russians nor anyone else, has the right to intervene in the internal affairs of another country.

Daily Record 31 October 1983

SOVIETS AND SATELLITES

Let Soviet Leaders Be Warned Now — Hands Off Poland

OVER 20 years ago, a Soviet aircraft flew in circles over Warsaw then Gdansk and Posnan. The plane was in radio contact with the High Command of the Soviet Army. Peering out the window at the Polish landscape was Nikita Khrushchev, First Secretary of the Communist Party of the Soviet Union.

For some reason he wanted to have a look before deciding whether to give the signal for the invasion of Poland by massive forces of the Red Army poised on the borders.

They would have crushed the upsurge and the movement of Polish workers against the regime. By the veritable hairsbreadth we missed what would have been the worst bloodshed seen in Europe since the Second World War. For a number of reasons, mainly historical and patriotic, Poles would have fiercely fought and defended every inch of their territory.

It's as well to bear this in mind when examining current events.

There are no moral or ethical considerations, such as a nation or a people's sovereign rights troubling the minds of the Soviet leaders, as they ponder. Will they allow genuinely independent trade unions in Poland? It would be the negation of the concept of "Party Hegemony", the absolute cornerstone of their creed. As the only democratic organisation in Polish society a free trade union movement would become an alternative centre of power, a focal point of national identity, a vehicle through which all popular grievances would find expression. This would be inevitable.

There are plenty of historical precedents. For example over 200 years ago the Kirk in Scotland was about the only institution offering even a semblance of democracy, and thus enjoyed great prestige for a period among the population and became a centre of social as well as religious matters.

A free and independent trade union movement in Poland would rapidly become the great mass organisation of the people.

Its growth would be in stark contrast to the perceptible bankruptcy, stagnation and isolation of the Communist Party. Poland would become a pluralist as distinct from a monolithic one-party society. It would cease to be a communist state in the terms conceived by Russian Bolsheviks.

Democracy in one area would highlight the lack of such civilised norms in the rest of the society. Freedom is contagious. It would spread throughout Poland and Eastern Europe. The elements for democratising the system within the Soviet Union itself would be inspired and strengthened.

The Soviet leaders will not willingly accept this prospect. They think in terms of a ring of buffer states with no rights of self determination, spheres of influence and domination and all the rest of the garbage that goes with a neocolonialist mentality. Big nation chauvinism, not socialism, governs their actions. The danger of Russian military intervention to crush the fledgling trade unions in Poland is very real.

The East German and Czechoslovakian borders have been virtually sealed. The Polish Prime Minister and Party Secretary were summoned to Moscow like vassals to report and be "advised" by their masters on how they will tackle the crisis. There is no doubt that the aim is to contain the present struggle of the workers and then at the most opportune time to restore the unquestioned, unqualified and uninhibited rule of the party.

The Judge dealing with the legal registration of the new unions insists that a clause involving the leading role of the Communist Party be accepted. Think of it. You cannot win the conscious, freely-given respect and adherence of workers after 35 years of absolute rule, so you command it by law. The hope is that the workers will accept this clause with assurances that would not mean anything in practice.

An independent newspaper and other concessions will be offered if only they accept the party's leadership as part of the agreement.

Thus will go the argument. The calculation will be that when the dust subsides and heady days of the factory occupations fade then the "independent" newspapers and the "independent" trade unions will toe the party line as agreed under the terms of their legal registration or else.

The Polish workers have been along this way before. Lulled by promises and guarantees into dropping their guard and then subsequently cheated of the fruits of their endeavours.

They seem to realise that the only guarantee of rights and real independence that will mean anything will have to come from their own unity, resolve, discipline, and vigilance. If these tactics of outmanoeuvring the workers fail then the movement must be crushed. This will have been made clear in Moscow. If the Polish Communist Party and State cannot discharge these responsibilities, then the Soviet Union as an act of fraternal assistance will do it for them.

"Loyal to the principals of proletarian internationalism, in response to a call from our Polish comrades, the Red Army have smashed the forces of counter revolution led by that agent of imperialism Lech Walesa." The text of such a Tass communique or a Pravda editorial could be written now.

Everyone acknowledges the real danger of Russian military intervention. It is no good waiting for it to happen and then protesting. Let the warning go out now to the Soviet leaders. Hands off Poland or face the severance of every contact and relationship with the Labour movements of all democratic countries.

In this respect the silence of certain trade union leaders, vociferous about the denial of civil and trade union rights in other parts of the world, is truly sickening.

If it had been the workers of Chile, Brazil or some other country outside the East European bloc that had occupied factories and courageously demanded elementary trade union rights, then the hills would have been alive to the sound of fury.

Last September at the TUC anyone near the rostrum would have ran the risk of being trampled underfoot by the stampede of certain trade union leaders anxious to express solidarity.

Instead they chose uncharacteristically to believe for a little while at any rate that silence is golden.

Why, you might ask, should there be any ambivalence? The issue after all is simple and clear cut. However, the Soviet Union, Poland, China, Cambodia, and some other countries, it is argued, are socialist and therefore any lack of freedoms should be seen in a different context than, for example, in a capitalist country such as Chile.

This raises a profoundly important question. Does the absence of capitalists equal socialism? If so, then it is a definition which would embrace the regime of Attila the Hun, and Pol Pot, all the societies of the Dark Ages and the rule of the Dalai Lama in Tibet, prior to the Chinese takeover, to name but a few.

Socialism in my view represents the extension of democratic norms into all aspects of life, including the economic and industrial spheres. It means the extension of freedom, not its curtailment or denial. A society or system which betrays fundamental human freedoms cannot in any real sense be socialist.

In defining our attitude to events in the Communist world we are clarifying our own concept of socialism. Those who remain silent, avert their eyes and by deed or omission act as apologists for these indefensible regimes, are also telling us something about themselves.

They are not to be trusted.

Glasgow Herald 5 November 1980

Walesa: The Enduring Symbol Of A Nation's Aspirations

IN Poland martial law prevails. An Army Junta rules just as in the fascist states of Latin America. It rules under the banner of "Socialism" and purports to be a "Workers' State". To safeguard this "Workers' State" it has felt obliged to jail workers and their leaders and to smash their trade unions. When it comes to "union bashing" the rulers of Eastern Europe and Soviet Russia make Norman Tebbit, Mrs Thatcher, and Ronald Reagan look like a bunch of amateurs.

In the name of proletarian power, the Polish working class is to be silenced. That at any rate was the intention on the 13th of December 1981 when the leadership of the Communist Party handed over the reins of Government to General Jaruzelski. That is a more accurate description of what actually took place than talk of a military seizure of power.

The die was cast much earlier, on the 9th of February 1981, when General Jaruzelski, already the Minister of Defence, was also made Prime Minister. The plan was then laid to suspend even those paltry norms of democratic accountability that exist within the structures of the one-party systems of Eastern Europe.

It took effect 10 months later. And anyone who thinks this happened without the collusion and endorsement of the Kremlin is a political simpleton. However, as history shows, the desire of a people to be free and a nation to be true to itself, are powerful notions, wisps of the night and the day, that cannot be contained by prison bars or dungeons.

So in recent weeks we have seen the Polish people in open defiance of those who have tried to destroy their fledgling freedoms. There were water cannons on the streets of Warsaw as thousands held aloft photographs of Lech Walesa, leader of the banned trade unions.

Crowds were also out, on the anniversary of the Warsaw uprising against the Nazis and sang a modified version of the National Anthem which included the words "March, March, Walesa".

The Communist bosses are furious. Mr Stanislaw Ciosek, Minister for Trade Union Affairs (that's like being Hitler's Minister for Jewish Affairs) gave vent to their feelings. "Why is the West obsessed with Walesa? What does it matter if he used a safety razor on his beard or eats mushrooms for dinner? Mr Walesa does not matter."

He matters alright and they know it. He matters where it counts in the hearts and minds of the Polish people. He has become a symbol of a nation's aspirations. There is nothing the ruling clique can do about it.

Kill him silently in the night and he would live forever in the collective consciousness of the people, a permanent indictment of those who murdered him. To bring him to trial is also difficult. What do they charge him with—that he organised a trade union in a Socialist Republic?

They would be delighted if he would "volunteer" to leave Poland. Mrs Walesa has told reporters "the authorities made us an offer to leave the country, and of course we refused". They could deport him, as the Russians do with some of their more prominent dissidents, but this wouldn't work either.

None of the Russian intellectuals who were kicked out of their homeland have anything like the base, and following among the Russian masses, as Walesa with the Poles. As a deported exile he would soon become a focal point of national resistance to the alien regime on Polish soil.

In a bit of a quandary they hold him in custody, without charge or trial, and hope that his spirit might break. This also isn't working so they have moved him to a shooting lodge near to the Russian border. What they will do with him next is anybody's guess.

What is clear is that this treatment of Lech Walesa is a violation of every known charter and code of human rights known to civilised man.

Meanwhile the country is in an absolute mess and things are getting worse. This was inevitable.

The centralised, bureaucratic control of the economy which is the fundamental characteristic of the Soviet model and which was imposed on the countries of Eastern Europe has failed disastrously wherever it has been tried. Initiative and the creative talents are strangled by bureaucracy in such a system.

Directives often wildly irrelevant to the actual needs or capacities of the particular country flow downwards into industry and the workplaces. The leadership of the party and the state cut off from the people and thus from reality govern by decree. Subjectivism triumphs. Fantasies prevail. Slogans become a substitute for thought and supersede analysis.

In 1929 Stalin spoke of ever expanding argicultural production through enforced collectivisation and the great five-year plans. In 1953 agricultural production was lower than in Tsarist Russia in 1913. In the Soviet Union this year the grain crop was so bad that no official figures have been published. Which is like the British Government banning the publication of the unemployment figures because they were embarrassing.

In industry a similar pattern emerges. In 1961 Nikita Khrushchev outlined a plan "to catch up and surpass the United States by 1980 in all fields of industry and economic development". These targets are all buried or recalled only as sick jokes in the Soviet sub-cultures.

The system doesn't work in the land of its birth or anywhere else. Gierek's grandiose plan for economic growth in Poland during the '70s was in the same mould, ludicrously unrealistic, and bore no relationship to the real level of economic development in the country. His "Plan" also collapsed and has left a trail of industrial debris and a crippling burden of debt.

Gierek has now been toppled and is castigated as the architect of all the nation's economic ills. He was not a cause but an effect. Gierek, and Stalin for that matter, didn't create the system—the system created them.

Poland's best hope lay in the reforms which could come only from the Government reaching an agreement, a negotiated settlement with Solidarity.

This could have led to that level of democracy which is essential for the solution of the country's chronic crisis. A process of democratic self management in commerce and industry might just have brought that realism and the release of local initiative without which there can be no economic solution.

Instead the regime chose repression. The result was inevitable. Production slumped even further.

People cannot be coerced into giving their best, in fact, it usually leads to their worst. This is not new. Slavery was always inefficient. The slave for obvious reasons was much less productive than a free labourer.

So Poland is slithering further into debt.

As you read this, Western banks are trying to put together a deal, to ease the burdens of repayment for 1982. Under the existing agreement the banks can call in these debts failing an understanding being reached by September 10. Part of that understanding should be the release of Lech Walesa and an end to martial law.

President Reagan tries to make West European Governments renege on their legal commitments to the Russian/West German pipe line deal to show the Russians what we think of their role in the suppression of free trade unionism in Poland. Yet he says nothing about American banks virtually subsidising Jaruzelski's regime.

It is argued that the West stands to lose its money unless it does so. The opposite is true. The continued absence of democracy in Poland will intensify the country's economic crisis and thus ensure that the debts will not be paid.

Anyway there are things beyond money that must be considered. I believe it to be a moral obscenity that British finance should be used to sustain a regime that imprisons people for trying to exercise those elementary freedoms that we take for granted in this country.

If we cannot help the Polish people for God's sake let's not help their oppressors. That is why the Labour Party Executive were right to cancel invitations to the party's conference extended to the political parties of the Warsaw Pact countries who all endorsed the suppression of Solidarity. The TUC were also correct to invite Lech Walesa to speak at this year's Congress. His enforced absence will give the British trade unions the opportunity of expressing their contempt for Jaruzelski's junta.

Of course we will hear the voices complaining that this is a return to the Cold War. Nonsense. Peaceful co-existence doesn't require that we stand mute with eyes averted as freedom and democracy are crushed in another land. Furthermore there are differences in the constraints on Government as distinct from political parties. For example a Labour Government in Britain would obviously want to maintain State relations with the Soviet Union.

It doesn't therefore follow that the British Labour Party should seek warm fraternal relations with the Soviet Communist Party. One involves recognition of a State with which one must live, the other implies moral approval. Given the current situation, democratic socialists in Britain must tell the Russians we are Poles apart.

Glasgow Herald 20 August 1982

Is The Old School Tie Our Secret Weapon Against Ivan?

LEO LONG. Say it quickly and it sounds like a Chinese takeaway. I'll have two sweet and sours, two chow meins and a leolong. But as we all now know, it is actually the name of a major general in British Intelligence recently uncovered, or should it be unfrocked, as a Soviet spy. Was he the fourth or fifth man, or the 224th?

I have lost count. After all this, Cambridge University is etched in my mind as the finishing school for KGB agents. The old school tie clearly carries as much clout in the Kremlin as it does at the Carlton Club or even the Foreign Office.

Before long Russians will be complaining about the elitist stranglehold on their spy industry. "I tell you Ivan, you can't get anywhere in this mob unless you've been to an English public school."

Mr Roy Hattersley, Shadow Home Secretary, wants an inquiry. He wants to know the full extent of the "cover up" of how many double agents are still being sheltered within the old boys' network. This seems a rather extravagant approach. It would surely be easier to establish those who didn't spy for the Russians.

There must be fewer in this category. The irony is that having absorbed all our secrets, the Russkies are also in a hell of a mess. Serves them right.

Apart from the particular problems of BL (Blunt and Long), it is interesting to note that all the best known spy leaders have been daft. They are either nut cases to start with or became so by the idiocy of their chosen profession.

For example, J. Edgar Hoover, who ran the FBI for decades, was a copper-bottomed, 24-carat, clod-hopping loony. Beria, boss of the KGB until Stalin's death, was another, psychopathic and perverted.

The wartime intellectual conscripts to British Intelligence were in general either appalled or hilariously amused by the stupidities of the service. Malcolm Muggeridge has written witheringly about his experiences. Even Compton Mackenzie, a man whose judgments were invariably gentle, was scathing and acerbic in describing the fatuous follies of the so-called secret service.

All of this should not surprise us. It's perfectly natural and even understandable. Think of the kind of mentality it takes to say "I am going to be a full-time spy".

You cannot treat such a person seriously. Sooner or later fantasy takes over and then it's Bonkers Away. Apart from anything else they are pretty useless. One good journalist who knows his stuff is worth 100 spies. Much less expensive, too, if you can keep the tabs on his expenses.

Glasgow Herald 7 November 1981

Simple Guide Through The Maze Of Kremlinology

THE only good thing about the speed with which Yuri Andropov was appointed successor to Brezhnev was that it saved us from a week of interminably boring and totally inconsequential interviews with the Kremlinologists, this weird assortment of media men, academics, retired diplomats and geriatric politicians who pose as experts on the inner world of the Soviet power structure.

Pravda articles would have been dissected. Every comma and full stop scrutinised for an inner meaning. Like the Red Army ceremonially marching past the plinth on Red Square, our "experts" would have been paraded before our very eyes every night on telly and every morning in the quality press. Linked like a human daisy chain, faces and words would have blurred into a featureless, meaningless, nothingness.

With a valuable stake in making a mystery out of the obvious they just love to pick at every morsel of news from Moscow and speculate on what might happen if this chap rather than that chap comes out with the top job.

Now, of course, we will have a week of Andropov assessment. These guys can't lose. The interviews and articles will spew out. Young Yuri's early life will be charted. We will be told for the umpteenth time how he clawed his way up through the party apparatus and whose coat tails he clung to, of his period as chief of the KGB and whether his fondness for modern jazz indicates a surfeit of liberalism. Should Reagan send Dizzy Gillespie to Moscow as his ambassador to "OO-Bop—She-Bam" our way to detente? Watch "Bluesnight" tomorrow night for the answer when in the studio will be a man who knew the nephew of an uncle of Andropov's father when he was a cypher clerk at Cheltenham before defecting to Britain.

His revelations will be analysed for their significance by Paul Coleslaw, expert on Soviet affairs who predicted that Stalin would die sometime, and Sir Anthony Sharp who was able to study Soviet life at first hand when an undergraduate at Cambridge in the 'thirties.

It is all a load of twaddle. The truth is much more simple. Russia has been ruled for hundreds of years by an autocracy. In 1917 the form changed, the substance of autocratic rule remained.

The Politburo of the Communist Party has more power, absolute power than any of the Csarist regimes. To speculate about how an individual might or could fundamentally change the Soviet system is a fundamental error in itself.

Like accepting the Kruschev argument that the "Cult of The Individual" was an adequate explanation for the terror associated with the period of Stalin's tenure of the leadership. This thesis attributes the whole panoply of Soviet repression, involving the party machine, the secret police, the judiciary, the army, the press and radio, the medical profession and particularly the psychiatrists, cultural and academic institutions, forced labour camps, etc, etc, to the personality defects of one man.

Such a theory and approach is an insult to our intelligence and I'm not talking about MI5. Stalin didn't create the Soviet system. He was its product as was Khrushchev and Brezhnev.

Every system has its own "logic". Objective processes are at work. The Kremlin watchers are so absorbed in the personalities they can't see the wood for the trees.

They argue that Khrushchev, by lifting the lid on what was going on, proved that an individual leader could change the destiny of Soviet Russia. This I believe is a superficial interpretation of the twentieth congress of the Soviet Communist Party. This was less a personal choice than is generally recognised.

Khrushchev and the other members of the Politburo felt threatened by the power accumulated by the secret police. First they felt it necessary to get rid of the KGB bos Beria. He was invited to a reception in the Kremlin with other members of the leadership. All except him were armed with handguns. The party went with a bang. They shot Beria.

The fears persisted. Control of the KGB had to be in the hands of the autocracy and not one of the autocrats. The exposure of Stalinism was intended to attack the dominance of an individual over the instruments of repression and not the instruments of repression themselves. They still exist. Ask Sakharov or any of the other dissidents or the inmates of the psychiatric wards for political deviationists.

Never in the whole of human history has so much power been concentrated in so few hands. All, too, in the name of collectivism.

But ever since the death of Stalin, it has been a group exercise in power. Like a bunch of elderly Mafia mobsters the Soviet leaders don't mind having a "Godfather" or a general secretary who can have certain trappings of office and even a little more say providing he doesn't control all the gunmen.

Brezhnev lasted so long because he didn't endanger his colleagues.

Changes in the policy of the Soviet Union will spring from the objective needs of the nation as perceived by this ruling clique. The changes will be quantitive and not qualitative and that's for sure. You see even this top group couldn't if it wanted to, change the system in a fundamental way.

There is another strata of Soviet society that is also important. The middle-ranking party cadre. The party apparachiks. The party secretaries at district and regional level. The party members who are the managers in industry and commerce, in the diplomatic corps, in the media, in the academic and cultural life of the nation. The party members who hold all the important positions in all the professions.

Their promotional prospects, status, affluence and privileges, which are enormous, are owed entirely to the party. These people have a tremendous vested interest in maintaining the status quo and constitute the most conservative element in Soviet society.

This is why attempts to read nuances of potential change into the proclivities of individual members of the Politburo can be so misleading. The irony is that Soviet Russia is one of the most stable societies on earth. The Russian people seem historically inured to autocracy and bureaucracy. Gogol's famous satire on the Csarist bureaucrat, "The Inspector General", could with slight changes be a comment on contemporary Russia.

It will take some diabolical collapse of the economy or system to rouse the Russian people. Their capacity to absorb injustices, oppressions and disasters seems almost limitless.

Anyway the character and nature of Soviet society, whether it can or should change is a matter only for the Soviet people.

The most important thing for us is that they want peace. No people has suffered more than the Russians from the cruelty of war. They still feel threatened by what they see as a hostile capitalist world. In the years following the revolution this fear was entirely justified.

The rise of Nazi Germany was encouraged by some of the most reactionary circles in the West who hoped Hitler's war machine would sweep East against Russia. This is part of the history taught in Soviet schools. Unfortunately it's true.

After the war Stalin's aggressive posture both internally and externally was fuelled by the fanatical unreasoning anti-Sovietism of American leaders like John Foster Dulles. Sometimes the death of a leader, while signalling no profound change in the nature of a society, can provide the excuse for a change of emphasis.

We in Western Europe should be doing all in our power to create the climate for a dialogue with the Russians on disarmament.

Their economy and our economies are distorted by the massive resources tied up in armaments. O.K. so we might not agree about heaven and many other things as well but surely we can agree not to make earth a hell. That's the theme the West should be playing in the weeks and months ahead. Before that we might have to deal with some of our own Hawks. A species by no means confined to the Kremlin.

Glasgow Herald 15 November 1982

THE MIDDLE EAST

Slaughter In Beirut: The Damning Case Against Begin

THE ghettos are littered with the dead. Corpses of young mothers clutch dead babies. Dead women lie draped over the bodies of children. Families massacred in their homes slouch in the unnatural postures of death. Old men and youths lined up against walls and shot lie slouched with hands still tied behind their backs.

Bulldozers have tried to scoop up the corpses and drag them away from the prying eyes of the outside world. Arms and legs stick through the debris of collapsed buildings. It isn't easy to conceal a carnage.

This could easily be a description of the "Holocaust", Hitler's "final solution" to what he saw as the Jewish problem. It might have been the Nazis' assault on the Warsaw Ghetto, but it wasn't. It took place in camps for Palestinian refugees located in West Beirut.

At the time of the massacre this part of the city was controlled by the Israeli army. Israeli soldiers occupied positions overlooking the Palestinian refugee camps of Sabra and Chatila. Last Friday the Israelis had turned these camps over to the Phalange, a military neo-fascist group, and to another extreme Right-wing Christian militia of Major Saad Haddad. These are the only Lebanese allies of Menachem Begin.

Either or both of these groups rounded up and killed every human being they could find. There was little or no resistance. The young Palestinian men had been persuaded by the United Nations to accept an American peace plan and to lay down their arms, leave the camps and go to various other countries. Promises were given that their wives and children and parents and grandparents would be looked after.

I want to weep for the betrayal of two peoples. The Jewish people have been betrayed. Young Israeli soldiers, children of those who survived one holocaust, are being used to create another. Menachem Begin, obsessed by some sense of guilt at his generation's failure to stop the Nazi slaughter of Jews, seems to feel his guilt or past impotence can be assuaged by slaughtering Arabs, particularly Palestinians.

This man has betrayed all that's best in Jewish culture. The questioning, tolerant, genuinely intellectual, liberal values personified by people like Einstein are besmirched by Begin's blind bigotry. This man is a fanatic. A few weeks ago he compared the Palestinian camps in Beirut to Hitler's Bunker in the doomed Berlin of 1945. The comparison was ludicrous and yet revealing.

It revealed a mind locked in the gas chambers of Auschwitz. To remember the horrors of the concentration camps is one thing. To remember nothing else is to take a demented view of mankind. Anyone who disagrees with him is a Nazi sympathiser or traitor to Israel, whether he be the Pope or the leader of Opposition in the Knesset. While those who support his strategy are friends even if they are fascists. His dementia is a danger to world peace.

Please think of this: how would you feel today if you were an Arab Muslim? Up till now it has been impossible to get unity among or between Arabs. They encompass such disparate and even conflicting social forces. The fabulously oil rich, feudal in outlook Arabs of the Gulf States have little in common with the Ba'athists of Syria and Iraq with their often meaningless but nonetheless socialist sounding rhetoric. That's apart altogether from Colonel Gaddafi and the Arab kings. These groups have nothing in common except that they are all Arabs. In certain circumstances however that common ethnic bond can transcend all else. Menachem Begin is creating such circumstances.

Today and tomorrow and next week the young Palestinians will be looking for arms. They will get them. The slaughter of Beirut will be a rallying call. Other Arab peoples will feel humiliated and guilty, the very emotions that have made Begin a zealot. Dignity and collective self respect are necessary for any ethnic group or race. Menachem Begin has heaped humiliation on top of humiliation for the Arab peoples.

The point is now being reached when all other differences are pushed aside and Pan Arabism will become a reality. Despite propaganda the state of Israel hasn't yet had to face a united Arab world. When it does it will be in circumstances of increasing isolation. Public opinion in the West is now swinging sharply against Israel.

There are even signs of latent anti-semitism surfacing. This must be combatted at all costs. Anti-semitism like anti-Arabism, like all racial prejudice, is a poison.

The Arabs will undoubtedly use their economic clout. They do not have to go as far as cutting off oil supplies. They could create chaos in the economies of the West by simply withdrawing their massive funds of petro dollars.

The pressure on the United States is legitimately immense. It was their plan after all that created the situation which has led to this massacre. Last week America voted in the United Nations to condemn Israel for advancing into Western Beirut.

The resolution gave Israel 24 hours to get out. Instead Israeli troops supported by the Christian Phalange were on the move in what was described as a "cleaning up" operation.

How in the name of Christ can these people be called Christian? The Arab world is looking to see what Reagan does now.

If he does nothing then American influence in the whole region will plummet. You see, even Sheikdoms have peoples or citizens whose opinions cannot always be ignored. Meanwhile the Russians are waiting. They need hard currency. The Arab world has plenty. The Russians can give them virtually unlimited arms. It is a recipe for disaster and has within it the seeds of a third nuclear war. And yet this I am certain the Russians and the Americans do not want.

I believe there is only one alternative. The Israeli army must be withdrawn from Lebanon or if necessary forced to withdraw and the United Nations peace-keeping force returned. The negotiations for a Palestinian homeland must be started almost immediately. Israel's agreed borders must be guaranteed. Unless this happens there will be no peace in the Middle East. The Palestinians will still be homeless and Israel's future will remain in jeopardy.

It would help enormously if the Israeli people would remove Menachem

Begin from office. It is difficult to see any way forward to peace with this man at the helm.

Glasgow Herald 20 September 1982

THE IRISH QUESTION

Do Scots Hold The Key To Ending Ulster's Agony?

WE Scots haven't said much, publicly at any rate, about the situation and plight of Northern Ireland. I suspect the silence is tinged with a little embarrassment and even a peculiar sense of guilt.

Behind a smokescreen of "Irish jokes" some of us must surely be grieving for our fellow human beings in Ulster. Many of us, I know, have a mixture of sorrow and despair. Many of our politicians, noted for volunteering their opinions on anything at the drop of a hat or at the slightest glimpse of a reporter's notebook or TV camera, are uncharacteristically reticent, when it comes to Ireland. The Tower of Babel becomes silent as the tomb, for you see bigots have votes here too.

The tragedy is that the Scots might just be the people best placed to help. There is no other part of the United Kingdom, for good or ill, that shares such common elements of history and social composition with Ulster as does the Central Lowlands of Scotland.

In fact, when the current "Irish Troubles" started some of us feared some kind of indigenous backlash here. Thankfully, it did not materialise, which is a testimony to the maturity and strength of the Scottish working-class community.

This is good. What is not so good is that the only Scots voices apparently heard in Northern Ireland are those of the bigots.

The silent majority tend to avert their eyes and would like to do the same with their minds when, or if, the subject is broached. Some are afraid to think about it, lest they rekindle the dying embers of their own bigotry.

The Rev. Ian Paisley, being interviewed on his proposal for a referendum in Scotland, England, and Wales to determine whether these peoples wanted Northern Ireland to remain part of Britain, forecast that the majority, if given the chance, would be for the retention of the status quo. I am not so sure.

The desire of many is to get "shot of Ireland". Some even want Britain to do a Pontius Pilate and wash her hands of what they describe as the whole sorry mess. Let the Irish sort it out among themselves seems to be their viewpoint.

The likely outcome of such a policy would be civil war. The two communities would polarise still further behind the banners of the rival extremists. A bloodbath would ensue with the minority Catholic community in danger of annihilation. The Irish Republic would be under tremendous pressure to intervene and thus possibly imperil the Protestant community.

Britain, in any event, could not stand aside and allow such carnage to proceed. It is too late to argue for Britain's non-involvement. Four hundred years too late. We, at the very least, helped create the mess and have the moral duty to help clear it up. There is no other civilised alternative. The problems will not go away.

Indeed, as the hunger strike in Maze Prison reaches a critical stage, as the Loyalists react angrily to the talks between the Irish and British Prime Ministers, tension grows and street violence escalates. One more martyr for old Ireland could spark off a catastrophe.

To argue, as some do in Scotland, that as we do not know the answers we are justified in abdicating our responsibility, is quite unprincipled. This, of course, is a luxury, unavailable to those living in Belfast.

If we always waited until we knew everything, before trying anything, we would end up doing nothing. That is the credo for moral cowards and those who constantly sit on fences. There is no doubt that the issues are complex and over-simple slogans can be worse than useless.

Yet to be over-conscious of complexities can paralyse the will. Always in every situation it is possible to isolate an issue on which agreement might be reached because of its self-evident importance. Surely, to defuse the immediate situation comes into that category. There can be only a negotiated political solution which, in turn, needs political initiatives. This means time and we're running out of that.

I would like other Scots to join with me in an appeal to the Catholic community and Republican Movement in Northern Ireland to use their influence to try and end this hunger strike. Too many young men have already died for Ireland, isn't it time we implored them to live for it?

We should also beseech the men and women of the Protestant and Unionist Communities to speak up for the path of conciliation. Some of those, who claim to speak on their behalf, appear to revel in the atmosphere of hate.

Please do not leave the arena to these people, but speak up and speak out for yourselves and for sanity.

To both sides of the great divide that has split this people asunder, it surely must now be obvious that they can neither bomb the way to a united Ireland nor re-establish a Protestant ascendancy in the secular government of the province. These options are not available and they must be told so, categorically.

Republicans can argue against the basis on which Ireland was partitioned. They can challenge what they claim is the artificiality of a border delineated for the sole purpose of creating an in-built Unionist majority based on Protestant sectarianism.

Even those sympathetic to this analysis will reject any attempt to rectify this by force. Another important point is being missed.

Northern Ireland, or six out of the nine counties of Ulster, has existed as an entity for 60 years, longer that is, than any of the emergent nations of Africa and

Asia. Even those who agree that the establishment of Stormont was wrong do not agree with a proposed solution in the 1980s that would mean herding, much against their will, the Protestants of the North into an all-Ireland Republic. This could be done only at bayonet point and that is not on.

What is on, however, is the responsibility of the British Government to create a democratic Ulster, with a charter that guarantees everyone their civil and political rights irrespective of religion. The ball would then be back in the Republican court. Their task would be to persuade the majority of their fellow citizens, Protestant and Catholic, that a United Ireland is just, would serve their interests and safeguard their rights.

In a democracy the only absolute pre-condition for change is that the majority will it to be. Therein lies the real challenge to the Republican movement.

It surely is by now clear to the Unionists and the Loyalists that there can be no return to the old regime. Furthermore, the principle of majority rule as understood by democrats cannot be equated with the permanent domination of any group based on religious sectarianism. And anyway, within a real democracy minorities have rights to. These vital questions were swept under the carpet by Stormont for more than 40 years.

The advent of the Civil Rights Movement in the late 60s spelt the long, overdue end of such abuses. No one in Britain outwith a tiny cabal of bigots, would even dream of restoring a regime that would condemn Catholics to a form of second-class citizenship.

So they can beat drums, whip up emotions around ancient battles or long dead kings, the reality is that sectarian rule enshrined in a Government is finished forever—and good riddance too.

Within these parameters the two communities must meet and forge new relationships of mutual trust, interdependence, and a fraternal sharing of power. The only alternative is mutual slaughter.

Once such relationships of equity and shared concerns have been established, then all constitutional issues of Ulster's relationship with Britain and Eire are in their hands, to be freely determined by all the peoples of the province in an atmosphere hopefully free of coercion and through the exercise of reason.

An old friend, the late Professor William Barclay, used to point out that the Lord's Prayer deliberately eschews the singular pronoun. It does not say "My Father who art in Heaven . . ." Nor my Protestant father, or Catholic father, nor even Christian father. It speaks of "Our Father" using the collective pronoun. It proclaims the universality of all human beings. Children of the one father or, as we Scots put it, we're all Jock Tamson's bairns.

Our plea should be to our Irish brethren to start again now as Christmas approaches, in a spirit of fraternity and not enmity. In the words of John Lennon: "All we are saying is 'Give Peace a Chance'." Why not?

Glasgow Herald 16 December 1980

Provo Gangsters An Insult To Honourable Rebels

RECENTLY on television for the umpteenth time was an old movie about the Mexican revolution led by the likes of Pancho Villa and Emiliano Zapata. The plot centred on the relationship between two characters, a reluctant Mexican hero played by Rod Steiger and James Coburn as the Irish republican whose expertise with explosives helped decimate the ranks of the hated "Federales". The latter character was portrayed sympathetically and as a romantic revolutionary.

Some years ago there was a highly acclaimed British film called "Odd Man Out" in which James Mason played the part of an IRA gunman on the run. Again the subject matter was handled sympathetically.

Fifteen years ago in "Folk" clubs all over Britain, Irish republican songs were sung and accepted as part of the "Folk" repertoire.

Quite a number of old stalwarts in the British Labour movement had, in "the early years" as they put it, been associated with Irish republicanism, and were proud of this association. It should be noted they were mostly non-Catholic.

I recall these things so as to establish that in years past the Irish nationalist movement enjoyed fairly widespread support or sympathy particularly among liberal minded people in this country and elsewhere.

Today the situation is profoundly different. The Irish republican cause has been besmirched. It's banner has been trampled in the dirt, ironically by those who claim to be the heirs of Robert Emmett and James Connolly. Nobody nowadays wants to hear, let alone sing a song in praise of the IRA except a few nutters who masquerade as Celtic supporters. There is no possibility of a United Ireland in the foreseeable future. The credit for this should go entirely to the Provisional IRA.

The Provos along with their blood brothers, the Protestant extremists also destroyed the Civil Rights movement in Nothern Ireland. In the 'fifties and 'sixties there was a growing realisation in Ulster and in Britain that the old Stormont regime could no longer be tolerated by a country which claimed to be democratic. Discrimination against Catholics was too manifest to be denied or ignored. The delineation of constituency boundaries and wards along with the power structures of the Protestant supremacists consigned Roman Catholics to the permanent status of second class citizens.

Many within the Protestant communities of Northern Ireland supported the Civil Rights Movement. Its aims were simple; one man one vote and an end to all forms of discrimination. There was overwhelming evidence that the great majority of the British people were in favour of these elementary demands which, however, in the context of Ulster would require profound social changes.

For many people these developments raised the cherished hope that at long last we might see in Ulster the bastions of bigotry on both sides crumble under the mass onslaught of reason, decency and democracy.

Alas, we reckoned without the element that has always existed in the Irish nationalist movement; the Authoritarians. At differing times they employ different political rhetoric. It can be of the far Right or the far Left, depending on the circumstances. Forty years ago they were neo-fascist and pro-Nazi. At that time this faction was quite influential within the Irish Government. It should be remembered that Eamonn De Valera and General Franco were the only national leaders to send condolences on the death of Hitler.

Today this element of Irish nationalism chooses to speak in the language of the ultra Left. Do not be deceived. Franco spoke like a Spanish Grandee and Hitler called himself a National Socialist. Phraseology was unimportant. They were both of the same ilk.

The Provisionals and extremists on the other side were dismayed by the growing unity in Northern Ireland and in Britain for a new deal in Ulster. They both wanted to destroy the Civil Rights Movement and succeeded. For different reasons they have a vested interest in the status quo. Love thy neighbour says their God, but they don't give a sod, for their 'god' is a 'god' of division. They fear political or ecumenical unity in Northern Ireland like Dracula fears the sunrise.

In the 1980s there is no romantic view of the IRA. The Provos aspire to the mantle of men such as James Connolly who, with his colleagues, raised the flag of an independent Ireland during the Easter rebellion of 1916. They occupied vantage points in Dublin such as the post office and fought the British Army. Whatever your opinions of their cause or the practicalities of their strategy, they fought and died for what they believed in, as soldiers, or more importantly as men. People throughout the world respected their courage.

The subsequent behaviour of the British Government such as bringing Connolly before a firing squad in a wheelchair further fuelled the sympathy many felt for the Republican cause.

Connolly, who by the way was born in Edinburgh, would have had nothing to do with terrorism, with planting bombs in public places to maim and kill indiscriminately. To commit such atrocities under the guise of being a rebel is to debase the very word. It is an insult to all those good and honourable men throughout history who have been in the real and best sense of the term, rebels, including George Washington, Mahatma Ghandi and a Galileean gentleman called Jesus Christ.

So when you look at the balance sheet, what in fact have the Provisionals done for the Irish republican cause? They have alienated public opinion in Britain except for the loony and diminutive fringe on the far Left. They have incredibly undermined support for a united Ireland in the Republic itself. I believe that a majority in the south do not want Ulster with its present divisions and hostilities, and who can blame them. In the north they have driven the Protestant community into the arms of the other gang of extremists. The Catholic population are sick and tired of the bloodshed and want an end to the carnage.

Only in the United States are there influential pockets of support. Of course the American Irish have always tended to be more Irish than the Irish. They pine for the "Ould Country" as if it were frozen in time, unchangeable and ossified. To them Ireland is Victor McLaglan fighting John Wayne with Barry Fitzgerald and Maureen O'Hara lurking in the background. Even in the "States" with every atrocity the support and the funds will diminish.

The strategy of the provisional IRA has failed as it was destined to do. Nobody with any sense could believe that the British Government, any British Government, could be intimidated by terrorist actions into forcing the people of Ulster into a united Ireland against their will. It is just not on. Britain's task is to establish democratic norms in the province within which those who are for a united Ireland can seek to persuade their fellow citizens that their cause is just and sensible. No change is valid or justified without the consent of the people. Those who think otherwise and would seek to impose change or preserve the status quo by force and terror are neither politicians or patriots—they are gangsters.

Glasgow Herald 26 July 1982

ON A NUCLEAR PRECIPICE

Time To Draw Back From The Nuclear Precipice

THERE is somewhere on my shelves a book called the *Wildlife of Scotland*. Despite the title it has nothing to do with the "Auld Firm". It is about the Auld Scotia's animal life. Produced by the Scottish Wildlife Trust and edited by Professor Holliday of Aberdeen University, chairman of the Nature Conservancy Council, the book was sponsored by Gulf Oil Corporation.

In it there are photographs of Scotland taken from a satellite, 570 miles out in space. It's beautiful. The various hues of green and brown denote the lowlands, the hills and the mountain ranges.

I have also seen photographs and films of the earth shot from a spacecraft. In these, Mother Earth is a jewel among the planets. Resplendent in her natural diversity and fecundity she sustains an incomparable richness of life. Right at the top of all the life she spawns, stands man, the homo sapien. The most marvellous of beings.

Of this planet it could truthfully be said time cannot wither nor custom stale her infinite variety. What time nor custom cannot do man seems hell bent on achieving. He, in an act of matracide, could wither Mother Earth, destroying himself and all other fellow creatures. From what we at present know there is no other planet within many light years that can create and nurture life as does the earth.

We human beings now have the capacity to turn this most glorious planet into a lifeless charnel waste floating in space. Just as arid or gaseous as the others.

78

To contemplate doing such a thing is a cosmic crime. A madness with no parallel in history. Yet there are those who think in terms of the "first strike", meaning they are prepared to be the first to unleash these weapons of global destruction. They pose as "hard headed realists" although apparently determined to make themselves redundant. Well I ask you—how can you be a realist when you have destroyed the only reality about which you can be a realist?

In 1983 my fervent wish is that mankind will draw back from the precipice and take the first albeit faltering steps towards the total abandonment of nuclear weapons.

It is horrifying to think that a nuclear war could start not from a malevolent consciousness but by an unmalevolent fluke. We already know that red alerts have been sparked off by computer error or through a flock of geese being wrongfully interpreted on a radar screen. If the circumstances that allow an error to be made are continued ad infinitum then sooner or later the error will occur. Let us assume there are a number of pieces of wood so shaped that they can be placed on a flat surface in such a way as to outline a house, then it might be a million to one that if thrown in the air they will land on the ground in the shape of the house. Pretty long odds but what if you are going to throw them up a million times or as often as it takes for this to happen?

I cannot accept that our generation has the right to gamble in this way with all the future life on this planet. It is outrageous arrogance to think that we have.

The nuclear arms race has to be stopped, the proliferation of these weapons has to end and a start made to a new process of nuclear disengagement and disarmament. The alternative is too horrendous to consider.

So far as the deterrent argument has any validity it can only apply to the United States and the Soviet Union. These two giants have the capacity to kill everyone on earth many times over. In this context Britain's nuclear weaponry is irrelevant.

It does however make us most vulnerable. A prime target. It also renders our country incapable of playing any part in trying to stop the spread of such weapons. How can we tell India, Pakistan, Egypt, or Israel that they should not acquire nuclear bombs. They would have every right to point out that the United Kingdom, a small offshore European island, already had such weapons and had therefore no right to lecture them on the moral or political merits of being non nuclear. For many geographical and historical reasons Britain could provide a lead on this issue. We cannot fulfil this role because we have the damned weapons ourselves.

The case for Britain ridding herself of the bomb is in my opinion overwhelming and can be argued within the framework of any traditional outlook. This alone would free our country to play a role in developing initiatives for world-wide multilateral nuclear disarmament. This could create the basis on which Britain might play its greatest and noblest role in world affairs as the peacemaker or the peace broker. Even if we fail we would be no worse off. In fact we have nothing to lose and a world to save.

In the last few years the healthiest feature of CND was the way it was reaching out to wider sections than ever before. It wasn't a trendy movement of the trendy Left. In a ceremony at the Glasgow City Chambers to launch a campaign against nuclear missiles in Britain all the churches were represented. Even more important in a political sense was the representative of a Conservative Party group opposed to Trident.

To someone who believes that nuclear disarmament is the greatest ever test and challenge to humanity then unity right across the whole spectrum of beliefs was most welcome. This cause is not something we can allow to be used or abused for other political ends. It is too important in itself.

Thus my intense anger at those on the sectarian Left who persuaded delegates to the last CND conference that 1983 should be a campaigning year around the slogan "Britain out of Nato and Nato out of Britain". If taken seriously this imposes as a condition of membership those whose political outlook is of the Left. It would exclude all others.

In fact it is worse than that. Many Left of centre parties in Europe are for their countries remaining in Nato while fighting for policies of disengagement and the simultaneous dismantling of both the Nato Alliance and the Warsaw Pact. Included in the parties that take this position is found the Italian Communist Party. So Left sectarians in Britain have persuaded the British CND to adopt a policy farther to the left than the Italian Communist Party.

These people are using CND to "politicise" in their jargon "the British masses". They use campaigns as a platform for their wider political aspirations. By now we should be familiar with this particular brand of political infantilism.

My appeal to all who want to banish the bomb from Britain is to unite on this single issue whatever our differences on other things. The survival of life is the essential precondition for an argument on how good or bad life could be, given the acceptance or refusal, of your particular panacea.

May the New Year be the start of a new beginning. Where a child may ask: "Daddy do you think there will be a nuclear war?" and you take her on your knee and look into that innocence that is at the core of humanity and answer truthfully and categorically, "No, my precious, there will be no war."

Glasgow Herald 28 December 1982

Peace And Nonsense

IN 1968, the Russian army invaded Czechoslovakia and arrested the government of that country who had been trying to build "socialism with a human face".

It was a classical, Mafia-style operation on the grand scale.

The Russians then installed their man to run Czechoslovakia. His name was Husak. He was put in power and kept there by Soviet tanks.

This year, the Husak regime sponsored a "peace assembly" in Prague. On balance, I believed it was a mistake for genuine peace groups in Britain to be associated with this particular conference.

It really is a bit much to get involved in a "peace assembly" in Prague.

However, certain good people in Britain argued such a conference nonetheless could help lines of communication with Eastern Europe that could be very useful to the cause of peace.

Though disagreeing, I could still respect their argument.

So while controversy raged I—and no doubt many other peacemongers with similar views—kept a diplomatic silence.

We didn't like to embarrass organisations like the CND that we otherwise support. Yet one can only take so much.

My breaking-point came last week when the Labour MP for Oldham, James Lamond, argued in the House of Commons that the assembly was not organised by the World Peace Council—which, as everyone knows, is a Soviet front organisation—but by the Czech Peace Committee.

This apparently important distinction made all the difference . . . or so implied Mr Lamond. This is a piece of nonsense.

The Czech Peace Committee, like every other organisation in that unfortunate land, can legally exist only if approved and endorsed by the Husak regime which, in turn, is sustained by Soviet arms.

Daily Record 11 July 1983

THE THIRD WORLD

The Inhuman Species

MODERN technology is an aspect of man's genius which, ironically, can show us man's stupidity and limitless cruelty.

Last week by satellite television, we were able to see men bidding for ownership of year-old horses at an auction in Kentucky. One horse sold for over £6 million.

Last week we also saw by satellite, a harrowing film of children dying in drought-ridden Africa . . . little emaciated bodies, arms and legs like sticks, little shrunken faces that made the brown eyes seem large as saucers.

The price of the horse could have saved three, four, five, six hundred thousand of them.

Now I am not singling out the livestock breeders for blame.

It's too easy that way, to shrug off our own guilt by pointing the finger at a few individual scapegoats.

My anger is for the human species.

What kind of animals are we that allow our own kind to starve unto death, while we have the food and the means of giving them life?

There is plenty of food in the world. If tomorrow Ethiopia discovered an abundance of easily obtainable oil or some other valuable mineral and each citizen became an overnight millionaire, then planes loaded with foodstuffs and medicine would pour into that country.

These people only lack food because they lack money. They die through their hunger and others' greed.

We are fond of talking about wildlife. On this planet, there is no animal wilder or more cruel than man.

"Come unto me, little children," said Christ. In today's world, so-called Christian governments in the Common Market and elsewhere with stockpiles of food are virtually saying:

"Come unto me, little African children, and if you have a few quid in your hands we will give you food—otherwise, you can starve to death."

You know something? If human beings could crawl under stones, it's just possible the worms might object to our company.

Daily Record 25 July 1983

On Society and Social Issues

WORK AND THE WORKERS

The Price Of Democracy

IN a democracy the assertion of rights by individuals or groups sometimes causes inconvenience and occasionally even hardship to others.

As social beings interdependent one to another it could hardly be otherwise. In addition modern industrial society has cast all of us in specific roles that interlock with such complexity that we do not fully realise how much we rely on each other until there is a crisis.

The fundamentally social aspect of our lives and our beings is concealed by illusions that we can be individually and totally self-reliant. That is a dangerous illusion. The self-made man: poor bastard, not only fatherless but motherless too, and other such myths bespatter our language like bird droppings. And then someone or some group decides for some reason that seems important to them not to play their designated role and bang, the balloon is up.

People who never gave them a thought suddenly are outraged. How dare they impinge on our comfortable lives. Sure it is a free country. You can go on strike for as long as you like so long as it does not effect me and mine, is essentially the cry.

In fact I heard a politician on television recently whose argument, once you stripped away the verbiage, was that people should only be allowed to strike if it affected no one except themselves. That is not only an impossible criterion but is a case for masochism not trade unionism.

This is the backcloth to the debate on the proposed amendments to the law as it applies to trade unionism. The division in the Cabinet appears to be, not should they clobber the unions, but to what extent.

I do not want to argue details of this or that piece of proposed legislation. Others are doing so. What I fear is that we will get too bogged down in details. In the present overheated atmosphere important principles concerning the nature of our democracy can be forgotten and even lost.

There is one truth of which I am certain. You cannot have an intolerant democracy. Tolerance enriches democracy. Democracy deepens our tolerance. Whatever our deficiencies as a nation, including the unacceptable secrecy that still surrounds areas of our Government, we remain one of the most tolerant societies in the world.

This is no weakness, but a strength of inestimable value to the true quality of life which can never be measured solely by economic indices. Yet there is no room for complacency.

Democracy is not indigenous to Britain or anywhere else. Historically it is still a very young and tender plant, even in our country which is among the oldest of the democracies. Our democratic rights were achieved after centuries of struggles and campaigns. They now represent our most valuable heritage and must be defended. There are forces at large that are anti-democratic, who sneer at the shortcomings of our democratic processes, who call for "strong leadership", a euphemism for authoritarian rule and dictatorship.

A stable democracy and its product, a mature, tolerant, self-reliant people, do not need personality cults or the great leader syndrome.

Part of the price we pay for democracy is that people have a right to be wrong. This, of course, is a matter of judgment or a difference of opinion. Such differences should only be resolved in a civilised manner. By persuasion, by appealing to reason, by argument or even by agreeing to differ. Democracy is by far the most civilised system yet devised by man.

Among the most basic of democratic rights is that of workers to organise and to negotiate collectively with their employer. The individual employee in any confrontation or difference with his employer has no chance. He is virtually at the mercy of his paternalistic or autocratic whim.

Without the right to withdraw their labour, workers even collectively are powerless. This right may not be invoked. It can even be placed in cold storage as long as this is voluntary and still be a constant factor in all collective bargaining procedures.

The only alternative to this is forced labour. You can outlaw strikes. You can leave it as a "right" hedged in with such conditions as to make it practically impossible. Hitler, Mussolini, Franco, Salazar and Stalin, strong leaders all, had no problems with industrial relations and strikes. That's some price.

Create a social, cultural and political desert and call it industrial peace.

In a democracy people have the right to seek to persuade others that their cause is just and merits support. This is a right that relates to religious freedom, freedom of speech, freedom of the press, freedom of assembly, freedom to organise and freedom to act in pursuit of what you deem to be just. These rights carry with them responsibilities. Action in particular must be within norms of behaviour that do not endanger the rights of others.

It is in this context that I challenge those who want to impose a legal ban on what is now described as secondary picketing. Workers on strike have, in my opinion, an inalienable right to try to persuade their fellow citizens, which includes their fellow workers, that their action should be supported up to and including supportive action.

We must defend the right of everyone to try to persuade others of the logic and justice of their cause as they conceive it. To do so gives us the moral, aye and even legal authority to assert that no body or group has the right to coerce others in our society. Physical intimidation or obstruction is not defensible. The existing laws of the land are adequate to deal with such transgressions in all areas of life. Democratic rights cannot be placed in separate compartments.

Like peace, democracy is indivisible. Attacks on the rights of workers and their trade unions cannot leave unaffected other sections of the community. With certainty it will evoke the call for recriminatory legislation from the other end of the political spectrum to that of our present administration.

I can hardly be accused of exaggeration if I remind some people that a Conservative Government is unlikely to be a permanent feature of British political life. The danger is that anti-democratic and intolerant extremism will be rendered respectable.

Mrs Thatcher and her Government are playing with fire. She might start a conflagration that will consume us all.

The Times 3 March 1980

A New Battle Of Britain In The Factories

IN the last century, when it came to manufacturing and industrial innovation, then Britain was tops. We ruled the world. This economic might and political stability made this country the world's centre for banking, insurance, and commerce. The "City" of London became adept at handling rather than producing wealth. Manufacturing industry ossified and the seeds of Britain's decline and current economic crisis were planted. This is not an argument against banking and insurance, both necessary in any balanced economy, but an assertion of an elementary truth—a society which neglects that which produces the necessities of life cannot progress and cannot ultimately survive.

The claim that Britain still lives in the past has a large measure of truth. The structures and patterns of our industry have been shaped in the nineteenth-century. You get some ridiculously ludicrous examples of this, like the factories where there are several different and separate canteens for executives, managers, foremen, clerical staff, and manual production workers. I have actually seen a foreign delegation looking at such a phenomenon with bewilderment and then hooting with laughter at the lunatic caste system still existing in British industry.

If it was only such weird and quaint absurdities then it would not really matter. However, it goes much deeper and wider. If a Member of Parliament is described as having a business background it invariably means that he previously worked as a stockbroker, an accountant, or an executive in a unit trust company. In this context, business is not the same thing as industry.

85

The professions or a professional person means a lawyer, doctor, university lecturer, and the like. The implication is that all the others are amateurs or that to be, for example, an engineer is not a profession but a job. This is not a question of semantics. It concerns attitude.

For years the middle class have thought of careers for their children almost exclusively in terms of the "professions". It's difficult to imagine a family conference in which young Ponsonby-Gore is being urged to go into industry as, let us say, a metallurgist or industrial chemist. Parents tend to be proud of children who become doctors or lawyers and less boastful of a son who becomes an expert on welding.

The aristocracy, of course, consider any venture into industry by their offspring as almost a family disgrace. Even a tycoon of the retail trade is likely to be viewed as a vulgar tradesman.

The son of an Earl can get behind a camera and become a photographer without besmirching his birthright. However, his social standing would plummet if he actually got involved in the making of a camera. One thing for sure, he would be much less likely to be featured in one of the colour magazine supplements.

The simple unvarnished truth is that people like welding experts are absolutely vital for Britain's future. For example, the technique of joining together steel structures that can withstand the rigours of the North Sea is an essential element in the new important technology for offshore exploration and production.

Youngsters are attracted to jobs that carry a status, social respect and approval. It's a fact that in this country a highly qualified engineer has less social prestige than a chiropodist and will have no brass plate either. Parents of daughters think of equal opportunites again in terms of access to the "professions". The pace of women's liberation is measured by the number of female advocates or television newscasters. The incidence of girl entrants to the Boilermakers' Society seems of no consequence.

Trade unions, their structures and attitudes, are also often the direct product of a division of labour that existed a century ago. Some unions are based on an apprenticeship system to a trade that no longer exists. Technology has disliked certain occupations and some youngsters are serving a four year apprenticeship to acquire a skill that could be learned easily on a three-month training course.

The apprenticeship system in some industries is a device to regulate, and give the workers some control over, the intake of new labour. You seldom have to prove qualification, merely provide evidence of having served your time. It's like four years of purgatory which then entitles you to be considered for a certain job. Even the terminology is revealing. "Have you served your time?" as a question tends to imply a sacrifice that brings an entitlement rather than the acquisition of a skill.

Before anyone starts shouting about "restrictive practices", let's get one thing straight. These attitudes by workers are not the cause of Britain's economic problems. They are an effect, a consequence of an industry that has stood still for so long that every group within it has petrified in the postures of the past.

The restrictive practices of the trade unions is a defence mechanism by workers who understandably view the future with fear and foreboding. It's an attempt, unsuccessful it has to be said, to give themselves some semblance of job security. A government and an industry that sought to generate confidence and full employment would create the climate which would enable such practices and attitudes to be discussed and then dispensed with.

I must confess to being fed up listening to people like lawyers rabbiting on about the negative attitude on the part of workers to new technology when they themselves belong to a profession totally steeped in restrictive practices which sometimes stem even from as far back as feudal times.

If you believe as I do that economics, social developments, and industrial strategy all inter-relate with the mental attitude and psychological outlook of our people, then it is possible to argue that there is no solution to Britain's ills which does not involve a complete reappraisal of work, its status and rewards, bearing in mind that rewards need not always be material.

We need to recognise that the present level of unemployment is in part caused by a structure in industry that is outmoded to say the least. Certain changes in Government policy might ease but certainly would not solve this crisis. It requires more fundamental change in the structure of our industry and in the mechanisms of our economy. It requires the political will to create a climate of opinion that will deliberately encourage and reward the flow of capital investment into the manufacturing sector of our economy. This would do more for Britain than all the speeches of all the politicians put together. There is, indeed, a new and urgent Battle of Britain that needs to be waged. It can only be fought and won in the factories and in the workplaces where real wealth is created. Yet we are busy demobilising the troops, sending them to the dole, and demoralising the diminishing number of those left manning our beleagured industrial front. It's crazy.

Glasgow Herald 1 March 1982

Enough Is Enough As Automaticity Prevails At TUC

AT last week's TUC, the hall resounded to the cry "enough is enough". It became the phrase of the week and was taken up at the fringe meetings. By the Friday finale I had had enough of enough is enough. It had even permeated the receptions and was widely interpreted by the catering staff as meaning that a sufficiency of drink had been dispensed—a reaction which shocked some delegates into a momentary state of sobriety. One celebrated imbiber sought to clarify this dreadful semantic confusion by shouting "enough is not enough".

The need to "translate" also got laldy. Resolutions we were told had to be translated into action. One trade union leader spoke of the need to "translate this resolution into words". As he was from a print union this was taken as a literal criticism of the text to which some of us who felt enough was enough murmured "Hear, Hear". Alas it was a verbal error by the speaker who had simply confused words with action, a not unusual phenomenon in the context of the TUC. Someone tried to explain this away by starting a rumour that the speaker once worked for the *Guardian*.

If enough is enough was the phrase of the week then "automaticity" was undoubtedly the word. It all started with Doug Grieves, the Scot who leads the tobacco workers. Doug could at least pronounce it but his less fortunate brothers with loose-fitting dentures were in a real pickle. Their pronunciation went aw tae pieces when they tried to say automaticity. This ugly word was used to describe the proposed change in the method of electing the leadership of the TUC. This was carried and means that from next year unions with more than 100,000 members will have their appropriate number of nominees automatically appointed to the General Council.

Opponents of this change argued that it would diminish the sense of accountability by TUC leaders to the Congress and place them more firmly under the control of their own union.

This is a very attractive argument to someone like myself who believes that sectional tribalism is the enemy of good trade unionism. However the old method was also based on tribalism. People were nominated by their union, which then worked and wheeled and dealed to get them elected. Once elected these people acted in accordance with the wishes of the union leadership which had been responsible for getting them on to the General Council. If they didn't do as they were told then they were not nominated the following year.

The only way the sovereignty of Congress could be upheld is by an electoral system where nominations were more widely based and included more nominations from union members than alloted to any trade section. Even then there would still remain the question of how the union vote is cast with the leadership obviously wanting to cast it for their favourite son.

All of this is basically concerned with the democracy of trade unions. At workplace level, trade unions are highly democratic. The shop steward is elected annually and can be recalled or removed at any time by the members he or she represents. They are subject to a continuous process of democratic control and accountability. The problem lies at other levels. Just think of this. TUC policy is for some element of workers' control or greater worker participation in the running of industry yet there is not one single rank and file worker on the General Council of the TUC.

Mr Frank Chapple, leader of the Electrical Trade Union, is somewhere on the Right of British politics. To place him more precisely on the political spectrum is difficult, for on some issues he is so far to the Right as to be out of sight somewhere over the horizon. Nonetheless Frank is now chairman of what is considered to be a Left-wing General Council because of what is known as the "Buggins Turn" system which gives the chairmanship to the most senior council member who hasn't yet held the post.

So far as I know this practice has seldom if ever been challenged despite the fact that on at least two occasions in my experience this has led to absolute nincompoops presiding over the TUC.

Last week Arthur Scargill of the NUM was prepared to break with this tradition and stand for the chairmanship. No one including Arthur doubted for one moment Frank Chapple's competency, it was his politics that were to be challenged. Michael McGahey was happy to nominate Arthur Scargill. They couldn't find a seconder.

This was no surprise to me. You see "Buggins Turn" sooner or later becomes "Muggins Turn". Some of those who publicly pour scorn on Frank Chapple are not prepared to upset the apple cart on which they are comfortably ensconced.

They too dream of sitting in that big chair, banging the bell and going on various delegations. Whenever such a "perk" is threatened, the ranks tend to close between the great ideological divide with all the clang of automaticity. The cry goes out. Enough is enough. General Council members unite, you have nothing to lose but the chains of office.

The tragedy is that trade unions desperately need to reform their structures which in many instances are rendered obsolescent by industrial and economic changes in society at large. The main obstacle to such change is the careerist self interest of cliques in control of certain unions and political factionalism not unconnected with the cliques.

In other words political factionalism can become a means of preserving and advancing personal careers on the Left and on the Right.

As an example of this we could take the amalgamation talks currently so widespread. These are often bedevilled by the crudest horse trading as to who should lead the new union or which set up can guarantee the best jobs and perks to the leading officials involved. Negotiations on union amalgamation have been sabotaged because some political faction is not prepared to submit to a democratic process. In all of this the real long-term interests of the work people are ignored.

At a time when trade unions need to stand back and have a long and objective look at their organisation and role, sectional and political subjectivity rules.

The democratisation of trade unions should be a fundamental issue in all discussions on amalgamation. It is not. In last week's *Tribune*, the paper of the Labour Left, there was an article which made the following point. "In addition, Duffy will need to drop his unrealistic demand that other unions must elect rather than appoint their full-time officials." This was a reference to the fact that sacrosanct in the engineering rules is the principle that all full-time officials should be subject to periodic election. This rule drawn up by the pioneers of the old AEU such as Tom Mann is gloriously and fundamentally correct.

A union leadership has no moral authority to speak on behalf of workers unless it is accountable to the workers through an electoral process.

It seems to me that the right of workers to control their union through a democratic process is not a minor tactical consideration that can be bargained away over the negotiating table. On the contrary amalgamations should be used for the rational restructuring and democratisation of unions.

There is of course a political dimension to all this. Unless you democratise the trade unions you cannot have a truly democratic Labour Party. The block votes of the unions are decisive. How those who fought and rightly so for the mandatory reselection of MPs can support the appointment for life of a trade union leader is a perverse contradiction beyond my comprehension. Yet at the TUC a splendid newly elected leader of a public sector union made a jocular remark from the rostrum about how he would hold his present position well into the twenty-first century. Many in the hall enjoyed the joke. I winced. It is by no means certain that such undemocratic practices can be permanently tolerated in a democratic society.

Glasgow Herald 13 September 1982

We're On the Eve Of Our Own Self Destruction

IN every organism there is a point of no return. A stage of decline when recovery becomes impossible. The condition is called terminal.

The Scottish economy is near that stage.

Manufacturing industry is the key element in any modern economy. It produces the wealth that funds everything else.

If there is no industry there will be no Health Service, social and welfare services, nor any of the other kind of services, including the armed services.

Since 1979 Scottish industry has declined by 15 per cent. At that rate Scotland will be an under-developed country by the 1990s, and you should start saving to send your kids abroad for there will be no future for them here.

We will go down in history as the generation that finally destroyed Scotland and its heritage.

The crunch is *here*. Further cuts at Ravenscraig will assuredly mean the end of steel production in Scotland.

Steel is called a basic industry because it is basic to the economy. Engineering, the mainspring of manufacturing industry uses steel.

Engineering factories are located near to where its basic raw material is produced.

No steel in Scotland and ultimately there will be no engineering industry.

Scottish shipbuilding is already down to the bone. There is no fat or meat to cut. Further cuts mean hacking at the skeletal framework.

The whole lot will collapse. Unviable and economically irrelevant.

This is why the savage attacks on all the Scottish yards and the plan to undermine Ravenscraig must be defeated.

The Government keeps telling us there is a work slump—we know that. It tells us that the demand for steel has fallen—we know that.

It tells us that the demand for ships has fallen—the biggest fool must know that.

On the upper reaches of the Clyde large tankers, moored and mothballed are a constant reminder.

The problems are complex, yet the issue is simple.

Government has a responsibility to ensure the nation's vital industrial resources are preserved through a slump so that when the upturn comes our economy can move forward to meet the challenge.

This Government refuses to acknowledge such a responsibility, which raises moral as well as economic issues.

Nowhere in the accountants' book so beloved by Mrs Thatcher is there a column which tries to evaluate the price or cost of a human community.

Hypocritically they talk about the importance of family life whilst pursuing economic policies that are destroying family life for millions.

If there is no industry, there will be no jobs.

If there are no jobs, our youngsters of necessity will drift away. Our communities will die.

The Chairman of British Shipbuilders told us last week that the Japanese and Koreans are so heavily subsidising their shipbuilding that nobody can compete.

This is not true.

We *can* compete if the British Government is prepared to back our shipbuilding industry through these difficult times.

After all, unlike the Japanese we are rich in mineral resources like oil, gas and coal.

What we lack is a Government with the political will to protect our people.

We Scots and our various organisations such as trade unions, political parties, employers associations and churches should unite around the twin issues of Steel and Shipbuilding.

This is our Alamo.

The choice is stark. We either lie down and die as a nation or we stand up and fight for our birthright.

Daily Record 4 April 1983

When Right Puts Us All In The Wrong

SOME years ago, when I was a young engineering shop steward in Govan, Glasgow, the semi-skilled and unskilled workers there went on strike.

Their action was justified, for only the skilled workers got a bonus, yet everyone had to work at the same tempo.

The lads on strike had a picket outside the main door. They stopped lorries and asked the drivers not to deliver to, or uplift anything from, the yard.

One day, they asked me to have a word with some people who had come in a lorry to collect some pistons for an ocean-going tug that we had been servicing.

I told the ship's engineer and his mates that, if they collected these pistons, the strike would be broken and the workers forced to accept ridiculously low wages, possibly for some years to come.

He didn't hesitate. Everyone on his ship was a trade unionist—and neither he nor his mates would cross the picket line.

We eventually found a formula for ending the strike and negotiated a bonus system that rewarded everyone's efforts.

Industrial relations in the place improved, and that was the last strike for many years.

It's doubtful today whether such action as we took those many years ago would be deemed legal.

My mates and I weren't on strike but were taking action in support of others.

The engineers from the tug weren't on strike, but were intent on solidarity with workers whom they considered to be victims of injustice.

Alas, such solidarity with others is now illegal in Britain as in Poland.

Let me make a prediction. Sometime, somewhere, the conscience of people will be roused by the plight of, or an injustice to, some group of workers.

Many will feel morally obliged to take supportive action, believing this to be an inalienable right of free men and free women in a free society.

They will, however, be breaking the law—yet the courts, owing to the numbers involved, will be unable to enforce the law.

According to all legal experts, a law which cannot be enforced is a bad law.

This Government's legislation on trades unionism, according to legal definition, is a bad law. And in my view, it is morally wrong.

Of course, mass picketing—uncontrolled and unlimited—can become physical intimidation, which is a crime. Trades unions cannot—or shouldn't—argue about that.

It should, however, be noted that had even two NGA pickets arrived at Warrington last week, they would still have been in breach of the law.

The issue, despite the hypocritical nonsense spewed out in Parliament, was not about mass picketing, but of the right of workers to take action in support of others.

Without such rights, trades unions are useless and will become completely ineffectual.

At the end of the day, this will be bad for good employers, good for bad trades unionists and a disaster for industry and for our democracy.

Daily Record 5 December 1983

Asbestos: It's Time We Knew The Truth

WORKING with asbestos has killed thousands over the years. Some were workmates and neighbours of mine. The material was widely used in shipbuilding and people worked with it completely unaware of the dangers.

A recent Yorkshire Television programme showed that the deadliness of this substance was known in South Africa more than 60 years ago. South Africa then was very much a part of the British Commonwealth. British companies dominated its economic life. Our civil servants virtually administered the country. It is therefore logical to assume that people in this country must also have known about asbestos.

The sparked off a recollection of a conversation with Jimmy Airlie about 10 years ago. He and I were then colleagues at the U.C.S.

Jimmy maintained that in the early 'thirties the British Government had received a report from a health inspectorate warning of the dangers of allowing anyone to work with asbestos. The report was never published. I contacted Jimmy Airlie last week to confirm my recollections. He now goes further and argues that the information was withheld until industry had found a cost-effective alternative.

All of this confirms my strong conviction that there should be a public inquiry into the use of asbestos in British industry. Was this information suppressed, and if so who were the people responsible? We have a right to know, for the suppression of such information will have led to the painful deaths of thousands of men, women, and children. We must also know the current dangers. Even if we banned the use of asbestos tomorrow there would still be problems.

Take just one example. There must be many thousands of boilers insulated with the substance. Sooner or later they have to be renewed or even removed. How do we ensure that this will be done without releasing asbestos fibres into the atmosphere? Don't forget that relatively small doses can kill. Women have died from asbestosis as a consequence of washing their husbands' overalls.

There is an asbestos dump at Dalmuir. Nobody knows how to move it without running great risks, so it is covered over. It is doubtful if anything can ever be built on this land.

We have a right to know all the facts. What are the dangers and the options open to us as a society? These matters cannot be left to the "experts". Such people sometimes play a tune called for by those who pay the piper. The only safeguard is to make sure that everything is brought out into the open. There should be a public inquiry into the whole question of asbestos, its dangers, its use and abuse.

Glasgow Herald 16 August 1982

Hard Work Can Be A Dirty Business

ARE workers never right? Isn't it just possible that sometime, somewhere, in an industrial dispute the workers might have justice on their side?

Not according to the Government, the Confederation of British Industry and the editorial writers in most national newspapers.

The dispute at British Leyland, Cowley, is the most recent example.

Sir Terence Beckett of the CBI compared the workers to lemmings, rodent-like creatures with suicidal tendencies.

This contemptuous remark passes without comment as if references to working people as rat-like maladjusted animals is fair comment.

The workers were condemned by politicians and pundits for jeopardising the future of the Maestro car over such a trivial issue as washing up time.

Not a word about the management who raised the issue in the first place and therefore could be more accurately accused of endangering the future of the company over such a "trivial" question.

Anyway, *is* it such a trivial issue?

I can remember, years ago, a painting of a miner black with coal dust who had fallen asleep in his chair from exhaustion as his family ate dinner.

The mother and children looked at him with a mixture of love and pity.

The message was clear—so that they might eat he worked at a hard dirty dangerous job which would probably and ultimately kill him.

The children, wise before their time, knew and understood.

More than 20 years ago, those employed in heavy industry came home from work with grimy hands and face and dungarees thick with grease and dirt.

Then people began to realise that this was totally unreasonable.

If you get dirty at work, you should get cleaned at work and the company should provide the time and facilities for a wash and, if necessary, a change of clothes.

In some extreme instances this can actually be a serious health problem.

There are recorded cases of housewives who died of asbestosis contracted from washing the working clothes of their husbands.

Basically, however, your attitude on such questions is determined by whether you have the respect for the dignity of those who work with their hands in conditions far removed from the executive suite.

The three minutes washing up time, so we are told, has existed at Cowley for nearly 40 years.

In industrial relations, custom and practice particularly over such a long period has the full authority of an agreement.

And agreements can only be changed through negotiations between management and labour.

At Cowley the employers decided that henceforth washing up time would end.

If one party can arbitrarily end an agreement then all agreements are useless. This is a formula for industrial anarchy.

Daily Record 25 April 1983

PRESS AND POLITICS

Tragedy Of This Toll

THE *Sunday Standard* is the latest victim of the economic jungle known as the newspaper industry. Over the last three decades, the number of newspapers in Britain has declined at an alarming rate.

A lot of people working in Fleet Street seem to believe powerful entrepreneurs will always be on hand to pick up the tab and pay out millions of pounds each year for the privilege of owning a prestigious newspaper like *The Times* or the *Observer*.

This is Cloud Cuckoo Land. Sooner or later, these guys will get fed up doling out money. The cost will exceed the prestige and they'll simply pull the plug. It could happen next week or next year.

One thing is absolutely certain: if present circumstances continue, it will happen.

The trend of newspaper closures will continue and that prospect is frightening to any democrat.

Democracy means the right to vote. It also means that people should have access to the information from which they draw conclusions as to how they shall vote.

Fewer newspapers means less choice.

Daily Record 11 July 1982

Fuelling Fleet Street's Anti-Union Bias

BY chance, a quirk of fate, I've become a scribbler. A fully paid-up card-carrying scribbler. It happened this way.

About four years ago someone asked me to write a television column for a Scottish newspaper for a period of two or three weeks. I did, and it lasted for two years. I was then approached to do something else, and then something else, and it has been great fun.

Writing is surely all about communicating and I've been doing that, or at any rate trying to do so, all my life and for nothing. To get paid for communicating what's in your mind, what you feel strongly about, is almost too good to be true. If my memory serves me right it's like being rewarded for making love.

Some people would consider that analogy most appropriate for those involved in journalism. I can remember many years ago a delegate to the national

95

conference of the Electricians Union (this was way back in the years BC, ie before Chapple) going to the rostrum, glaring up at the Press table, and saying Fleet Street is the biggest aggregation of male prostitutes since the decline of the Roman Empire.

One got the feeling he was not referring to the compositors, maintenance electricians, and other supposedly heterosexual horny-handed sons of the proletariat who earned a bob or two from the ill-gotten lavish coffers of the Press barons.

His loathing was obviously for the scribblers, and the prostitution inferred was intellectual rather than sexual. His main complaint was that journalists had been less than friendly to him and his colleagues. At the time I wondered why.

Without in any way underestimating the scandalous—and overwhelming anti-trade union—bias of the British Press, a simple truth has to be acknowledged. British trade unionism for many years didn't give a damn about how, or if, their case was presented to the media.

In many industrial disputes trade union leaders would emerge from meetings in the proverbial smoke-filled rooms and mutter gruffly something like: "My members want five quid per week", and then shuffle off feeling they had fulfilled their responsibility to the dissemination of information within a democratic society.

In those days a lot of strikes rarely hit the headlines. A factory could be locked in a dispute for weeks and hardly merit a mention, even in the regional Press. The general public were not all that interested, and seldom are unless a strike impinges on their everyday life.

Thirty years ago British industry was less inter-dependent than it is today. Things have changed dramatically, and yet some appear not to have noticed. In modern societies industry and commerce are so interlocked that a strike of relatively few workers can dislocate entire sectors of the economy.

In one sense this could be seen as enhancing the industrial clout of the workers concerned. It hasn't. Other workers affected by the industrial action can become antagonistic. Public opinion mounts against those on strike. The hand of the employers or the Government is thereby strengthened. The strikers can become isolated, and thus ultimately defeated. Today no trade union can possibly win a major industrial battle without first of all securing the support of those others directly affected by their action and enlisting at least a fair measure of public sympathy.

The victorious miners' strike of the early 'seventies vividly illustrates this point. Edward Heath's government had stock-piled sufficient coal to have kept British industry going for six months and more . . . long enough, so it was reckoned, to break the strike.

At that time, however, the miners enjoyed widespread public support. Their wages were, in fact, disgracefully low given the nature of their work. Other groups of workers refused to use, or move, or allow to be moved the stockpiled coal.

The Government's strategy was in tatters, destroyed by the extent of sympathetic action by others on behalf of the miners. Hence the current legislation, making illegal such supportive action by trade unionists.

What it boils down to is this: in the 'eighties public relations is a decisive requirement for successful trade unionism. No section can go it alone and win. Those days are past. The old style of trade union leadership is worse than useless in the reality of today's industrial and economic climate.

If and when a group of employees decide on the ultimate sanctions, the collective withdrawal of their labour, then the case for such action, the carefully worked out arguments and analysis that proves it is just and fair, must be prepared and articulated, not just to the workers involved but to the public.

This was brought home to me very forcibly during the campaign to save the shipyards on Upper Clyde. We had occupied the yards, and kept on working and producing ships even though many of us had been declared redundant.

We knew from the outset that we couldn't win, whatever we did inside the yards. The real battle was for the minds of our fellow citizens in the United Kingdom.

So we set out to run a public campaign of explanation. Trade union jargon was declared taboo. We were determined to speak and write in whatever language was most appropriate to those we were addressing. We also sought to give our particular cause a wider social significance, one that people from different walks of life could identify with and endorse. We won public opinion and thereby beat the government.

This is surely what is meant by legitimate extra-parliamentary activity within a democratic society; not a minority obstructing a government's legislative programme, but a majority telling our governors that a particular policy no longer enjoys, if it ever did, popular support.

That experience and its lessons are deeply embedded in my mind. It might give you some idea of how I feel when some trade union leaders go to Press conferences, and onto television and speak in the gobbledegook of trade union bureaucracy, obviously having made no attempt to make their union's case presentable and understandable to the wider reading and viewing public.

I've seen longstanding friends of mine in important trade union posts being interviewed on television and speaking as if they were addressing a mass meeting of militants.

I've seen them shortly afterwards in the company of their mates, being slapped on the backs and told: "Well done Charlie. You sure socked it to them". Charlie had, in fact, blown it. As you watched and listened to him on the box you could almost hear the minds of everyone, except a handful of trade union activists, clanging shut. His task, if he is serious, is to open minds, to plant seeds of potential support, to win allies . . . not to please his cronies.

97

I believe it is actually a good thing for trade unionism and trade unionists that modern circumstances dictate that we obtain a wider mandate for our actions and aspirations. Such a mandate is the only democratic way of validating the changes we wish to bring about.

All of this requires trade unions responding to a much wider range of social responsibility. It means training and helping officials and delegates to communicate beyond the rarified circle of union activists.

The Press in this country is biased against the Labour movement. There is no sense in feeding and fuelling that bias, in making it easier for them to exercise their prejudices. Some trade union leaders project such a distorted image of trade unionism that no-one has to add or subtract anything to make them, and the movement they purport to serve, look ridiculous.

Journalist October 1983

BOTH SIDES OF THE LAW

Like The Birdman Of Alcatraz Without The Birds

AS a film about aspects—terrible aspects—of the human condition, *A Sense of Freedom* must be judged a success.

The standards of production, direction, script writing, camera work and even the sound, often neglected on TV films, were exceptionally good. The acting, particularly by David Hayman in the lead part, was outstanding.

It showed once again the resilience of the human spirit to survive and even triumph within a brutal regime.

Lest anyone start protesting that our prison officers are card-carrying pacifists incapable of any act of physical violence against one of their charges, let me immediately establish that my definition of the regime as portrayed here as brutal is based entirely on the admission that a prisoner spent 19 months in solitary confinement. About this there was no dubiety. The prison authorities and everyone else acknowledged it to be a fact.

In the discussion about the film *A Long Term Solution* someone from the prison service remarked that this was a mistake. A mistake! What kind of mistake?

An oversight—a nineteen-month oversight of their most notorious prisoner? Inconceivable. It could only be a premeditated attempt to crush a man's mind. As a society we have abolished capital punishment. The mind is precious and sacred, and indeed more so than the body.

To preserve the latter and then give anyone the power to try to destroy the former is barbaric. We know that such prolonged periods of solitary confinement occur in authoritarian and totalitarian systems. I never knew that it could, and actually did, happen within the British penal system. It must never be allowed to happen again.

The story was about a swaggering, insensitive young hoodlum that anyone who lived in the slums of Glasgow or any other city would recognise at first sight. This particular specimen also had what the military would describe as "leadership qualities". He was a brute, or at any rate more brutish than his compatriots. Maybe in his patch of jungle he had to be, to keep the mantle of leadership.

The scenario was based on the life of James Boyle. It told us very little of what made him a psychopathic killer. It showed us nothing of the environment of the special unit at Barlinnie wherein this man developed, according to all reports, into a highly intelligent, rational, sensitive and compassionate human being, and where his latent artistic talent found expression.

Films about two-bit mobsters and gang warfare and the unbroken spirit of the tough guy when he goes "inside" are 10 a penny. Hollywood used Cagney, Bogart, Garfield and many others to flog this theme to death. If this was the only period in Boyle's life to be portrayed then "Legs Diamond" or the "Kray Twins" or even "Cut The Lugs Riley" from Govan would have provided better material.

It was like filming *The Birdman of Alcatraz* without the birds. What was it all about? It wasn't really about Boyle, for all the things that make him significant were absent. I came to the conclusion that it was a film about the sub-culture of Glasgow slumdom.

If so it was totally lacking in balance. This "culture" had many strands. For example there were many non-violent groups whose exploits evoked mirth and respect within the community.

One such group climbed into the local greyhound track and greased four of the starting traps laid out for the next day's racing. Hoping their handiwork would pass unnoticed they backed the dog occupying the ungreased trap in the first race.

As the gates flew open, four dogs fell flat on their faces and the other had an unassailable lead at the first bend. They collected their "winnings" and disappeared.

The hard men, on the other hand, were looked upon as "headbangers", as scroungers, often tapping rather than loaning money. Generally considered to be a penny short of the shilling: in other words, somewhat mentally defective. They were not the object of reverence, except in the main from youngsters who were similarly disadvantaged.

Some of these young tearaways grew up into fairly decent citizens and neighbours. Others grew into old tearaways, drunken bums and street brawlers, shunned rather than feared, and certainly not respected. The sub-culture also had its amazing humour which provides even to this day the material for most contemporary Scottish comedians. Within this humour the hard men are lampooned.

The Glasgow slums were terrible—a source of disease that could cripple mind as well as body. They were also a testament to the human spirit. They were communities that shared. Life had to be lived. They could laugh and joke and sing. There were strong bonds of friendship, mutual help and even love.

The environment did produce fighters, people who fought for an end to the squalor and degradation. This film portrayed a people and a community cowed by a pimply-faced hooligan. That aspect is an insult to people, and there are many, whom I knew, who lived and loved in the Gorbals of that time.

All the pertinent questions about Boyle were ignored in the film. Profound, important questions about the human spirit, about the effect of the environment on a person's outlook, and many other aspects left out by its concentration on one period of his life.

The trouble is that Jimmy Boyle is no longer viewed as an individual but as an issue. There are those who believe in "bad men". In their book Boyle is a bad man and cannot possibly be anything else. They believe in predestination. Environment has nothing to do with it, according to their dogma.

Others seem to be able to live with the thoughts of a man who is damned. Their minds can encompass damnation but the thought of redemption, that the damned man might have redeemed himself, seems to be beyond their conceptual powers. Those people who want to introduce what amounts to torture into our penal code, against violent criminals, do so because deep in their subconscious they have problems somewhat akin to those they would like to punish.

On the other side, among many well-intentioned and helpful friends, the Special Unit has suffered from being "adopted" by those carpetbaggers of good causes who search for a new social issue like entomologists trying to add to their bizarre collection of rare insects.

Only recently I heard from a television director sympathetic to the Special Unit that he was present when a cultural party from the United States, part of a commercial tourist package, had on its schedule a visit to the unit to discuss with the inmates "the nature of art".

This unit has taken our worst and most vicious criminals, has treated them as human beings, and they have responded. Their success rate of rehabilitation has been phenomenal. They will certainly have failures.

A belief that within every human being there is a spark of humanity which must be nurtured if possible into a flame of compassion is the very essence of a civilised society. Without that belief we can all become beasts.

I expected this to emerge, albeit implicitly, from this film. It didn't. Maybe my expectations were too high.

Glasgow Herald 21 February 1981

Why Meehan Should Not Have To Prove His Innocence Again

HOW'S this for a theory—42 people could have been involved in the robbery that led to a brutal killing in the town of Ayr 13 years ago. Two were on the inside, the other 40 whose skills covered every conceivable felonious need were probably waiting round the corner in a privately hired bus in case their services were required.

There is, of course, no evidence for this theory just as there is no evidence for Lord Hunter's that four men might have been involved. Yet his Lordship seriously advances this hypothesis and explicitly suggests the still possible guilt of Mr Paddy Meehan.

Put aside for a moment the fact that terms of the inquiry specifically excluded his Lordship from making a judgment on Meehan's guilt or innocence, which in the circumstances was hardly surprising as he has already received a royal pardon.

Simply think of this—Mr Meehan now has to prove to the public at large that he is not guilty of murder. The presumption of innocence until proven guilty, a fundamental cornerstone of elementary justice in any democratic society, has been cast to the winds by the Hunter Report.

This is not a legal technicality that can be left to legal technicians. It affects all of us. Once this principle has been abandoned the door is then open to smears, discrimination, and the abuses and paraphernalia of the witch-hunt. It is a scandal. I have never met Meehan and have no particular axe to grind. It is a matter of justice. If there isn't the evidence to prove a person guilty of murder, then no one has the moral or legal authority to publicly impugn his innocence and that includes High Court Judges.

It would appear that law lords in Scotland can do what they like when placed in charge of an inquiry. They apparently can ignore the remit or venture beyond it and go where ere their fancy might lead. With hindsight it is somewhat surprising that his Lordship in this instance didn't take the opportunity to express in the report his views on the current controversy as to the legal powers of water bailiffs in Scotland, or give his opinions about Jock Wallace's training methods on the Gullane sands.

On a lighter note but still concerned with the majesty of the law, let me tell you another true story. It goes back to the days of the old burgh councils. In this town somewhere in Argyllshire the ruling party decided that at the next local elections they would give a safe seat to an old stalwart or hack, as political opponents would put it, as a reward for his work over the years for the "cause".

He was duly elected and the party decided that as he was getting on a bit, in years that is, they would make him a magistrate right away. Within a matter of days the old boy, who I should add was not very bright, had to stand in or should it be sit in, for a younger but more experienced magistrate.

The first case to come before him was the old town worthy charged for the umpteenth time with being drunk and disorderly. He pled guilty as always. The old magistrate was very excited and sought advice from a depute town clerk, a lawyer by trade, who always sat to the right of the bench and kept the incumbent informed on matters of legal etiquette and detail.

Out of the side of his mouth the old boy hissed to his mentor: "What shall I give him?" The depute town clerk replied: "Give him the maximum." The magistrate responded by sitting upright and looking most magisterial. He peered at the accused who was now, of course, convicted, cleared his throat and then intoned "Your long record of similar convictions leaves me with no alternative but to impose the maximum penalty under the law. I sentence you to death."

The old drunk whose only thought a few seconds previous had been how soon he could get a drink, looked up at the magistrate, saw his unyielding face, then fainted. Elsewhere in the court pandemonium reigned. The depute town clerk had by this time lost his cool and was shouting: "You silly old bachelor (this is as near as I can get to what he actually said. It is after all a family column and he was indeed an old bachelor). You silly old country yokel—it's £20 or 14 days."

By this time someone had helped the drunk to his feet where he slouched and sipped a glass of water and with eyes downcast awaited his fate. The magistrate was meanwhile trying to retrieve the situation and threatened to clatter the depute town clerk with his gavel or charge him with contempt.

He called the court to order and looked once again at the hapless victim in the dock. "This Court," he proclaimed, "as an act of clemency reduces your sentence to a fine of £5 or 10 days in prison with 30 days to pay."

Now I am opposed to capital punishment or the death sentence, yet honesty compels me to admit that on this occasion it sort of worked. The old drunk became teetotal. On the other hand the depute town clerk developed a drink problem and after a few years working with the old magistrate he started to look like Herbert Lom playing Inspector Clouseau's superior in the Pink Panther movies. The magistrate to his dying day was known, behind his back mind you, as "The Hanging Judge".

Glasgow Herald 9 August 1982

Alarming Pronouncements By Judges On Rape

A MAN who twice raped a six-year-old girl was sentenced to four months imprisonment in the Leeds Crown Court. He actually served 25 days. Bank robbers can get 25 years for a crime that I consider less despicable.

Last week in summing up another rape case, Judge David Wild said: "Women who say no do not always mean no. It is not just a question of saying no. It is a question of how she says it, how she shows and makes it clear. If she doesn't want it, she only has to keep her legs shut and she would not get it without force and there would be marks of force being used."

I suppose, according to this logic, the best evidence of rape is when the woman resists until she is battered near to death. It would certainly make it easier for the courts.

Over the years pronouncements by some Judges on the subject of rape have given cause for alarm. Their approach to women is like that of a barrack room philistine. I seem to recall that one Judge actually admonished a rapist because imprisonment might have jeopardised his career prospects in the regular Army.

I think that too many of our Judges come from too narrow a social base. In 1978 about 80% of the Judges of the High Court, the Court of Appeal, and the House of Lords had all gone to the same few schools and then onto Oxford and Cambridge. This could imply that the selection owes more to the "Old Boys Network" than to either excellence of mind or professional expertise.

It would be interesting to know how many women or coloured Judges there are in this country?

Glasgow Herald 13 December 1982

Crime: Imagine What It Must Feel Like To Be 18 With No Hope

MENTION law and order, and like the conditioned reflex of Pavlov's renowned dog, some people start to salivate or even foam at the mouth.

A few years ago I witnessed this phenomenon during a debate at the Labour Party Conference. It surprised me, for banshee howling about an "eye for an eye and a tooth for a tooth" was something I associated with the conferences of that other political party. It's just occurred to me, that if society really lived by this precept then those involved in the manufacture of white sticks and dentures would be on to a good thing.

In this particular debate, some delegates wanted to smash all criminals into submission or even oblivion. Absolutely typical of the vigilante species and wracked by emotional spasms they offered ideal raw material for the script of a Charles Bronson movie.

Others came to the rostrum and argued that criminals were simply the products of capitalism. End it, they implied, and criminals and crime and the need for prisons and the police force would disappear. A pity no one told Stalin.

In general it was a debate not to be touched with the proverbial barge pole. A great time was being had by one and all and anyone injecting a tincture of reality would have been resented as a churlish spoilsport. Like most debates on this matter it was absolutely unrelated to reality.

In the real world, if you came across a group of young men booting almost unto death some old fellow, it would be most unlikely and certainly unhelpful if you simply raised with all concerned that the assailants were probably the demoralised products of a bad social system. Even if the elderly victim, above the thud of the boots both heard and was convinced by your argument, the likelihood of him responding by exonerating his tormentors because he now realised that it was in fact "capitalism that was actually putting in the boot" is to put it mildly highly improbable.

He would expect you to try to stop the assault, by whatever means were necessary, including the use of force. You would want these young thugs kept in custody, at least in the short term, for the protection of other vulnerable citizens.

However, to view such a complex question as law and order exclusively in terms of punishment and physical restraint is equally ludicrous and ignores the vitally important question of the causality of criminal behaviour. This would be like treating measles by scrubbing vigorously at the spots and thus exposing a mass of frayed nerve ends. A cure much worse than the original sickness.

Criminal statistics as Mrs Thatcher found out last week must always be treated and interpreted with care and caution. For example, the London Metropolitan Police for the first time ever published the racial identity of those involved in street offences such as muggings. Not surprisingly, if you know contemporary London, it showed a high percentage of black youths were convicted for this type of offence, which accounts for something like 3% of the total crime rate in the capital. Fraud amounts to 5%. A racial breakdown of those involved in fraud would show a preponderance of whites.

Would this then imply that white Anglo-Saxons are more fraudulent or bigger frauds than other ethnic groups? Hardly, it probably means that in our society blacks are less likely to be in positions of responsibility with access to the goodies or in charge of the cash box.

Similarly petty crime will be more prevalent in Drumchapel than Bearsden. Does this mean that the Scottish working class has an inbuilt genetic propensity for such crimes which is absent from the make up of our middle classes? The truth is more prosaic. A business man is unlikely to "do in" his gas meter. Apart from the fact that he probably doesn't have one, he will also be inclined to view the sums involved as paltry.

On the other hand the businessman is much more likely to abscond with his good-looking secretary and the company funds to the sunny climes of South America. The unemployed bricklayer is less prone to such a crime for he lacks not so much the imagination as the opportunity. For starters it's difficult to run away with your secretary when you haven't got one.

Let's take another angle. A youngster in Bearsden is on average much more likely to enter the professions of commerce and business at managerial level than his counterpart in Drumchapel. He will also more likely be a partcipant in such sports as tennis, squash, skiing, horse riding and sailing.

The home will probably have a piano and he is more liable to have been to music lessons. These and other seemingly small things will cumulatively mean a much better quality and expectation of life as compared to the youth of Drumchapel.

The current recession has of course affected everyone but to the already deprived youngster it has transformed prospects already bleak into a hopeless and forlorn future. And here in my opinion is the most critical factor. A society must provide its people but particularly its youth with the hope that life can be better.

This is the psychological basis by which society secures from its citizens respect for its laws. In a democratic society law and order can emanate only from the willing consent of the people. If significant numbers become convinced that the society offers them no hope then that society's law and order will cease to have any moral authority in their minds.

Just try and imagine what it must be like to be 18 and to feel that your entire life is to be one of unemployment, interspersed with brief bouts of work at various unskilled, menial, low-paid jobs. It must literally be soul destroying. Youth has a right to dream but how can we ask, or have we even the right to ask, these youngsters to uphold the values of a society that has so cruelly dashed their dreams.

Unless our country, and that means you and me, can bring hope to our youth then social disintegration especially in our cities is a distinct possibility within this decade. In this context, talk of Borstals and prison regimes and floggings and the death penalty is irrelevant. There is no judicial solution.

The crime which must be tackled urgently is that which condemns our young citizens to a stunted and diminished life either through an accident of birth or because some politicians are more obsessed with political dogma than people. In the midst of the current controversies some fundamental truths need re-statement. In a democracy we live by the rule of law to which no one is superior including the police. The recent speech by the chief constable of Manchester was dangerous coming from one of the country's top policemen.

Respect for laws stems from consent and not coercion. This indeed is the very cornerstone of civilised society expressed in the rejection of arbitrary power by a single person or group and its replacement by rule or legal principles by which we agree to conduct our lives and business. The law and its appendages should be stripped of all mystique. The police do not exist, as some would have it, to police the community but to act on behalf of the community in upholding those laws endorsed by the community.

The actual law itself, for far too many, is shrouded in mystery and is also invoked as if it sprung from some divine authority. God, with the possible exception of the 10 commandments, has had nothing much to do with framing legal systems. Laws are man-made and can sometimes reflect the greed and self-interest of specific groups.

There have been bad laws as in Nazi Germany. Hitler after all was very strong on law and order. On his law and his order.

In Britain the main corpus of law as it affects ordinary people, in their everyday life, is tried and tested and enjoys overwhelming approval because it seems on balance to be reasonable. However, these concepts cannot be abstracted from social circumstances which, if allowed to decline, can undermine the broad base of public consent without which no law is operable within a democratic society.

I will leave the last word with Lord Macaulay speaking about consent or force in Government (on October 10th, 1831) in the British House of Commons: "Be bold; be firm; defy intimidation; let the law have its course. Sir, we have heard this blustering before, and we know in what it ended. It is the blustering of little men, whose lot has fallen on a great crisis. Xerxes scourging the waves, Canute commanding the waves to recede from his footstool, were but types of the folly.

"The law has no eyes; the law has no hands; the law is nothing—nothing but a piece of paper printed by the king's printer, with the king's arms at the top—till public opinion breathes the breath of life into the dead letter."

Glasgow Herald 22 March 1982

Why Does The Law Protect The Ritual Of A Cub Hunt?

LAST week a gang of youths in the East End of Glasgow scoured the neighbourhood collecting all the kittens they could find and then took them to an enclosed back court. Dogs that they had already goaded into a frenzy were let loose and literally tore the little kittens to pieces. The youths seemed to enjoy the carnage and even permitted young children to watch the horrendous spectacle.

They have been charged by the police and will come up for trial within the next few weeks. Like me, you no doubt wonder what kind of monsters these young men must be. What a reflection on our society that it can produce sick minds that actually derive pleasure from such wanton cruelty. At the very least the court should keep them in custody pending a psychiatric report.

The foregoing is fiction. It didn't happen. But last Monday a letter appeared in the *Glasgow Herald* explaining the ritual of a cub hunt. The vixen is chased away, the young fox cubs are dug up and unearthed. Unable to run off like the adults the fox cubs are set upon by a pack of hounds. Adults and children encircle the massacre and kick back any cub that tries to escape. Policemen are present to protect not the cubs, but these sick human beings as they go about their fiendish business. Such cruelties are obscene to contemplate let alone perpetuate.

No one, including the police, has tried to refute the allegations as contained in that letter. If it is true then some questions must be asked.

Why is cruelty against animals by youths in, let us say, Easterhouse deemed illegal and considered quite rightly to be outrageous, and yet precisely the same kind of cruelty by well-heeled adults in the Houston and Linlithgow areas condoned and even protected by the law? The law in this instance is clearly an ass and should be changed.

Society must be able to protect fox cubs and other forms of animal life from the ravages of such demented individuals. We must also be compassionate and think of how we must help those fellow human beings. To enjoy such cruelties is a form of perversion. A malady of the mind. The condition is surely not genetic and yet it is equally difficult to comprehend how these communities could spawn such mentalities. Do they look normal? Surely such fiendishness must have a physical manifestation. Do they have fangs? Coming from a pacific, well-adjusted, civilised area like Govan, I just wouldn't know.

Glasgow Herald 31 August 1981

Throw New Light On Police Powers

IN a city centre on a crowded street a car is caught up in a traffic jam. In the car there are two men and a woman. Suddenly, without any warning, a group of unidentifiable men with handguns start to pump bullets into the car. The driver, hit many times, falls out of the car and slumps on to the roadway.

I can see it in my mind's eye. We can all see, for this is a typical Hollywood scenario for a Mafia operation. We would know that it couldn't be the police, for even in trigger-happy America the coppers are supposed to shout out things like "Freeze" before being allowed to blast away like Babyface Nelsons.

According to Starsky and Hutch and a host of other screen upholders of law and order American-style, you then make the suspects lean with outstretched arms on the car and legs well apart, then you frisk them. You then slip on the "bracelets" and take them down to the precinct for questioning.

Presumably this sensible ritual is designed to safeguard everyone—the innocent, the police and the guilty, from an unnecessary, premature death.

So there is no doubt, given the circumstances as described in the opening paragraph, this would have to be a gangland job, probably in Chicago or Las Vegas or in some Sicilian town like Palermo.

To the great alarm of all who value the special standards of policing associated with the United Kingdom this took place in London last weekend and those who fired the shots were policemen.

The police thought the driver of the car was David Martin, who is on the run having escaped from Marlborough Street Magistrates Court on Christmas Eve. He is accused of attempting to murder a policeman. In fact the driver of the car was 25-year-old Stephen Waldorf, a television film editor.

Some of the reports lament that this was a terrible case of mistaken identity as indeed it was, which tends to imply that if the driver had been Martin then the conduct of the police would have been justified.

This is a terribly dangerous attitude. The man has yet to be tried. Even more to the point, if he was a convicted runaway criminal he cannot in a civilised society be considered a suitable target for shooting practice. We cannot shoot human beings, though they may be villains, as if they were mad dogs. And, just for the record, we do not try to terminate the lives of mad dogs in public places.

As I write, young Stephen Waldorf lies in hospital in a critical condition, when you read this I hope and pray he is out of danger.

There will be reports and probably an inquiry. In the last few years the Metropolitan Police have had more inquiries etc., than Liz Taylor has had husbands. Any benefits or improvements from these deliberations are difficult to discern.

The whole question of the powers of the police are bedevilled by the politically entrenched positions taken up by some people. There are those on the Right who would give the policeman on the beat a bazooka to intimidate drunks at closing time in Brighton if requested by the police federation. There are some on the Left who view every policeman as a neo-fascist. They usually come from well-heeled, upper, middle-class backgrounds and consider it trendy to refer to the police in terms such as "Pigs".

There is the story of the shipyard worker during the campaign to save the yards on Upper Clyde who was asked by an earnest Left-wing young lady doing an article for a university magazine if he had during his years of struggle for the oppressed ever been picked up by the "Fuzz"? The old guy looked at her and said: "Naw hen, but I imagine it would be sore."

To say there are some swine in the police force is not to denigrate the police. There are swine among clergymen, lawyers, accountants, politicians, journalists, shipyard workers, and university lecturers. I knew a school teacher whose swinishness was such that it was a gross insult on the poor respectable pig to call him a swine.

For a whole number of reasons the police in a democracy must be answerable to the institutions of democracy. Not to the Government of the day but to the structures of our democratic heritage.

I go further and will argue that the hallmark of a mature democracy will always be the extent to which the forces of law and order are themselves subject to the principles of law and order as decided democratically by the people. Where these agencies are above the law or are not subject to democratic control then you have a fairly accurate definition of a police state.

The real worry about the shootings in London is not whether the officer in charge or the policemen involved made some errors, or misjudged the situation, but how many policemen are there with access to firearms, which, no matter the restraints imposed, are a licence to kill.

In certain circumstances with terrorists and armed thugs it is unreasonable and impossible to expect policemen to confront them with truncheons.

It is all a question of control and accountability. It is now widely suspected that there are too many policemen who might think they belong to some elite force not subject to the usual norms of control within the force.

I have greater trust in the judgment of the ordinary policeman on the beat in a crisis than in the snap reaction of some specially-trained operator whose para-normal training and para-normal occupation just might create some para-normal behaviour and thinking. This elitism could breed the John Wayne mentality at least as expressed on celluloid.

I, for one, do not want scapegoats from among those who were actually involved in this particular incident. It is Parliament and Members of Parliament and the Government who must be held responsible. MPs must insist on a full parliamentary debate about the number of special groups, their powers, who is in charge of those policemen issued with firearms, are they subject to democratic control by someone or some committee acting on behalf of Parliament, and, most important of all, are special groups necessary?

Members of the police force could be given special training. Enough, so trained, that in a place like London sufficient could be on stand-by each week for a day to deal with anything that might arise requiring their special services. The rest of the week they should be on normal police duties, which is more likely to bring them into contact with the ordinary public, and, so to speak, help keep their feet on the ground.

You see, there is a lot of evidence to suggest that in areas such as espionage and counter-espionage and with those who are always dealing with the real hard nut, violent villain or terrorist, that after a while the methods and even the values of those involved can become blurred. "The hard-headed realist" will argue in justification: "You must fight fire with fire." If everyone fought fire with fire, then we would all be incendiarists and the fire brigade would have to be recruited from arsonists.

Mr Pitt, Liberal MP for Croydon North-West, whose general remarks on this issue were excellent, observed that: "London is not Belfast or Chicago." I can accept that law and order in Chicago doesn't exactly come within his remit as a British MP. Belfast does. Is it now the attitude of Members of Parliament that standards for the protection of British citizens totally unacceptable in London are somehow acceptable for Belfast?

You know, what we really need is an Inquiry into the performance of Parliament. Though there already is such an Inquiry. It is called a General Election. Unfortunately too many of us take if far too lightly.

Glasgow Herald January 1983

Shoot First, Then . . .

THERE was this bloke being driven through London. With him in the car were two others. They got caught in a traffic jam.

Suddenly a man approached with a pistol in his hand. He shot one of the tyres, thus immobilising the vehicle.

He then started pumping bullets in the general direction of the bloke. He's quickly joined by his partner who started doing the same thing.

It was like the shoot-out at the OK Corral transferred to London . . . with one slight difference. In this particular shoot-out, only one side was armed.

The bloke was hit by five bullets. He slumped and fell face down in the road, half in and half out of the car.

As he lay there, one of his assailants proceeded to lash at him with the butt of his revolver with such force as to fracture his skull.

Before the bloke became unconscious he must have been wondering what the heck was going on.

His attackers couldn't be robbers. Robbers stick a gun at you and say something like "Your money or your life".

The police are duty bound to give some kind of variant on the theme "freeze" or "stick 'em up", and then one of them spreadeagles you against the car and frisks you.

There could only be one explanation—for some unknown reason, someone had taken out a "contract" on him.

These guys must be paid assassins. There could be no other explanation.

Ah, but there was. These men were members of the London Metropolitan Police.

They had thought the bloke was a dangerous criminal which presumably, in their eyes, justified everything.

The next time I'm in London I'll have to be careful.

You never know, they might mistake me for Lord Lucan.

Daily Record 24 June 1983

CHRISTIANS AND MARTYRS

Too Many Protestants, Too Many Catholics, Not Enough Christians

A FEW years ago, my two eldest daughters rushed excitedly into the house. They had come from the local church youth committee. Their Saturday night dance had become so popular that the doors were being closed at nine o'clock. The proposal from the elders was that the Catholic youngsters who were attending should be banned.

My daughters opposed the proposal. The committee threatened to resign unless the proposal was withdrawn. It was. They asked my opinion. Had they been reasonable? Being very moved, I mumbled agreement. Whatever our deficiencies as parents my wife and I had children who were non-bigots. That's something to be proud of in Glasgow.

After Hampden, the Scottish "Establishment" once again trots out its usual rag-bag of phoney excuses. Not enough police—too much booze—inadequate caging, euphemistically called fencing. Anything but face the truth.

Were there more police at Wembley? Were the Arsenal and West Ham supporters all stone-cold sober? Of course not. The difference was that at Wembley there was an absence of the blind, unreasoning, beast-like bigotry that is the real social cancer in our community.

The drunken morons who invaded the field on Saturday are a consequence, not a cause. Symptoms, not the disease. They are the demoralised dregs of the Clydeside working-class. In their own way victims, vicious victims attracted to the frenzied atmosphere of an "Old Firm" game.

To hold the clubs responsible is also to hypocritically seek scapegoats. Of course, they are not blameless. Rangers in particular are caught in a trap of their own making. Never having employed a Catholic, they can hardly lecture their supporters on the virtue of religious tolerance. Rae Simpson and his colleagues on the present board inherited this situation. I believe they genuinely want to end it. Without going into detail, the practical problems of doing so are immense, not least getting the first Catholic player prepared to face the "music".

Anyway, Celtic have employed Protestants for decades. This hasn't stopped bigots from describing a Celtic team that included a majority of Protestants as the "Pope's Eleven".

If the problem was merely a football game, then how simple the solution would be. The argument about banning this fixture would then be worthy of consideration. It is a very much more serious problem. I know it. Politicians know it. Businessmen know it. Trades union leaders know it. Church leaders know it.

We have too many Protestants, too many Catholics, and not enough Christians. Hatred, intolerance, and bigotry are not compatible with the teachings of Christ as contained in the New Testament. Some time ago the Rev. James Currie was going to lead Christmas carol singing at Ibrox. He was persuaded not to do so.

I privately expressed the opinion to Jimmy that he was likely to hear some unusual lyrics from the terracing that had nothing in common with the sentiment of peace on earth, good will to all men.

Yet shouldn't the leaders of the Protestant churches, either from Ibrox Park, the pulpits, TV, or any other platform, launch an attack on those bigots who profess to be part of their community and tell them bluntly that the hatred in their hearts is the hallmark of the anti-Christ? We should treat bigots as pariahs.

Surely the vicious anti-Christian mentality of many Celtic supporters puts them in the deepest spiritual sense outwith what Catholics consider to be the Mother Church. A Catholic whose heart is full of hate for fellow humans must be committing a blasphemy if he goes to receive the sacraments of his church.

It is many years since I last attended a Rangers versus Celtic match—for reasons which should be obvious. I do recall one episode from the distant past. A Celtic supporter urged his team to "get stuck into these Protestant bastards". His attention was drawn to the presence of a priest just behind him. He apologised to the clergyman for his bad language. Neither seemed to think it necessary that he should apologise for his bad and hateful thoughts.

The events like those last Saturday are like intermittent eruptions from the active volcano of bigotry that is a part of our pattern of life in the West of Scotland.

It is my contention that the essence of the problem lies not with Saturday's drunken hooligans but in apparently more "respectable" areas of our community.

As racism in the Deep South of the USA was expressed most overtly and obscenely by the lynch gangs of the "poor white trash", and yet was really sustained by the power structures of the ultra respectable, not to say sophisticated, in that society.

So here in Scotland the open practitioners of the "Billy and Dan" syndrome are our equivalent of the "poor white trash". With growing unemployment, their ranks could increase. For some it is good that the most deprived have some other group on which to vent their frustrations and spleen. It diverts them from thinking about the real cause of their barren lives.

The real problem is that in the West of Scotland religious sectarian bigotry is given a certain mantle of respectability to a degree that exists nowhere else on the mainland of the United Kingdom. It's the only place in Britain where matrimony involving two white Caucasian Christians can be described as a "mixed marriage".

Denis Law once told me that he didn't know he was a Protestant until he went to England and met footballers from Glasgow. It's the only place in the UK, outside Ulster, where the religious denomination of a candidate can be in certain constituencies, a marginal factor in elections. I have seen trade union positions being contested on a straight Catholic/Protestant basis.

It's all swept under the carpet. A conspiracy of silence descends. If we don't talk about it—it might go away is the attitude of many well-intentioned people. Bigotry thrives in darkness—the darkness of ignorance. In the light of reasoned and open debate, it shrivels up. I know from my involvement with some of the clergy and active laity of Protestant and Catholic communities that many are prepared to raise their voices and fight the bigots in their midst. I pray that Saturday's riot may prove to be a catalyst.

Theological differences cannot be allowed any longer to obscure the more fundamental Christian commitment of both sections. I appeal to our Catholic friends to consider some form of integration in our school system, even by defining those areas they wish to preserve but which might still be consistent with all our children going to the same school.

Tiny tots playing happily together for years should, on the day they start school, set out hand-in-hand to face this new adventure in the same school.

It's true that separate schools didn't create this bigotry, but they do not help to destroy it.

No one is born a bigot. Every child is born innocent. Bigotry is a social product. The teenagers of last Saturday are products of bigoted parents, or a bigoted social environment, or a bigoted local church, or all three.

Let's have an all-out drive against bigotry. Television warnings against smoking and drinking are sometimes brilliantly contrived. Why not similar warnings against bigots and bigotry, which are damaging to our social health?

A spirit of true ecumenism among the Christian community will also reach out to embrace our fellow citizens of all religions and cultures. Tolerance and mutual respect are necessary within communities and between them.

Next week at Hampden when Scotland play England, whenever the mindless morons start up their chant of "If you hate the English, clap your hands", it would be nice if just for once all the rest of us booed the bampots, not the English. So a week on Saturday, if you hear a solitary boo at this juncture, you will know who it is.

Glasgow Herald 15 May 1980

The Hills Are Alive To The Sound Of Hatred

IN other times or in another place Senator Joe McCarthy would have been recognised for what he was, a cheap little two-bit chiseller. Couched in the breathless prose of the libertarian private eye, so often played by Humphrey Bogart, this evaluation of the man would nowadays find wide if not universal acceptance.

He was the sort of guy from whom you wouldn't buy a second-hand chamber pot, even if recommended by Arthur Negus. A liar who invented a fictitious heroic war record for electoral purposes. Yet for a few years he was the uncrowned king of America. As chairman of the Congressional Committee on Un-American Activities, he unleashed a witch hunt that terrorised millions and destroyed thousands.

The United States was suddenly pitchforked back into the Middle Ages. People bore false witness against their neighbours and colleagues. An hysteria gripped the nation. Some would "indict" others to prove they were "loyal Americans". When reason flees, madness and the dark forces of ignorance prevail.

Arthur Miller, the doyen of American dramatists, was one of the few to emerge from these years with immense dignity. He defied McCarthy and wrote *The Crucible*.

McCarthy's name is now a term of contempt. A few months ago there was talk of Labour MPs being asked to sign or take an oath of "loyalty". This was condemned as McCarthyism and immediately sunk without trace. This play on the other hand is revered by all who cherish freedom.

It is based on the witch hunt that engulfed the village of Salem, Massachusetts in the year 1692. The scenario was fundamentally similar to McCarthy's Hearings. A group of girls led by an amoral young woman is whipped into an hysteria which is then interpreted as the influence of the devil. Under her prompting they point the finger at other members of the community as being the source of this evil.

The accused are then given the choice—admit to being a witch and be reprieved or be killed. Understandably many are tempted. John Proctor, the upstanding young farmer, actually signs a "confession" then tears it up, choosing to die with his wife rather than live with this abasement of his integrity and intellect. Glory, Glory Hallelujah. These are the people who help distinguish us from the beasts.

Miller also used this play to revile dogmatism. Absolute certainty is the mark of the fool, the posture of the fanatic, or the guise of the charlatan. He is right. I know of no large-scale atrocity perpetrated by consciously evil men. Always these monstrous crimes against humanity were committed by the self-righteous. Those convinced beyond all doubt that they and they alone were licensed to act on behalf of God, or were the custodians of some secular truth that made them the true agents of history.

This play was aimed at McCarthyism. It is equally valid if applied to Stalinism. The Moscow trials of the 1930s with the fabricated evidence, false confessions, torture and consequential "legalised" murder were all essentials similar to the medieval witch trials.

This play also raised for me once again the horrendous form that Christian fundamentalism can sometimes take in parts of the United States. "Christians" who hate Blacks, Jews, Catholics and any other Christian who doesn't accept their doctrine. They also hate science, homosexuals, literature except approved "classics" such as *Black Bess* and their own tracts.

In fact they hate everyone who doesn't share their hates. They seem to believe that the injunction in the bible to "Love thy neighbour" was a misprint.

Current Account was about religious extremists in our own midst. Most of the Protestant Loyalists on the programme appeared to worship Dr Ian Paisley who it is interesting to note obtained his doctorate in divinity from a theological university in the United States.

George Reid, the presenter wisely let them talk uninterruptedly. Words and phrases like "scum" and "back to the gutter where they belong" abounded. The team filmed a meeting of IRA supporters on a piece of wasteground in Blackhill while the Loyalists watched from adjacent high ground. The hills were alive to the sound of hatred.

It was interesting to note the similarities between the Protestant Loyalist and Catholic Republican marching bands. Both cavorted around in ridiculous mincing steps with guys knocking hell out of bass drums as if they were surrogates for the Pope and King Billy. All were working class. Not a cheep from Bearsden or Kilmacolm. Maybe bigotry is expressed more discreetly among the middle class.

The overall feeling was of people who knew nothing about Christianity, whose "religion" was in fact a form of tribalism, determined through an accident of birth, which simply codified prejudices and gave them something to hate and someone to look down on.

How ironic that the Christ, whose message of love, tolerance, and forgiveness should be in all our minds this weekend should have His name invoked by those who represent its very antithesis.

Glasgow Herald 18 April 1981

Why Hold A Thanksgiving Service?

AS someone who believed that Britain had really no alternative but to send a task force to the South Atlantic, I nevertheless find all this talk about a Thanksgiving Service for the Falklands war to be deeply disturbing. What is God to be thanked for? Is he to be thanked for the war or for a British victory? We are told that God made man in his image. That presumably applies to the Argentinians. If he is to be thanked for a British victory then he must also have willed an Argentinian defeat.

114

Should they then be organising a No Thanksgiving To You Service. Was it the Lord's finger that directed the torpedo which sank the General Belgrano and caused the deaths of so many Argentinian youths? And who pray tell me was guiding the Exocet missile that cost so many British lives?

Christ is proclaimed as the prince of peace so for Christ's sake stop this hypocrisy.

Robert Burns once saw some clergymen participating in a march to celebrate a military victory and wrote.

> "Ye hypocrites! are these your pranks?
> To murder men, and give God thanks?
> Desist for shame! Proceed no further:
> God won't accept your thanks for Murder."

Apparently someone suggested that in the "service" a prayer should be said in Spanish for the Argentinian dead and Mrs Thatcher dismissed the idea disdainfully. If true, this is even more disturbing.

The chap who commanded our land forces in the Falklands returned to Britain last week. On television we saw him being greeted by a band playing "Jesus Christ Superstar".

This whole assumption that God is an ex-officio member of our armed forces is a blasphemy. Clergymen should only participate in a service of thanks that the fighting is over and prayers offered for those who died on both sides. Politicians who want something more should be told to stop using the Church for political rallies.

Glasgow Herald 26 July 1982

Opus Dei

STAN KENTON, the American band leader, was decidedly lacking in modesty. This showed in his choice of titles. Some of his records feature compositions called "Artistry In Rhythm", "Artistry In Blues" and the gloriously egomaniacal "Concerto To End All Concertos". When I first heard of Opus Dei, I thought it was Kenton's reply to "Opus One", the big band swing number by Si Oliver. It is, as everyone now knows, a Catholic organisation which grew to some prominence in Franco Spain and is considered by many in the church, including priests and bishops, to be unacceptably authoritarian.

The Pope is to give this organisation a personal prelature which seems to involve an enhanced status. The theological implications of this we can leave to our Catholic friends as it concerns them directly. There is however something else about this society that does intrigue me. Members of Opus Dei subject themselves to a remarkably strict regime which includes, so we are told, physical self-abasement by the use of a lash and a spiked chain.

Now if someone was to set up a club or form a closed society in Glasgow

115

where such implements were to be used to induce pain, then we all know how it would be described—kinky. Followers of the Marquis de Sade and tuppence ha'penny masochists would be queuing up to join. What I really want to know is this; is God appeased by such practices?

Glasgow Herald 30 August 1982

The Reluctant Revolutionary

HISTORY is festooned with reasonable, well-meaning reformers who end up as reluctant revolutionaries through the rigidity of those who defend the status quo. Such was Martin Luther, born 500 years ago this week.

Augustinian monk, theologian and biblical scholar, Luther developed from his scriptural studies a Roman Catholic critique of Roman Catholicism. He anticipated a dispute within a single Church rather than a war between separate Churches.

Luther proclaimed that divine authority resided solely in the gospels; that the human institutions of the Church in Rome had no such authority unless they were in accord with the gospels. He argued that the Church was in error and in many aspects corrupt. Yet he saw himself as a loyal member of that Church and wished to proclaim the gospel as a member of it.

That was not to be. This devout Roman Catholic was to become the first Protestant leader of what became a revolution but of which the original and limited aims were explicit in the title. Reformation.

In the weeks ahead, we can expect a Lutheran avalanche. Historical theological re-assessment will cascade on to our screens and the pages of our "quality newspapers". Many will claim him as their very own. Such is the fate of great historical figures, their theme often cynically manipulated by opportunists to buttress and justify their own positions.

Against such a background, I urge you to watch *Heretic—The Making of Martin Luther*, a filmed drama that tells us more about the man than any documentary.

Luther's life has all the ingredients of a cracking tale: innocence, corruption, courage, cruelty, death threats, kidnapping, courtly intrigue and, in the midst of it all, the hero, a monk in search of human salvation. A quest that unleashed primeval forces. Any modern scriptwriter would be stretched to produce a more thrilling scenario.

It must have been tempting to hone in on the sensational aspects of Luther's life at the expense of the issues that have made him an important historical figure. But William Nicholson's script avoids this pitfall. The high drama and meaning of Luther's life, superbly characterised by Jonathan Pryce, are skilfully interwoven into an entity that illumines and enthrals. An excellent production which, with its authentic medieval settings, vividly conveys Luther's time.

All the main points of Luther's life are explicitly dealt with or implied. When he pinned his theses on the church door at Wittenberg, it was no more than a conventional invitation to fellow theologians to discuss the matters raised. Instead, within weeks Luther became the talking point of Europe. Why this happened is skilfully implied in the film.

The history of religion cannot be abstracted from contemporary social conditions. Luther lived in the German lands of the Holy Roman Empire in times of political and social unrest. The potential conflict of interests between the three pillars of the empire—pope, emperor and regional princes—together with the corrosive pressures for change from the outside world are now from hindsight easy to discern.

Any challenge to this social order meant challenging the authority of the Church. Luther's dissenting voice on a matter of scriptural interpretation therefore became a rallying point for the disaffected in general.

Luther lived in a world of plagues which was keenly aware of death. And after death what next— damnation? Not surprisingly, he was obsessed with guilt and feared the punishment awaiting him on judgment day. Nicholson highlights this aspect of his earlier life splendidly and with a delicate touch of humour. Maurice Denham, excellent as Father Superior John Staupetz, says to his fear-ridden young monk "I'm told you were in the confessional yesterday evening for six hours". Luther: "Yes, father." Staupetz: "Doesn't that strike you as . . . greedy?"

He agonised over man's means of redemption and found his answer in Paul. Only through God's mercy could man be saved. Redemption through faith was the only salvation.

This interpretation of scripture was a direct challenge to the thriving trade in papal indulgences. For cash you could, so it was claimed, buy yourself, or a loved one, out of purgatory and into heaven.

The Dominican Friar John Tetzel (played here by Clive Swift) flogged indulgences by the thousands in Saxony. You might think that Nicholson and Swift have overplayed or hammed up this part. Not so. Tetzel was much worse and used "jingles" such as "As soon as the coin in the coffer rings, the soul from purgatory springs".

Due to the constraints of time, the film is only able to hint at other issues such as those reformists who could almost be described as theological Trotskyists who aligned under Luther's banner. But he argued vehemently against these extremists who dismissed the entire history of the church as a long unrelieved chapter of papal heresies and corruption.

Luther escaped the stake and went on to marry, had six children and adopted four orphans. Friends and students thronged around him and he loved to argue and debate. He was no religious fanatic. His culture was wider than is generally understood. In 1554 he wrote on his idea of a good library. In addition to the scriptures, he advised collecting books of "poets and orators, regardless of whether they were pagan, Greek or Latin. After that would come books on the liberal arts".

It would be wonderful if on this 500th anniversary all the Christian churches would try to re-assess Luther objectively—the man who was both Roman Catholic and Protestant. Maybe from such a reappraisal would come the badly needed stimulus to ecumenism among and between the Churches. Christians, by redefining their differences, might also establish the broader ground of common agreement.

This would be good for Christians and non-Christians. If you don't believe me, just go to Northern Ireland.

Sunday Times Magazine 6 November 1983

ON APARTHEID

You Can't Reason With Racists Sir Richard

SIR Richard Attenborough seems to believe that if white South Africans see his film *Gandhi* then they may abandon their racial prejudices.

WHAT A HOPE!

If racists could be influenced by reason then they wouldn't be racists. To try and categorise human beings on the basis of colour is an absurdity.

It's as logical as trying to classify people by size of nose or some other irrelevant, physical characteristic.

The black Africans I know all have different personalities. Some are placid, others volatile. Some pacifist by nature, others more aggressive.

In fact they are just like us. Black jocks.

Imagine trying to classify the rest of nature by colour. Let's say that all things yellow were to be considered as belonging to the same group. It would include mustard, daffodils and even some lions.

Such a grouping would have nothing in common except the triviality of colour—and would therefore be a nonsense.

To classify or group human beings by colour is equally nonsensical.

To then argue that one such group is superior to another is dangerously nonsensical.

From experience we know that such prejudices always end in lynch parties, concentration camps and apartheid.

There are no inferior or superior races. The features that mankind has in common are more numerous and important than the trivial differences. As we Scots say "We are all Jock Tamson's bairns".

Try and tell that to the white Afrikaaner. He doesn't need Sir Richard to tell him that Asians and blacks are treated like dirt in South Africa.

It's him that's dishing out the treatment.

And mixed audiences at charity showings of the film in South Africa will make little difference. That is merely a cosmetic for the outside world.

The Afrikaans community will not change of its own free will. It believes, through the Dutch Reformed Church, that Christ wanted them to rule over others whose skin, like His, was darker.

It's an idiotic belief but then racism is essentially idiotic.

In the meantime, all decent men and women throughout the world must do nothing that will bring a shred of credibility to such a cruel and irrational regime as that which exists in South Africa today.

Daily Record 18 April 1983

ON DRUGS

I'd Show No Mercy To Those Beasts Who Deal In Death

ONE of my daughters came home in some distress. She had met a friend whom she hadn't seen for a year.

The lass and her boyfriend had at that time saved more than £6000 and were planning to get married. Then, somewhere, at some time along the way, they had become hooked on drugs.

The drug pedlars had taken everything. As addicts they now desperately scramble through every day trying to raise the money for a 'fix'.

Unless they get help, the girl will almost certainly be forced into prostitution. Both will probably be dead within a few years.

The addicts are the innocents. The criminals are those who exploit human frailty and make a business out of the misery and death of countless youngsters.

So far as I am concerned, the guys who got away with seven million pounds without injuring anyone are saints as compared to the beasts who peddle drugs.

This crime should be treated as seriously as murder. In fact, in many respects it's worse.

Most murders are committed in the heat of the moment, they are not premeditated.

Those who organise drug trafficking are perfectly aware of what they do and of the disastrous consequences for those who fall into their clutches.

They do it because money is more important to them than human life. They should be hounded mercilessly and punished severely.

Daily Record 18 April 1983

ON CHILD ABUSE

It's Never Cissy To Love Your Children

AS a kid I dreaded a Friday night. In a household nearby a terrible ritual was enacted.

The father, a morose and moronic individual would come straight from work (some of the other men stopped at the pub).

He washed himself meticulously, changed from his working clothes, and was then ready for the weekly chastisement of his children.

His wife brought the weans to him one by one and "reported" the misdemeanours of the past week. The father then passed sentence.

"Six" he might say. The child was then held down over a chair by the mother and lashed six times with a heavy leather belt by the father.

The howls could be heard in the next block.

These memories were prompted by the campaign launched last week by Strathclyde Regional Council against child abuse.

This is something we must all support.

People who think they can do what they like with their children are confusing parentage with slavery.

Cruelties are inflicted on young children within the home—and neighbours who either know or suspect do nothing about it.

They don't want to interfere, is the excuse. Or do not want to be known as a "copper's nark" by reporting their suspicions to the authorities.

This is a piece of nonsense, and reeks of the school playground and cries of "tell tale tit".

To bring to light the abuse of a defenceless child is honourable. It can liberate the child from a life of terror and also help the parents.

Let's face it, anyone who regularly and systematically thrashes and beats up their children must be sick and in need of treatment.

Evidence shows that non-accidental injuries to children in Strathclyde is linked to poverty, deprivation and alcohol.

I believe there is another factor for there are poorer communities in Europe that do not have this particular problem.

We Scots have a heritage of which we can be proud.

There are also some aspects of our traditions which are bad and harmful to the development of the human personality.

Scottish parents, particularly fathers, are often afraid to show affection to their children.

There are many thousands of Scots who cannot recall in childhood ever being kissed or cuddled by daddy.

Thus was born the image of the stern, unapproachable father figure of Scottish folklore that in modern times has tended to degenerate into the "A'm boss in ma hoose, a'h kin haud ma drink, hard man", syndrome of the cities.

In addition to food and shelter the most fundamental things that children require are love and affection.

Too many Scotsmen think that such emotions are cissy.

The real cissies are those who have to prove their so-called masculinity by acting like tyrants in their own homes.

Daily Record 11 April 1983

ROYALS AND ROYALTY

Engaging Variety Of Performances

SCHEDULES went haywire. Extended news programmes told us in detail about the forbears of Lady Diana Spencer. Various still photographs of Prince Charles and some film from the archives took us through his childhood, adolescence and early manhood.

We also got flashes of the other young ladies with whom, according to the press, he has skirmished. I noticed something that everyone else had apparently missed—not one came from Drumchapel. Has the Prince got something against the "Drum", I pondered.

They seem a very nice young couple and my wish is that their marriage be happy and their children, and yours and mine, will inherit and live in a world at peace.

Naturally we can expect vast television coverage from now until the great day. The most terrifying moment of the week was a voice-over. Some sadistic swine, no doubt, who informed us that Di's stepgrandmother was, wait for it—Barbara Cartland. Stepgrandmother? Never even heard of the term. It seemed like some fiendish plot engineered by Willie Hamilton to undermine the standing of the Royal Family among the lieges.

Surely, with the real Momma back in town and the real Papa and stepmother plus a supporting cast of thousands it is hardly necessary to inflict on an already suffering populace a dose of the "Galloping Cartlands". A people can only take so much.

Glasgow Herald 28 February 1981

The Nice Young Lad From The House Of Windsor

THERE is an MP who has probably made more money from the Monarchy than the Queen. He has almost made a profession out of baiting royalty. The Royals are an easy target and generally cannot reply to their critics. That is one reason why I have never made critical remarks about the Queen, her immediate family, and the innumerable cousins, once, twice or even thrice removed.

Recently, however, on a radio programme I felt compelled to make a critical observation on a speech made by the Duke of Edinburgh. The Prince Consort, addressing the "lieges" in Glasgow, said: "Nobody owes anyone a job." This is a highly contentious statement. It also implicitly rejects the post-war consensus whereby British Governments, Tory or Labour, were committed to the principle of full employment.

Now the Duke, since coming to this country has done rather well for himself. He had, of course, good connections. He has fared much better than most other immigrants. Surely, he should be more circumspect, when lecturing others less fortunate than himself, on matters such as unemployment. This is by way of establishing that I am no sycophant to the House of Windsor, the House of Usher or any other House.

Where, you may ask, is all this leading? A good question with a simple answer. Prince Charles is my television personality of the week. Both channels carried speeches by this young man on the network news. His attack on bigots—on the closed mentalities that cannot envisage the possibility of being even marginally wrong—made at a university in the United States, was quite outstanding. He can also depart from his prepared text with reasonably witty asides. Despite the disadvantages of his upbringing, he seems a genuinely nice bloke with whom you could imagine having a "crack" over a pint.

The news broke that some journalist claimed to have the tapes of his telephone conversations with his lady love. A German magazine has since published them. The Palace rightly described the whole business as "despicable".

In last week's column I made some references to television's responsibility to scrutinise public figures in their conduct of public affairs. This scrutiny should be piercing providing we also recognise their right to a certain privacy in their personal lives.

To put it bluntly, a journalist in television or the press has no right to ask a politician how often he exercises his conjugal rights and what are his sexual propensities. But he has the right, and indeed the duty, to question any public figure about, for example, his financial interests and whether these might compromise or influence his dischargement of his public duties.

Often you will have noted over the years a television interviewer asking a worker in an industrial dispute how much he or she earns. Seldom if ever do they put the same question to the managing director or any of the "big wheels" in business or politics.

Glasgow Herald 9 May 1981

Koo's Wrong Choice Of Friends

ACCORDING to press photographs, Koo Stark is a stoatirr. She makes the daughters of the English aristocracy look unlovely, but then so does Molly Sugden.

Prince Andrew is obviously wise to prefer her company to that of the horsey brigade, some of whom would not look out of place being unsaddled at Aintree.

It is therefore with some reluctance that I critise Koo. Let's face it, with a name like that, the lassie has enough problems.

Koo went to a "do" last week in New York. It was a party thrown by Adnan Khashoggi—there's another brammer. Is there nobody in that "do" crowd called Fred?

The shindig cost £70,000. At the same time we saw on our television screens the soup kitchens for the unemployed poor in American cities.

In this situation such conspicious consumption is immoral.

Mr Khashoggi makes his millions by selling arms. He has a good line in guns.

Koo should keep away from such people, they make the Mafia look decent.

Daily Record 21 February 1983

ALIENATION

ALIENATION is the precise and correctly applied word for describing the major social problem in Britain today. People feel alienated by society. In some intellectual cirlces it is treated almost as a new phenomenon. It has, however, been with us for years. What I believe to be true is that today it is more widespread, more pervasive than ever before. Let me right at the outset define what I mean by alienation. It is the cry of men who feel themselves the victims of blind economic forces beyond their control. It is the frustration of ordinary people excluded from the processes of decision making. The feeling of despair and hopelessness that pervades people who feel with justification that they have no real say in shaping or determining their own destinies.

Many may not have rationalised it. May not even understand, may not be able to articulate it. But they feel it. It conditions and colours their social attitudes. Alienation expresses itself in different ways by different people. It is to be found in what our courts often describe as the criminal anti-social behaviour of a section of the community. It is expressed by those young people who want to opt out of society, by drop outs, the so-called maladjusted, those who seek to escape permanently from the reality of society through intoxicants and narcotics. Of course it would be wrong to say it was the sole reason for these things. But it is a much greater factor in all of them than is generally recognised.

Society and its prevailing sense of values leads to another form of alienation. It alienates some from humanity. It partially de-humanises some people, makes them insensitive, ruthless in their handling of fellow human beings, self-centred and grasping. The irony is, they are often considered normal and well adjusted. It is my sincere contention that anyone who can be totally adjusted to our society is in greater need of psychiatric analysis and treatment than anyone else. They remind one of the character in the novel, *Catch 22*, the father of Major Major. He was a farmer in the American Mid-West. He hated suggestions for things like medi-care, social services, unemployment benefits or civil rights. He was, however, an enthusiast for the agricultural policies that paid farmers for not bringing their fields under cultivation. From the money he got for not growing alfalfa he bought more land in order not to grow alfalfa. He became rich. Pilgrims came from all over the state to sit at his feet and learn how to be a successful non-grower of alfalfa. His philosophy was simple. The poor didn't work hard enough and so they were poor. He believed that the good Lord gave him two strong hands to grab as much as he could for himself. He is a comic figure. But think—have you not met his like here in Britain? Here in Scotland? I have.

It is easy and tempting to hate such people. However it is wrong. They are as much products of society and a consequence of that society, human alienation, as the poor drop out. They are losers. They have lost essential elements of our common humanity. Man is a social being. Real fulfilment for any person lies in service to his fellow men and women. The big challenge to our civilisation is not OZ, a magazine I haven't even seen let alone read. Nor is it permissiveness, although I agree our society is too permissive. Any society which, for example permits over one million people to be unemployed is far too permissive for my liking. Nor is it moral laxity in the narrow sense that this word is generally employed—although in a sense here we come nearer to the problem. It does involve morality, ethics, and our concept of human values. The challenge we face is that of rooting out anything and everything that distorts and devalues human relations. Let me give two examples from contemporary experience to illustrate the point.

Recently on television I saw an advertisement. The scene is a banquet. A gentleman is on his feet proposing a toast. His speech is full of phrases like "this full-bodied specimen". Sitting beside him is a young, buxom woman. The image she projects is not pompous but foolish. She is visibly preening herself, believing that she is the object of this bloke's eulogy. Then he concludes— "and now I give . . ." then a brand name of what used to be described as Empire sherry. The woman is shattered, hurt and embarrassed. Then the laughter. Derisive and cruel laughter. The real point, of course, is this: in this charade the viewers were obviously expected to identify not with the victim but with her tormentors.

The other illustration is the widespread, implicit acceptance of the concept and term, "the rat race". The picture it conjures up is one where we are scurrying around scrambling for position, trampling on others, back-stabbing, all in pursuit of personal success. Even genuinely intended friendly advice can sometimes take the form of someone saying to you, "Listen, you look after number one". Or as they say in London, "Bang the bell, Jack, I'm on the bus".

To the students I address this appeal. Reject these attitudes. Reject the values and false morality that underlie these attitudes. A rat race is for rats. We're not rats. We're human beings. Reject the insidious pressures in society that would blunt your critical faculties to all that is happening around you, that would caution silence in the face of injustice lest it jeopardise your chances of promotion and self-advancement. This is how it starts and before you know where you are, you're a fully paid-up member of the rat-pack. The price is too high. It entails the loss of your dignity and human spirit. Or as Christ put it,

"What doth it profit a man if he gain the whole world and suffer the loss if his soul?"

Profit is the sole criterion used by the establishment to evaluate economic activity. From the rat race to lame ducks. The vocabulary in vogue is a give-away. It is more reminiscent of a human menagerie than human society. The power structures that have inevitably emerged from this approach threaten and undermine our hard won democratic rights. The whole process is towards the centralisation and concentration of power in fewer and fewer hands. The facts are there for all who want to see. Giant monopoly companies and consortia dominate almost every branch of our economy. The men who wield effective control within these giants exercise a power over their fellow men which is frightening and is a negation of democracy.

Government by the people for the people becomes meaningless unless it includes major economic decision making by the people for the people. This is not simply an economic matter. In essence it is an ethical and moral question, for whoever takes the important economic decisions in society *ipso facto* determines the social priorities of that society.

From the Olympian heights of an executive suite, in an atmosphere where your success is judged by the extent to which you can maximise profits, the overwhelming tendency must be to see people as units of production, as indices in your accountants' books. To appreciate fully the inhumanity of this situation, you have to see the hurt and despair in the eyes of a man suddenly told he is redundant without provision made for suitable alternative employment, with the prospect in the West of Scotland, if he is in his late forties or fifties, of spending the rest of his life in the Labour Exchange. Someone, somewhere had decided he is unwanted, unneeded, and is to be thrown on the industrial scrap heap. From the very depth of my being, I challenge the right of any man or any group of men, in business or in government, to tell a fellow human being that he or she is expendable.

The concentration of power in the economic field is matched by the centralisation of decision making in the political institutions of society. The power of Parliament has undoubtedly been eroded over past decades with more and more authority being invested in the Executive. The power of local authorities has been and is being systematically undermined. The only justification I can see for local government is as a counter-balance to the centralised character of national government.

Local government is to be re-structed. What an opportunity, one would think, for de-centralising as much power as possible back to local communities. Instead the proposals are for centralising local government. It is once again a blue-print for bureaucracy, not democracy. If these proposals are implemented, in a few years when asked "Where do you come from?", I can reply: "The Western Region." It even sounds like a hospital board.

It stretches from Oban to Girvan and eastwards to include most of the

Glasgow conurbation. As in other matters, I must ask the politicians who favour these proposals—where and how in your calculations did you quantify the value of a community? Of community life? Of a sense of belonging? Of the feeling of identification? These are rhetorical questions. I know the answers. Such human considerations do not feature in their thought process.

Everything that is proposed from the establishment seems almost calculated to minimise the role of the people, to miniaturise man. I can understand how attractive this prospect must be to those at the top. Those of us who refuse to be pawns in their power game can be picked up by their bureacratic tweezers and dropped in a filing cabinet under "M" for malcontent or maladjusted. When you think of some of the high flats around us, it can hardly be an accident that they are as near as one could get to an architectural representation of a filing cabinet.

If modern technology requires greater and larger productive units, let us make our wealth-producing resources and potential subject to public control and to social accountability. Let us gear our society to social need, not personal greed. Given such creative reorientation of society, there is no doubt in my mind that in a few years we could eradicate in our country the scourge of poverty, the underprivileged, slums, and insecurity.

Even this is not enough. To measure social progress purely by material advance is not enough. Our aim must be the enrichment of the whole quality of life. It requires a social and cultural or, if you wish, a spiritual transformation of our country. A necessary part of this must be the restructuring of the institutions of government and, where necessary, the evolution of additional structures so as to involve the people in the decision making processes of our society. The so-called experts will tell you that this would be cumbersome or marginally inefficient. I am prepared to sacrifice a margin of efficiency for the value of the people's participation. Anyway, in the longer term, I reject this argument.

To unleash the latent potential of our people requires that we give them responsibility. The untapped resources of the North Sea are as nothing compared to the untapped resources of our people. I am convinced that the great mass of our people go through life without even a glimmer of what they could have contributed to their fellow human beings. This is a personal tragedy. It is a social crime. The flowering of each individual's personality and talents is the pre-condition for everyone's development.

In this context education has a vital role to play. If automation and technology is accompanied as it must be with full employment, then the leisure time available to man will be enormously increased. If that is so, then our whole concept of education must change. The whole object must be to equip and educate people for life, not solely for work or a profession. The creative use of leisure, in communion with, and in service to our fellow human beings can and must become an important element in self-fulfilment. Universities must be in the forefront of development, must meet social needs and not lag behind them.

It is my earnest desire that this great University of Glasgow should be in the vanguard: initiating changes and setting the example for others to follow. Part of our educational process must be the involvement of all sections of the university on the governing bodies. The case for student representation is unanswerable. It is inevitable.

My conclusion is to re-affirm what I hope and certainly intend to be, the spirit permeating this address, which is an affirmation of faith in humanity. All that is good in man's heritage involves recognition of our common humanity, an unashamed acknowledgement that man is good by nature. Burns expressed it in a poem that technically was not his best, yet captured the spirit. In "Why should we idly waste our prime . . ."

> "The golden age, we'll then revive, each man will be a brother,
> In harmony we all shall live and share the earth together,
> In virtue trained, enlightened youth shall love each fellow creature,
> And time shall surely prove the truth that man is good by nature."

It is my belief that all the factors to make a practical reality of such a world are maturing now. I would like to think that our generation took mankind some way along the road towards the goal. It's a goal worth fighting for.

Rectoral Address, Glasgow University 1972

TECHNOLOGY AND SOCIETY

TECHNOLOGY is the new scapegoat responsible, so it would seem, for a multitude of sins including alienation, football hooliganism, unemployment, the rise of neo-fascism and almost all manifestations of anti social behaviour. No doubt someone is currently busy trying to establish a link between it and legionnaire's disease.

Industry prior to the advent of modern technology is lauded as a place where the human dimension was uppermost. This of course is nonsense, like the myth about primitive man as a noble savage, serene and secure in his human relationships, at one with nature and with no Freudian hang-ups or hang-downs. He was in fact assailed by fears, disease, ignorance, superstition and above all a bloody primitive standard of life. The contemporary view of labour intensive industry as more in tune with the human psyche and therefore socially more desirable is also a myth and in Britain of the 1980s a dangerous myth.

Man is unique to the extent in which he uses tools and instruments to prise from nature more and more of his requirements of life. The flint and the silicon chip differ only by degree. Both are tools, more or less complex, at our service. These appendages helped homo sapiens to a totally dominant position relative to all other species. Development has been a constant feature and has been, so to speak, the "engine house" of social progress. The speed or rate of change has

127

varied. When a multiplicity of technical developments emerge, overlap and inter-relate in a given period of time it can then become an industrial or technological revolution.

Man cannot deny this pre-condition of his dominance on this planet. How well we fulfil this role will be determined by the ecological and other considerations that should be part of the criteria which guide us in making decisions. We cannot abdicate from this responsibility.

One problem would appear to be that the pace of technological change often outstrips the tempo of social change. The tension created by this contradiction can express itself as a blind rage at the advanced technology and not the backward sociology. This is not a new phenomenon. The Luddites are simply the best known of those throughout history who blamed machines for the crimes and mistakes of men. To view technology as horrendous in itself is like having a concept of electricity based exclusively on the electric chair. It can bring warmth and energy, or it can electrocute, either by design or accident. Electricity is strictly neutral: how we use it determines whether it brings light or the darkness of death. The decision is in our hands. This is true of all the tools, resources and elements discovered, devised or invented by man.

The only real issue for debate is how we should apply our expertise to nature, and what principles should govern the distribution of the largesse so extracted. Unsubstantiated assertions abound. Where for example is the evidence for the widely held belief that technology equals unemployment? The slump in the thirties was characterised by the aborting of the process of technical improve-ment, by the destruction of productive resources, not by their utilisation. In today's world, countries with a greater level of investment in high technology are by no means the worst affected by unemployment. Within Britain the first casualties in the present recession were generally those sectors of industry most dependent on an outmoded technology. The television advert showing a pro-duction line "manned" by robots has tended to confirm fears of total job displacement when new techniques are introduced. In real life, jobs are moving from the actual productive process to the preparatory stages of production, to research and design, servicing and maintenance. This again is nothing new and to my certain knowledge has been a consequence of technical innovation for at least the last 30 years and probably for much, much longer.

My main argument is that technology must have social objectives. Hitherto the objectives have been too narrow. Profitability and cost efficiency alone are too limited and provide no social criterion whatsoever. Many tasks currently done by human beings are dirty, tiresome, boring and dangerous. Technology can release people from such drudgery and should have such an objective. It should also have the goal of freeing human beings from extensive and protracted hours of labour. By the end of the century we should be working a 25 or even a 20 hour week.

This raises the question of educating people for the creative use of leisure time and the provision of facilities for recreation and culture. These services would need to be funded and staffed from the wealth generated by a manufacturing industry based on modern equipment. In broad general terms technology should liberate everyone from physically hard, unclean, repetitive, non creative toil, while enabling them to contribute in accordance with their particular abilities to the general well being of all through constructive work or service. This plus the creation of a sufficiency of wealth to satisfy all reasonable needs and tastes is within our productive capacity. The danger is that as a society we might well choke on our own greed. Social need we can meet. Limitless private greed is insatiable.

An acquisitive society obsessed with commodity consumption, creating artificial demands and expectations and producing goods with inbuilt obsolescence must eventually become a rat race, wasteful and ultimately destructive to our environment, both physical and moral. The crude grasping hands of greed cannot be entrusted with the delicate instruments of science. In such a grip every discovery becomes a new weapon of enslavement. Value judgements become expendable. Eventually everything is soured and the true potential of human ingenuity is nullified. How else do we explain that at a time when we have the capacity to create an abundance the talk is of austerity, sacrifice and hardship? This is further confirmation that our economic ills are social and political, not technological.

In past centuries men spoke of Political Economy. Adam Smith, Marx and Ricardo studied Political Economy. Today we talk of the economy, of economists studying economics abstracted from everything else. Monetarism is but one example of this truncated approach. Like every fallacy it has a grain of truth which gives it a certain and totally unmerited credence. Of course the indiscriminate printing of money is bad. But to sweepingly conclude from this that by regulating the money supply all human activity relating to the production and distribution of wealth will conform in some undefined way to a more intelligent pattern is outrageously illogical. It is ironic that this century the dogmatists of the Right and the Left have reduced Political Economy to a crude vulgar theory of economic determinism operating mechanically and independently of man's will.

Any theory on any subject unrelated to the social reality of which it is but a part must be wrong. Each aspect of reality can only be understood in the context of its relationships and interdependence with all others. There are no exceptions. It applies to technology, science, economics and sociology.

For example I think it is impossible to evaluate the real significance or role of the new technology without considering its impact or likely effects on the relationships between the developed and under developed countries. One in every three humans on this planet is undernourished or dying from malnutrition. The moral imperative that should govern all our activities should be to end this tragic circumstance. Population growth coupled with economic stagnation and

129

decline, super-imposed on vast areas of the world already unable to provide even subsistence for many spells disaster. A catastrophe of such proportions cannot be confined to certain geographical tracts. Technology has made the world a smaller place. Even in the most industrially backward nation there is an awareness that in the West there is a problem of obesity.

Herein may lie the greatest threat to world peace. The seeds of war can be sown in the minds of a people rendered desperate. A parent whose child is dying from starvation could understandably have an overwhelming compulsion to find food for the child or die in the attempt. This tendency could be projected into the collective will of a nation or an entire people.

The Brandt Commission and its report has been of great value in putting this question before every government and people. To leave productive capacity unused or undeveloped in the midst of such painful human need is obscene. Technology must be used to generate a surplus sufficient to finance a massive programme of aid to the Third World. As Brandt argues, such a programme totally justified in itself on humanitarian grounds would also open up vast new markets which could provide the stimulus so critically needed by the economies of the West.

In other words ethics and our economic interests coincide. This creates another problem. Our politicians and economists have been conditioned to react with hostility to ethical considerations almost as a matter of principle. Aid programmes for the Third World to engender trade would be acceptable if only we could separate them from any humane motivation. Aid for trade is good, aid for people is bad; that would appear to be their credo. That the two should coalesce is considered unnatural.

This mentality is the outcome of divorcing value judgements from economics. The potential of modern technology in terms of production and social repercussions is so vast that such a distinction is no longer tenable. Apart from anything else it is surely now evident that we can destroy the environment on which we depend for survival. We can unleash terrible forces and power that could break a vital link in the chain of life that sustains ourselves and other species on earth. Technology has to be applied within the framework of a wider understanding of social and environmental causality. No man is an island, nor is technology. Nowadays the social application of science must conform to principles that only the people can define. This cannot be left to the "experts". There are none.

What we need is a philosophical discussion which is difficult even to suggest because ideas and language have become trivialised. Philosophy is looked upon as a rarified indulgence for octogenarians cocooned in the cloisters of some institute of higher education. It is simply a word to convey the assertion and investigation of generalisations which exceed the boundaries of any science or combination of sciences. It concerns moral values and ethical judgements, the nature of logic and scientific methodology. It might sound complicated but all of us live in accordance with such generalisations. We have never lived without one. The mind cannot embrace such vacuity. The only question is whether our philosophy is valid.

Look at some of the events, facts and personalities of this century. Two world wars and innumerable lesser ones like Vietnam, colonial enslavement, Hiroshima, the cobalt bomb, race hatred, communal massacres, religious persecution, terrorism, mass unemployment, slumps, poverty, starvation, Hitler, Stalin, Belsen, burning books and people, the Gulags, show trials, napalm, Amin, Franco and Pol Pot, radiation sickness, chemical warfare, Senator Joe McCarthy and thalidomide. These are just some of the negative products of our world and of our philosophies. Of course it is not the whole picture. Some positive things did happen. There were good men too. However I think this incomplete inventory of the twentieth century's chamber of horrors is enough to prove that the philosophies that have prevailed thus far are somewhat inadequate.

We need to re-appraise the generalisations, the values by which we have lived, the institutions political and economic by which we have agreed to be governed. It is possible that structures devised for the steam engine might be unsuitable for the requirements of micro-electronics. To obstruct necessary change can only defer the inevitable and in the long run is more painful and traumatic. We suffer from a surfeit of social inertia. We should try consulting the world instead of our prejudices. It would blow away the cobwebs and open our minds to new information which may help our judgement.

The Institute of Data Processing Management Members' Yearbook, 1981

Culture High and Low

HELPLESS AS A TINNED SARDINE WITH MY HEAD IN THE CLOUDS

THE modern aircraft is the most boring mode of transportation yet devised. You sit there well above the clouds, encapsuled and as helpless as a tinned sardine. Something to read is essential particularly if the journey is too short to do any work.

On longer journeys I can get a lot done. Unlike the train when you look out the window there is nothing to distract your attention. It's the short hop without a book, newspaper or magazine which brings on an intolerable tedium. In such circumstances I tend to raid the pouch on the back of the seat in front and force it to disgorge its secrets.

The spew bag as we used to call it in the RAF is of no use to me for I simply cannot regurgitate on a plane which is rather unfortunate for it might help to pass the time.

Then there is the glossy in-flight magazine that is so nauseously nice as to make pornography intellectually respectable. The writing seems clearly designed to generate a need for the aforementioned bag.

The best reading of all is to be found in the safety manual. You can, for example, learn how to put on a life jacket as you fly overland across mountain ranges. The thought that you won't drown if the plane plunges into the side of Ben Lomond is most comforting.

Last week I flew back from London and found myself searching frantically through a pile of newspapers looking for something, anything that I hadn't already read. In desperation I seized a *Times* supplement called *Preview* which is really a sort of entertainment guide to what is going on, particularly in London.

What first caught my attention was a blurb about a festival on "The Sound of Women". As someone who despite the evidence to the contrary still stubbornly adheres to an idealised concept of women, I was more than happy to hear for instance that female sounds are nicer and gentler than male sounds. Where we might gurgle, gurgle, slurp, blurp, gurgle, the ladies would in all probability go plink, plink, plink, pleep, pleep, plink. Such a welcome discovery was not to be. It was the title of a festival of music played and performed for women.

One lady will present a programme under the heading "From Monteverdi to the Beatles". Really, what is one to think of a person, no matter the gender, who would leave the sunshine of Monteverdi and come to London to sing some Beatles songs.

Another lady performer we are told ". . . is a composer, singer, researcher, guitarist, at present working on a complete opera for Rome". Amazing! Does Rome and its citizens know? And more importantly who are those that by implication are working to produce an incomplete opera?

Yet another lady ". . . sings in half a dozen languages". Simultaneously? And yet another ". . . a fifth generation member of a circus family, is a dancer, acrobat, juggler, singer, clown" and is accompanied by another on "the dulcimer, lute, guitar and Vosges harp". Who does this harpie think she is using Vosges' instrument and does the poor guy know?

And yet another one will play "compositions by Kagel, Crumb and Cage". Despite the fact that this trio sounds like a London firm of solicitors I still want to hear this lot.

I then turned to the section on films and was thrilled to read "*Mephisto*: Istvan Szabo's majestic and spectacular adaptation of Klaus Mann's 1936 roman-a-clef." Well that's a must. One can't miss an adaptation of anyone's roman-a-clef.

The French Lieutenant's Woman was described as "Karen Reisz's screen version of John Fowles's novel, scripted by Harold Pinter, finds cinematic equivalents to the literary experiment of the original. The period reconstruction is often breathtaking; and Meryl Streep is revealed as a pre-Raphaelite beauty in the role of a Victorian heroine who forces a way to liberation from the sexist, social and moral constraints of the age." Cor. Imagine that. Can you get a season ticket?

Under concerts we are informed that "Giacinto Scelsi's *Canti de Capricorno* are performed by Michiko Hirayama with highly unorthodox vocal techniques. The music of remarkable Italian composer is only now getting a hearing, though he was born in 1905". He would probably have had even greater difficulty getting a hearing if he hadn't been born in 1905.

Under "Jazz" you are informed "Taj Mahal: This intimate pub room should be packed and jumping for the appearance of a great folklorist who takes on more kinds of black music than you could shake a stick at, and makes it cohere". What a guy—he can actually make things cohere without a stick.

In the same section we are told that "De Egelentier is a baroque group who play a Rameau, Haydn, Mozart and two Forquerays" which sounds a bit strong to me. There is also a recital by "Steven de Groote, who plays Bk2 of Brahms's *Paganini Variations*, Bk2 of Debussy's *Etudes*, Liszt's *Dante Sonata*, Schubert's *D568 Sonata*."

I suppose for an encore he might be prepared to have a go at "Boeing's 707". Under "Theatres" you can read of "The Peoples Show No 87" with Emil

Wolk, Mark Long, George Khan and Chahine Yavroyan, in a new show which combines newly-found comic and acrobatic skills with the traditional poetic invention of the Peoples Show". I like that 87, does it refer to the variety of their wares as with canned food manufacturers.

It's funny how there are no actors in London with names like Fred Abernethy or Sid Doyle or Whuggie McGonnigle or an Aggie Shaw. Instead according to this publication the West End Theatre is festooned with names like Dinsdale Lansden, Paolo Dionisotti, Nick Edmett, Francis de la Tour, Matyelok Gibbs, and Derren Nesbitt.

My attention drifted to the page that sought to promote galleries and exhibitions. We read "Dorian Ker, a painter who goes his own way yet seems somehow in the super-realist swim. Excellent oils on gessoed panels—crisply mysterious flowerpieces, landscapes seen with a surreal (or pre-Raphaelite) clarity—suggest comparisons with Meredith Frampton or the turn-of-the-century Birmingham tempera painters". Now there is another name to conjure with—Meredith Frampton.

It could be the title name of a television soap opera. "Meredith Frampton M.D." or "Meredith Frampton D.A."

There is also a blurb for "Chaime Soutine" . . . "Elaborate retrospective devoted to the Russian-French painter captures his expressionistic violence of colour and subject-matter; even the calmest landscapes seem liable to leave the wall and eat one up. And some of the portraits and still-lifes suggest Bacon before the letter".

There can be little doubt that we were safer with the Wally Dugs and what is meant by this reference to Bacon? Is it Sir Francis or Streaky? On the same page there is notice of a photographic exhibition "The Thirties and After". It shows the Jarrow marchers and "slum dwellers in London's East End".

It is funny how you can only dwell in a slum. Nobody talks of mansion dwellers, bungalow dwellers or semi detached dwellers. Mick Thick the latest punk rock sensation is hardly likely to say "Eh well, you know like, what I mean, I'm you know a penthouse dweller".

Actually the language deployed by many involved in the so-called cultural life of this country is a dead giveaway. They are dilettantes comfortably cosy in the cloying confines of their esoteric little worlds. Invariably egocentric, they tart up their self promotional ploys in a language which tries to convey an impression of artistic creativity.

They are mostly the purveyors of a phoney culture.

They assemble up here at the Edinburgh Festival and are the main reason why I have given it a body swerve. You can easily imagine the discussions in the Festival Club. "You know Nigel, I must confess that I do find Vivaldi a trifle twee." Either that or they reject all values as bourgeois except the value of money. "Marcuse my Dear is definitely in this year." "Marx is too bourgeois for me, really he is Dahling."

Maybe it is about time the Scottish people (or for that matter the British people) laid claim to the Edinburgh Festival and challenged these poseurs. There is a lot of good stuff there, maybe we should go and support it. Anyway Vivaldi is a bit twee.

Glasgow Herald 2 August 1982

GEE WHIZ, WHAT A LOVELY WAY TO SPEND FRIDAY

YOU will remember that a few weeks ago I stumbled upon a veritable literary treasure house called *Preview*, a weekly guide by the *London Times* to the cultural hanky-panky going on in the country at large. Since then it has become compulsive reading. It brightens my every Friday.

Last week the Tate Gallery retrospective of the Swiss Sculptor Tinguely is reported as follows: ". . . his mobile and kinetic art tends to take the form of slightly Heath Robinson machines which behave in an erratic and unpredictable way while making loud noises, squirting water, throwing balls, destroying themselves or even producing abstract paintings . . ."

By an exercise of great self restraint, I will refrain from observing that this is a fairly accurate description of some abstract painters. Instead, let me suggest that making loud noises, squirting water, throwing balls, etc., is a very accurate picture of a pre-school play group.

Then we read: "A Prelude to Death in Venice written and directed by Lee Breuer, acted by Mabou Mimes, New York's leading experimental theatre group. A 3ft. wooden dummy is the hero, with dazzling wordplay and some remarkable images." Gee whiz, Mister, that is just what some constituency Labour Parties want as parliamentary candidates.

And then: "Welsh National Opera. The season opens in Cardiff tomorrow night with a new production of Verdi's Un Ballo in Maschera conducted by WNO's music director, Richard Tamburlaine makes the journey down from Edinburgh to Cardiff for a trio of performances."

Well, the best of luck to him. I ended up stranded overnight in Birmingham when last attempting that journey. It's a peculiar name that, innit? Tamburlaine. He must come from Morningside.

Now, why shouldn't we all write in the prose style of this kind of blurb? Just think of how a report of a Rangers/Celtic match would read.

"This 'Old Firm' retrospective was most memorable and showed that the division between overbearing religiosity and frustrated sexuality is slight. The histrionic chants of the fans have Freudian overtones and are linguistic expressions of desensitised men seeking a short cut out of a cycle of despair and deprivation. This can only be understood as a scream of outrage from a humiliated Oedipus.

"The sectional singing was marvellously contrapuntal. An evocation of the anguish embedded in the deep recesses of the psyche which assumed Dostoyevskian proportions when Celtic were given a late and disputed penalty. The chord sequences in the songs were surprisingly close to those in Blacher's Paganini Variations. This has led to some interesting specualtion. Was Blacher a Bluenose or a Tim? The controversy still rages among musicologists at the Anderston Festival.

"The individual performances by some of the players illumined the light and shade of the human predicament as a Rangers defender showed when he embraced Celtic's little number 7 around the throat.

"The volcanic atmosphere was an inter-relating mixture of Sophoclean values and the essentially didactic humour of Groucho Marx.

"This show should not be missed by anyone who wants to understand the Clydeside of 1910."

Glasgow Herald 6 September 1982

THEY'RE ALL OUT TO MAKE A BIT OF HISTORY

THE Hitler diaries are forgeries and this is a great embarrassment to the newspaper that paid a lot of money for them.

More serious than the money is the loss of credibility. I'm not interested in crowing about the *Sunday Times*. It won't be the last newspaper whose desire for a scoop overwhelms caution.

No, my concern is about history and historians.

Hugh Trevor-Roper (or Lord Dacre) is acknowledged to be one of Britain's foremost historians. He "authenticated" the diaries after perusing them for a few hours.

The average bloke would take longer to examine a second-hand car before purchase.

Again, I'm not interested in disparaging Trevor-Roper for there is a much wider and more important consideration. Every "con job" depends on the desire for what is being offered inducing gullibility.

Trevor-Roper, as someone who has specialised in the life of Hitler, wanted the diaries to be authentic. But then isn't all history written by people who want things to be as they would like them to be?

The victors write history.

Hitler re-wrote Germanic history on the basis of a screwball theory of an Aryan master race.

In Russia, Stalin defeated Trotsky and promptly wrote him out of Soviet history except as a bogey-man.

Even photographs were changed to remove Trotsky from the side of Lenin and replace him with Stalin.

Stalin died, Khrushchev exposed his terror—and Soviet history was again re-written to diminish Stalin. Khrushchev got the heave and Stalin was partially rehabilitated and Soviet history was once more re-written.

The official histories of our own country are not all they are cracked up to be.

When I went to school, our history was taught as being the pedigree and family-tree of kings and queens. The people were passive spectators as the nobility shaped our destiny.

I had to find out for myself about the Chartists and how common people fought that we might all have the right to vote.

Modern democracy, the greatest achievement in the history of this country, was largely created by working men and women.

The nobility, who now claim it as if it was their idea, were bitterly opposed to democracy.

In 1831, Edinburgh judge, author and conservationist Lord Cockburn wrote: "I fear that our boasted constitution must soon sink into that democracy which seems to be the natural result of every government where the people have become politically free."

Then another Scottish lord by the name of Braxfield said: "If they hae ability, low birth is not against them. But that they hae a richt to representation in Parliament I deny."

I am by no means certain that my interpretation of history would or could be neutral. I would tend to favour the people.

As my favourite Scottish hymn puts it:

> "When wilt Thou save the people,
> O Lord of mercy, when,
> The people, Lord, the people,
> Not crowns or thrones, but men."

Daily Record 9 May 1983

LIBRARIES: AN ESSENTIAL SERVICE

LET me come clean with you at the outset.

When I agreed to do this talk, The Woman had not made up her mind about the General Election, and I had visions of meandering down to Peebles through the Borders and staying overnight, a nice, relaxed and leisurely preparation for speaking to you this morning. Well, it has not quite worked out that way. You understand that I have more than a fleeting interest in what is about to happen to this country tomorrow, with the result that I have travelled up this morning with nothing prepared. So, I am going to talk "off the top of my head", if you like, about my interest in libraries and why I think they are indispensable. Libraries played a very important part in my own education, if you can call it an education. In terms of formal scholastic qualifications I have none—not even an "O" level.

137

Not because I was a total "bampot", as they say, but I left school at fourteen and, to tell you the truth, we did not take exams at that time. I passed my eleven plus. We still had the eleven plus in those days. I think it was out of 150, and I got 148½, which was not a bad pass mark. I am not indicating anything here, because I did not think much about the eleven plus at that time. When I grew to maturity I thought even less about it as any kind of guide for measuring the intelligence of human beings, because people, particularly children, develop at different levels.

Anyway, I passed the eleven plus. I don't know what it is like now, but they streamed you in those days, and in Govan we were streamed into the academic stream that was based on Oxford and Cambridge. I did Greek, French and Latin, but my expectations never involved higher education. I did not know anybody who went to university from the streets of Govan. You normally assumed that at the first opportunity you were out to work. I must confess I never found a smattering of knowledge about Latin verbs of great assistance in the shipyards, but do not knock it for that reason.

I must also add that I have no recollection of my formal education, particularly at secondary school, stimulating or generating the slightest interest in any subject, in any subject at all, yet at the age of twelve or thirteen I was a voracious reader and pestered the life out of the woman in Govan Library. She swore blind that I could not be reading all the books I was taking out! Now, I was not exactly a bookworm—I used to play football and do all the other things with the lads. The truth is that for whatever reason, I started reading and by the time I was thirteen or fourteen had read everything that Shaw had ever written, including his novels (which were not very good) and, to this day, I am still a voracious reader.

The importance of the library to me then was considerable. But there is another factor which I want to raise with you this morning which I think is important. The best way of raising it is to ask you to jump forward in time to about 1972–73. I went down to London to do a literary programme for London Weekend Television and Jonathan Miller was there. I introduced the question of the decline and fall of the novel. All the evidence suggests, in my opinion, that that particular literary art form has gone over the apex of its development. I am saying that now, more in sorrow than in joy, because to me it has made a colossal contribution to human knowledge. Anyway, we went into this in detail and after the programme, having a drink, he said to me, "Where did you study English Literature?" I said, "Govan Library", and he said, "Ah, come on. The library?" And I did realise then that because I had not been reading in order to increase job expectations, or career prospects, or to pass an examination, there was a catholicity in my reading for which I am eternally grateful.

There was another question which Miller raised which I want to raise with you this morning. Miller and Bennett and some of the others from Beyond the Fringe years ago bought a Church of Scotland manse that was being sold off by the Kirk in Perthshire. He loves going up there, with three or four others, where they are away from all the pressures of the big city. Miller told us that they went down to the local pub with their big woolly jumpers on. (That is what intellectuals do. When workers come home they take off the woolly jumpers and put on a pin stripe suit. When they take off the pin stripe suit they put on big woollies!) Anyway, Jonathan had the big woollies on and was down in the local pub when a wee guy wearing a bonnet, rolling a fag, came over and said "Are you Jonathan Miller?" and he said "Yes, I am." And the wee guy said "I must say I disagree with your interpretation of Marlow." He was a maintenance engineer in a local distillery, and his critique was more effective than anything in *New Society*, the *New Statesman*, the *Guardian*, or *The Times*. The wee guy said it all, and Miller had to listen to him. There is nowhere in Britain where you are more likely to get working class intellectuals than in Scotland. It could never happen in the East End of London.

I will tell you why I am raising this with you. There is a tradition, sadly, I think, diminishing, but still extant when I was a youth, a tradition of literacy amongst the Scottish people that goes back some centuries. The reason Scotland has a ploughman as its national bard is because two hundred years ago the ploughmen in Scotland were more likely to be literate than the ploughmen in England. At that time we were amongst the most literate nations in the world. I do not know the historic reasons for this. Perhaps it was the Kirk, with its demand for a school in every village and a college in every town. But it is not without significance that at a time when Scotland had a ploughman as the national bard the equivalent south of the Border was more likely to be Lord Shelley, Lord Byron or Keats. Not because English ploughmen lacked potential literary merit, but because it was just a bit difficult to express such merit if you were illiterate.

I think the point I am making here is that literacy became a characteristic and a feature of the Scottish working class in the industrial era. I told Miller that there is another place in Britain where I have detected that characteristic, and that is in South Wales. There, the miners in 1880 and 1885 were deducting a half a penny and a penny a week to build their own libraries. Everyone in the Labour Movement quotes Bevan now—people who would have spat on him if he was alive. They are always saying "as Nye said", and everybody invokes his name as a kind of Holy Ghost that will bring Benediction to whatever interpretation of socialism they are advancing. But Bevan's rhetoric, analysis and manner and mode of speech sprang from a broadly-based culture that was achieved in a working man's library when he was in his late teens. Now there are all those young boys in London trying to emulate Bevan by reading all the political memoranda, whereas Bevan's secret was his broad literary base.

In Clydeside, when I left school, this tradition of the pursuit of knowledge as a good thing in itself was still alive and I remember when I was fourteen or fifteen going to a place in Renfrew Street in Glasgow called the Workers' Open Forum. It was a bit of misnomer because there were some guys in there who were fairly successful businessmen, but all of them were either working class or working class in origin and they were all a bit pedantic, and they loved arguing, particularly about philosophy. I would sit and listen, and someone would talk about Nietzsche. I would think "Nietzsche? Get his name down!" and down I would go to the Govan Library to swot up about Nietzsche!

I came through that period between fourteen and sixteen when my education, for what it is, took off because I was stimulated and generated by that then extant, tremendously important, Scottish tradition of valuing the pursuit of knowledge for itself which was very prevalent in the area where I grew up. Maybe I was of the generation at the tail end of that tradition.

I read and read, and if I got a good book, I could be up to three of four in the morning because I couldn't lay it down! It was a tremendous feeling, like a voyage of discovery every time you went to the library. And I pursued everything. Someone mentioned Marx, and I was away down to the Library to see what Karl had to say. Now I hear people on television, trade unionists, saying "I am a Marxist." I know them personally. I know one guy who said, "I am a Marxist," and I tell you he hasn't read Heidi never mind Marx! You can be a communist without having read Marx but I don't see how you can call yourself a Marxist without having read Marx! It is like calling yourself a nuclear physicist without ever having examined or studied nuclear physics. I think people are getting away with murder, particularly in politics, by making claims to perceptions and knowledge which they cannot possibly possess, because they haven't done even the elementary homework to acquire the information. That alone would give them the authority to claim to be what they say they are.

All I am saying is that my knowledge was obtained outside the formal educational structures. It came from life, I suppose, the old cliché about the university of life or life being my university. The library was there for me, and to this day I believe that it is a fundamental element when people talk about establishing a society within which there is an increasing quality of life representing something beyond the rat race. That is my view of the importance of libraries, and why I think that a public relations job has got to be done for them.

First of all, in Scotland we should rekindle a respect for that tradition of which I have spoken. Too many youngsters, and students in particular, are encouraged to read only within an academic syllabus to get themselves academic qualifications. I have met too many well-educated people now ever to make the mistake of confusing a good education with understanding or intelligence. It is possible to have a highly educated, highly intelligent, highly perceptive person. It is equally possible, and I know it from my own experience, to have a highly educated, not so highly intelligent, and by no means highly perceptive person, and you can get an ill-educated, not so highly intelligent and by no means highly perceptive person. In other words, the equation of educational excellence with

140

intelligence is wrong. I have met professors who, outside their own discipline, could hardly tie two bits of string together. Now, I am not saying that they are all like that. By no means. There are a few of them that are almost as intelligent as some boiler-maker shop stewards I used to know! The point is that we have got to regenerate and rekindle the interest in that tradition and maybe even take a pride in it.

The second reason is because of one of C. P. Snow's arguments about the two cultures. The most alarming thing in the post-war educational establishments of this country has been the divergence of sciences and the humanities. It seems to me that the anthropologists have the only meaningful definition of culture. They use it to describe the totality of a human civilisation. They talk about a culture meaning everything, meaning the economics, the law, the jurisprudence, the socio-economic character and features of that society. They aren't talking about something for the Arts Council, something esoteric. They mean the totality, and I do not believe that anyone, in the latter part of the twentieth century, can genuinely be equipped in the humanities unless they have some knowledge of the technology. How can you understand the sociology of modern society without having some appreciation of the technology? Similarly with the science students. I have experienced some appalling examples of crass philistinism in faculties of science, and I am fearful of people with scientific qualifications who have no appreciation of the humanities. We should be insisting on the humanities as a basic for science disciplines, and a knowledge of science as an indispensable factor in the humanities. It seems to me to be an unanswerable case.

Because what is happening? From a working class labour movement point of view, I believe we have been criminally neglectful in failing to draw attention to a very vital area of deprivation—cultural deprivation. You know, at the end of the day, that cultural deprivation can be more pernicious in stunting development of the human personality than lack of proper nourishment from food. Many working men and women are seared with a lack of self confidence that stems, in my opinion, from a cultural deprivation. That seems to me to be a tragedy which we must overcome, and the library system is a vital cog in that process.

Let me tell you about another form of deprivation which I have noticed only over the last ten or fifteen years. I am talking here about people I know—good people. You go into their houses, and clearly they have done well for themselves. Their houses look like a shop window in Buchanan Street—the big furniture is all there, with the Tretchikoff, the clock on the wall. There is not a book in sight. Instead of books they have expensive, glossy magazines costing about two and a half quid, usually presenting a kind of predigested pap so that you can take a short cut to some area of knowledge. The kids are brought up in a house without books. There is a cultural deprivation becoming more and more evident amongst an emerging middle class whose education has focused almost exclusively on being equipped to make a few bob, and not for an appreciation of the qualities of life, which cannot be enjoyed without a cultural dimension to your upbringing, to your attitude, to your outlook and to your concepts.

Therefore, to me, a library system is not a luxury that should be subject to government economies. There are certain services which are fundamental and crucial to the development of proper social relations and the development of people, and I really do put libraries in that context. I think that libraries are not promoted as they should be. I think an emphasis on books, and a re-orientation to an educational system which tries to engender an interest in books and literature as one of the colossal delights of human life is essential. That, related to the availability of books through the library, is a very important cog in human society in the latter part of this century. If we are not to have a mass, permanent pool of unemployed, we can only find means of averting it by thinking of principles and concepts of work-sharing. That will mean, for many people, leisure time on a scale never previously conceived. If you could negotiate a thousand pounds a week take-home pay and a fifteen hour working week for some men in our society, you would be virtually signing their death certificate. It isn't their fault. They have been given the most minimal education for work and no education at all for the enjoyment of life and for the creative use of leisure time. If you are serious about maximising the social benefits of modern techno-logy, then it has got to be associated not only with education but the re-education of people for the creative use of leisure time. That is an impossible concept unless it relates, very substantially, to opening people's minds through the delights of reading.

I also believe that the library system in the new technology age has other important tasks to perform. Why should people be going to shops for videos? Why shouldn't there be an expanded library system in this area? Public services have to be accepted as much more desirable than privatised services. I do not see people queueing up to privatise the sewage system, although if they thought they could make a few bob from it they might do that as well! The important thing here is that public services have got to be excluded from market forces, because once market forces are applied I think any element of public service disappears. Of course, you then get the search for the lowest common denomi-nator, the opposite of excellence.

As you can gather, because of the Election I have come totally unprepared to speak to you today. I will not pretend that my remarks are in any way some substantive, coherent contribution to your deliberations this week, but then I did not create the circumstances of the last couple of weeks in which, for obvious reasons, both professionally and otherwise, I have been very much involved. You have my thoughts. They have come from the top of my head but they are, by and large, based on and stem from my own experiences. If you are fighting for the library service, then I want to tell you that in me you not only have an ally but a zealot, because I believe that libraries are fundamental to the kind of society that I want to live in and in which I want my children to grow up. I think your service is, indeed, absolutely essential.

This text is edited from a recording of the speaker's informal and unscripted Conference Address. Wednesday, 8th June 1983

MUSIC

Bottom Of The Pops

THIS week was the 900th anniversary of "Top of the Pops" and the Post Office didn't even print a commemorative stamp. It really does seem as if it's been around since the Battle of Hastings.

But it was at least comforting to be reminded by clips from the past that the worst of pop music has always been unbelievably bad. The common thread that runs throughout is a contempt for the customers' intelligence. Nowadays the pop industry is funded by the teeny bopper's purse.

The promoters, through a form of brainwashing called plugging, create a demand for their product and then justify the asinine quality of the product by quoting the demand. "It's what the kids want," they intone. In a slightly amended form this could be a rationale for drug pedlars.

Don't misunderstand me. Popular music is both necessary and enjoyable. The Beatles, The Cream, The Electric Light Orchestra, and Blue Mink are but a few of the genuine talents that even I can recall and appreciate.

It's the lower depths of the commercial pop scene that appal. The cynical manipulation of young minds and tastes.

The irony is that the BBC, so pristine pure about straightforward advertising is the main vehicle for the pop pedlars. The radio disc shows are decisive in making a "hit". When the potential hit record is "plugged", it isn't in an advertiser's slot but on a programme. It's the ad man's paradise. An advert disguised as something else. "Top of the Pops" is about the only television programme that comes in this category.

Highly competent and talented musicians make a good living as what are called "session men". I actually know some who have played on hit records that have gone under the name of a pop group.

When it comes to live concerts the promoters have a difficulty in ensuring that the lack of musicianship within the group is concealed or drowned by noise levels, by flashing and clanging, and by screams, above all screams.

On "Top of the Pops" there is no problem. All they have to do is flap their mouths like ventriloquist dummies. There are groups in heavy rock etc., that are genuine and talented but at this bottom level the pop scene stinks.

143

The BBC should detach and distance itself from this racket by dropping this show.

Glasgow Herald 11 July 1981

Portrait Of A Youth Forgotten

THEN there was "The Big Time", which told the story of Sheena Easton. This beautiful Scottish girl was singing, semi-professionally, at little functions and dinner dances when picked for an experiment that was to be filmed for television.

Could a young girl like Sheena be "groomed" and "moulded" into a pop star?

Irrefutably the answer is—Yes. There are the hit records to prove it. She was voted Britain's top female singer and appeared at the Royal Variety Show. The distinct impression was that they could do the same for any pretty girl who wasn't tone deaf.

The graphic artists discussed her appearance. One said: "Baked beans have an established background. No one knows Sheena Easton."

The point being that they had to give her an "image" different from, but as effective as, baked beans. She had to be packaged like any other saleable commodity.

The recording studio was without musicians. They had clearly been taped earlier. The gadgetry and electronic equipment would have bewildered the crew of the space ship Enterprise.

It seemed more of a technological than a musical happening. The record thus made was then "promoted" which mainly seemed to consist of nobbling disc jockeys and persuading them to give it an "airing".

Somebody called Simon Bates made it his record of the week and "aired" it five times which more or less made it a hit. What power has this man!

Hooray for the new Lord Chamberlain. He and his pals have apparently become the arbiters, nay, the gauleiters, of popular musical taste. Even a genius would demur and feel nervous at the prospect of such power. But not this merry band.

What worried me is that some of them in their programmes plumb the very depths of banality and you find either mentally defective or, even worse, reasonably intelligent men treating the listeners as mental defectives.

The whole set-up stinks. Sheena sounded better as she auditioned for the recording experts and before they had moulded her vocal talents into their concept of commercial success.

My fervent wish is that the girl becomes a star in her own right without the "Svengalis". My fear for her was expressed most succinctly by Sheena herself near the end of the programme. Talking of this "success" thrust upon her, she asked: "When do I pay for all this?"

I hope the "price" is not too great. She seems a nice kid.

144

By the way, the producer was Esther Rantzen, the research by Linda McMullen, and the excellent director was Patricia Houlihan whom I remember a few years ago doing research work for the Michael Parkinson Show. It's good to see women getting a chance at the big jobs in the BBC.

Glasgow Herald 25 April 1981

There Is No Defence Against An Amplified Fiddle

THAT splendid fellow and dear friend Jim Craig wrote in the *Herald* last week about the Edinburgh Folk Festival and brought memories of my exile in London flooding back.

Jim, as you may recall, revealed a growing conflict in the folk-song world. The instrumentalists apparently were acting like marauding guerrillas and waging a kind of decibel war against the folk singers.

The singers are cheesed off and threaten massive retaliations. If pushed far enough they might even accuse the folk instrumentalists of being popular.

It should be understood that to the aficionados of the folk music world, to brand anyone as "popular" is the ultimate insult. Lord Haw Haw or Burgess and McLean are the essence of fidelity compared to a folk artiste who becomes commercial.

The lines of this new battle are now apparently drawn. It is folk music versus folk song. This may seem a rather fine distinction to fight over, but let me remind you that fine distinctions have caused more trouble than all the big differences put together.

There are plenty of examples. Contrary to popular belief, Trotskyites are in no way anti-Conservative. They are far too busy hating other Trotskyites, with whom they have microscopic disagreements on the interpretation of the gospel according to Leon, to have any hate or time left for Mrs Thatcher and the Government.

Ayatollahs might rave about infidels but they are much more likely to fight over Muslims with a slight variant in the concept of the Koran. Then there are the Christians whose inclination towards murder as a means of resolving theological differences with other Christians is a matter of historical record.

And so it was in the folk world of London in the 'sixties. The ethnics fought the non-ethnics. Fisticuffs were not exactly unknown. The intensity of feeling was bewildering, particularly for someone like myself who couldn't understand what all the fuss was about.

To let you into a secret, in Govan, the hub of my cultural development, folk song wasn't recognised as a separate category. At a party, as you would expect, "Ra pale moon was shahiningah" got laldy.

Someone, usually a lady of ample proportions and strident voice, would assume responsibilty for trying to ensure silence. "A bit of order for Erchie— wan singer, wan song."

145

"My Yiddisher Momma" was another favourite and got more airings than "The Sash". A consequence of this was that anti-semitism had no chance in a community where most children thought their grandmothers were Jewish.

Then somone might sing, for example, "The Four Marys". It wasn't introduced as a folk song. It was accepted on its merits as Auntie Jean's party-piece. Unknowingly we were probably subscribing to Big Bill Broonzy's theory that "All songs are folk songs—I ain't ever heard a horse sing." Either that or there were no folk in Govan, only people.

In London at that time you would hear someone introduce a folk song and tell the audience that he had collected it from a remote island community in the Outer Hebrides and had thus saved it for posterity. For some reason one of them wasn't the least bit pleased when I told him he needn't have travelled so far for there was a bloke in Govan who sang it every Saturday night as he weaved his way home from the pub.

People were also tape-recording in all the rural fishing villages in the south and east coast of England. A 93-year-old East Anglian fisherman would be taped singing the song peculiar to his area. Not surprisingly the voice was liable on occasions to lapse into an asthmatic wheeze.

Young clerks from Fulham would learn to sing this song and include the asthmatic wheeze as proof of their ethnic integrity. The vision of young bank clerks and solicitors who changed from the work-a-day pinstripes into heavy boots, rough corded trousers, and rough knitted sweaters, as purchased from a surplus army store, trying to simulate the voice of a geriatric suffering from asthma, is still fresh in my mind.

Even within the ethnic group there were differences in the degree of commitment to what was called folk orthodoxy. Some repudiated all new technology.

Like some religious sects in North America who will not use electricity, a few folk singers rejected the microphone as a devilish contraption. Others said it was all right, provided you didn't use it too expertly like the contemporary crooner.

It was all rather painful to see my friends bickering and fighting over something that seemed to me, in my ignorance, unimportant. I would try to assuage feelings by suggesting that Robin Hall and Jimmy McGregor shouldn't be blamed too much for being successful. We should blame the BBC.

Maybe it was all an Establishment plot to undermine the pristine purity of our ethnic folk music. The trouble with that argument was that the BBC was being simultaneously attacked for undermining our ethnic folk music by not giving it sufficient airtime.

As a veteran observer, or even war correspondent, from the previous conflict which tore the folk world apart, might I suggest that conciliation is the best course?

You know, it is possible for musicians and singers to be on the same side. A few weeks ago in the City Hall, Candleriggs, there was evidence that this is not simply a pipe dream. Instrumentalists and singers did blend together in a musical synthesis composed by a bloke called Beethoven. It was his Ninth Symphony sometimes called "The Chorale".

Okay, so old Ludwig never sang at a "Hootenanny", and had never attended a seminar organised by the Society of Folk Music. That doesn't necessarily mean he was a musical ignoramus. It's at least arguable, even in the folk song world, that he proved that both sides, singers and musicians, can work together.

Peaceful co-existence should be the aim. This is basically an appeal. As one who lived through the last conflict, I urge you not to plunge the young generation into the horrors of an all-out war where folk fight folk. People should realise that there is no real defence against an amplified folk fiddle.

The very thought is shocking and should spur us into action in a campaign for musical disarmament. In the meantime, does anyone fancy Mantovani?

Glasgow Herald 6 April 1982

No, They Don't Write Them Like That Anymore

SOME months ago a U.S. Army General, seconded to Nato, was seized by Italian terrorists. To the relief of all civilised persons he was liberated by the Italian security forces.

At a press conference following the release the General explained how his captors had begun exposing him to modern "pop" music.

This was a chilling revelation and could signal a new diabolical refinement in the weaponry of psychological warfare. Is there no limit to man's fiendishness? What would then be the next stage? Surely nobody has yet been born so utterly devoid of human feelings as to force a fellow mortal to listen continuously to the disc jockeys on Radio 1.

Well, you all better get one thing clear. See me, I would shop, squeal, inform, shoot the gaff on everyone and in general be a regular little tell-tale tit rather than endure such intolerable pain. Every man has his breaking point and I know mine.

The music these gentlemen purvey is horrendous and yet that is nothing as compared to the absolute cruelty of their deadly chit chat. They milk an audience almost as brutally as Barry Manilow who, of course, in performance must be the ultimate sanction.

The very thought of him teetering about the stage on his platform heels like an elongated claw hammer is enough to give anyone the heebie-jeebies particularly if afflicted by vertigo. His act is justification in itself for crunching into that old standby the strychnine capsule.

Of course music is in the ear of the listening beholder and one man's "Prom" can be another man's poison. There is plenty of evidence to support this assertion. For example I knew a bloke who worked in the joiners shop at John

Brown's, Clydebank, whose wife was absolutely dotty about Frank Ifield. No kidding.

His records blared throughout the house from morning till night. She used to swear by Ifield, and so, when I come to think of it, did her husband. The poor bloke eventually did a bunk, ran away to Arabia and found work as an orderly in a veterinary hospital specialising in the treatment of camels whose bowel movements needed some adjustments.

He was back in Scotland last year on holiday and told his old mates that after listening to Ifield for all those years he found his present environment to be idyllic.

Live and let live is my motto with regards to music and everything else. Though, it has to be admitted that this tolerance is pushed to breaking point by Adam and his Ants, Judas Priest and other groups of musical muggers whose aural assault and battery would be legally questionable in any place that came within the provisions of the Safety At Work Act.

These feelings are tempered by the realisation that others might take umbrage or offence at my musical tastes.

I happen to like the work or works of the old Broadway/Hollywood song writers like Cole Porter. His classic "Kiss Me Kate" was recently on the telly. Ann Miller, the lady with the long tapering shapely legs that start in the region of the cloth pelmet that usually surrounds her pelvis and stretches all the way down to the floor, sang: "I'm always true to you darling in my fa-shun."

She was smashing. Will today's young men look back to Toyah or Alice Cooper with the same warm nostalgia?

However, even the lithe and luscious Ann had to play second fiddle to Keenan Wynn and James Whitmore as the two Runyonesque gangsters who performed "Brush Up Your Shakespeare" as an old vaudeville song and dance routine.

How about this, "If she doesn't respond when you flatterer. Tell her what Tony told Cleopatterer". They don't write lyrics like that nowadays. At least not intentionally.

There is another favourite of mine currently being featured by George Melly called: "My canary's got bags under his eyes". Then there is that splendid song which is now making a bit of a comeback and is entitled "Is you is or is you ain't my baby". To guys who wrote such lyrics syntax just like any other tax was something to be avoided.

These songwriters had a penetrative eye for the social humbug. A wry, dry, ironic, sense of humour which is often the most effective and sometimes the only way to make the point. Some people claim that "Buddy can you spare a dime" was the best popular song of the inter-war depression. Nonsense. It smacks of the band of hope brand of pseudo proletarian politics where things weren't laid on by a trowel but a bleeding great shovel.

Much, much better was a song called: "There's a gold mine in the sky far away". Just think of being unemployed in the 'thirties, languishing on the Means Test or waiting in the queue at a soup kitchen and hearing someone singing in saccharine sweet tones: "Far away, far away, we will find it you and I some sweet day, We will sit out there and watch the world go by, when we find that long lost gold mine in the sky." Yes, I could easily imagine listening to that and then enlisting in the next hunger march.

Now that's a real protest song. In the 'sixties lots of people were talking about Dylan. "What do you think of Dylan," they would ask. "His 'Under Milk Wood' is a minor classic" I would reply. "Twit" would be the response. "Bob Dylan not Dylan Thomas."

The problem was and still is that I can't understand a word the man sings. In projecting a lyric he sounds like a toothless Jocky Wilson chewing a bolt while trying to engage in an argument with Eric Bristow.

What it all boils down to is this; words are fundamental to a song. A good song needs good words otherwise it can't be a good song. And a good singer has to be able to project the words otherwise he or she can't be a good singer.

In Scotland or at any rate on Clydeside we have in my opinion many good word spinners, lyricists in the vernacular who exude in particular the spicy, spiky, outrageous sense of the comic so characteristic of our community.

One of my prized recollections is of Fran and Anna singing a song written by Cliff Hanley entitled "Voulez vous ra noo". It's a glorious spoof, all the better for being sung absolutely straight by our dynamic duo.

Matt McGinn could also pen a nifty lyric and will some day be recognised as one of Scotland's best ever songwriters. He had a rich comic inventiveness which also found expression in monologue. I will never forget hearing him in concert telling the saga of a town in France called Effen.

It was plagued with a swarm of oversized bees. The Effen police had to wage on all out war on these big Effen bees and Matt told the story with relish to the great enjoyment of the audience.

Tom Leonard, Liz Lochhead, Tom McGrath and others are currently writing great stuff. It seems a pity that they can't be teamed up with equally talented composers who might be able to give their words an appropriate musical form or structure. This whole scene could develop into a new urban, witty, indigenous Scottish school of popular music with an appeal well beyond our borders.

Who knows it might contribute to the reinstatement of words to popular music and maybe even result in those who seek to conceal their dearth of talent behind a barrage of decibels being put in their place—you know a padded cell would tend to drown the noise.

Ah well, now that the article is finished I will pour myself a drink, get the feet up and watch the end of the London Marathon. "Here, look at that bloke. His tactics are all wrong. Instead of staggering all over the place he should put in a sprint finish. At least that's what I would do. Fancy a fish supper?"

Glasgow Herald 10 May 1982

The Anti-Hero Cult

POP music has always had its stupid conventions but today it has reached a new low or high. I watched bemused and bewildered as a rock group performed this week on the telly. It really is now the cult of the anti-hero. Ugliness is in. The lead singer was massive and shuffled about the stage like the Incredible Hulk stricken with chronic constipation.

He sometimes stopped to let his hands and head loll downwards until they nearly touched the ground. His long hair, matted and moist with sweat, stuck to his face like bootlaces. Through the hair the face glistened, the mouth puckered into a snarl as he delivered the lyric. He and the supporting group lunged about the stage as if demented.

When the concert finished, searchlights raked and roved the auditorium. The audience, who were all standing, clapped in unison with hands meeting above their heads. It seemed familiar and then I remembered. Just like the old newsreels of the Nuremberg rallies.

Tony Bennett and Sammy Davis and even Jimmy Durante were dead jammy. They would never make it today. They sang in key and delivered and phrased the lyric so that all could understand. These diabolical deficiencies would have been their downfall. Who wants a singer who can sing? Anyway, apart from all that, they were too good looking. Mind you, Lon Chaney would probably have been a smash hit.

Glasgow Herald 22 February 1982

They All Get On My Wick

I once belonged to an elite. To the illustrious few who hadn't seen *The Sound of Music*.

You boasted: "See me, I've never seen *The Sound of Music*." When entering a company you could hear the whispers: "See him, he hasn't seen *The Sound of Music*."

It was easy not to have seen this particular movie. Miss Goody Goody Gumdrops, otherwise known as Julie Andrews, got on my wick.

Her screen persona always brought to mind Groucho Marx's crack about having known Doris Day before she was a virgin.

One day during the festive period *The Sound of Music* was being shown on the telly for what seemed like the 800th time.

My grasp on what was going on around me was somewhat tenuous and so I sat through The Sound of Music.

On more sober reflection it wasn't too bad. I still had many other claims to fame.

For example I have never bought or possessed an Elvis Presley disc nor seen one of his awful movies.

I know they are awful because I've caught snatches of them on the box.

His light baritone voice was tenth rate. He couldn't swing, and his face and personality reflected a mind permanently caught in the grip of infantilism.

I also do not own a recording by the Glen Miller Orchestra, though to be fair it has to be acknowledged that, as a band, they were much better than Elvis as a singer.

However, as a composer/arranger, Miller was never in the same class as Duke Ellington, and, as a band leader, wasn't in the same league as Count Basie.

Then lots of people started raving about Bob Dylan.

He sounded like an asthmatic tom cat recently "dressed" by the vet.

I have also never appreciated Charlie Chaplin.

So for years I concealed as something shameful my failure to see anything tremendously funny in the antics of the wee man and preferred instead, Laurel and Hardy and even the Three Stooges.

Now we come to Barry Manilow.

He will shortly be appearing in Scotland, and looking at the size of his high heels, you could say he was very, very shortly appearing in Scotland.

He teeters about the stage like an animated claw hammer, exuding as he goes a treacly candyfloss substance.

This purports to be charm and tends to ooze off the stage, threatening to engulf the impressionable women in the audience.

So, obviously, Barry's fans are searching for a safe experience as a substitute for the real relationships of life.

Daily Record 8 August 1983

TELEVISION

Waiting For The End Of Part One

> "The girl that I marry will have to be,
> soft and as pink as a nursery,
> the girl I call my own,
> will wear satin and lace and will smell of cologne;
> her nails will be polished and in her hair
> she'll wear a gardenia and I'll be there,
> instead of flittin' I'll be sittin'
> next her and she'll purr like a kitten;
> the doll I will carry, the girl that I marry must be."

In these words of Irving Berlin's song of some decades ago is defined the ultimate role of woman as perceived by the conventions of the time as described by pigs of the male chauvinist variety. Then came Germaine Geer and some other Che Guevarras of women's lib.

The more fair-minded men accepted their main arguments while learning about trying to proceed beyond the bounds of biological possibility. This consensus led to translation which, however imperfect, was in principle favourable to the wants of women in society.

Now savour this lyric:

> "My man takes what he wants from life,
> my man walks off the ground,
> and oh the world looks good to me,
> when my man's around,
> when we split a pinta and share it rim to rim,
> I know that I'm sharing,
> the goodness of the world with him—pinta man."

The singer is soft and pink and wears a lace blouse and shorts. A kind of sexed-up Mary Poppins. She apparently spends her time waiting for her man, who is obsessed with hang-gliding, to come down to earth so that she can ply him with milk. As he once again soars off into the wide blue yonder clinging to an oversize kite she heads back to the dairy for another pinta for her man.

This is an advert on British television in 1981. It is in classical pristine form the stereotyped concept of the totally-dependent woman. Content to sample adventure or the excitement of life at second hand, as precariously derived from her man's activities. The point to note is that women must identify or the advert would have been discarded as a failure. Does such an advert reflect or condition minds? Maybe it does both.

One thing is certain, advertisements are technically the most brilliant productions on television. Nothing is skimped. How many times have you had to reduce the volume when the adverts come on. It's simply to make sure you don't miss the message. Great care is obviously taken with enunciation. Despite the wide use of regional accents every word is understandable in all parts of the country.

A dear friend, who for many years was one of Britain's outstanding female vocalists, once told me of the painstaking effort that goes in to the recording of a jingle. It was for a washing up liquid and contained the line "the hands that do dishes . . ." At first it sounded very, very slightly like: "The hands that judicious." Nothing would suffice until the diction and recording was absolutely 100% correct.

A line of Shakespeare might be fluffed on telly but never a jingle that might implore us to make our armpits charmpits by using a brand name deodorant called "Brutus" or something.

Those who tell themselves and others that they are in no way influenced by adverts are simply the victims of self-deception. Hard-headed businessmen do not spend millions for nothing. Advertising pays for and attracts a wide range of outstanding talents including psychologists, psychiatrists, writers, musicians, composers, actors, film directors *et al.*

Remember how the fortunes of a company manufacturing beef cubes were transformed by a television advertising campaign. This related the product in the public mind with an attractive young suburban housewife called Kate. She had the irresistible combination of respectability and sexuality and showed millions of women viewers how to give a meal man appeal.

Personally I find some of the adverts immensely entertaining and resent the trashy serials, quiz games, and programmes on current affairs that interrupt the commercials. On the other hand, some adverts are in shocking taste, without wit or charm and pandering to the worst in people.

There is one currently to be seen promoting a brand of crisps. A young Geordie lad has a paper round. He greets a younger boy just outside a block of multi-storey flats. "Hey, Jock," he cries, "deliver them and I'll give you a canny bag of crisps." The youngster accepts. Meanwhile "Wor Geordie" smugly smirks and says: "Pity the lifts are out of order." Ugh.

The image is of a selfish, self-centred, unattractive little twit who will never create wealth but might make money. Potentially a clever Dick, smart asset stripper or a machine politician.

Then we have that wonderful duo, the grandad and grandson with a liking for canned soup. The old boy's tall tales, the wide-eyed innocence and trust of the child are underpinned by an affectionate warmth. I consider their acting to be outstanding.

As you would expect the drink trade do very well. The grouse-beaters are now part of our everyday language and might even become a part of folklore. I haven't seen it this week but the advert for our other national drink rarely fails to raise a chuckle.

Then there is the one promoting a lager that features a repulsive smart alick who is always outwitting his pal or girl companion or getting off with some stranger's girlfriend. This advert ends on a note that is either flat or sharp. This is apppropriate as the whole thing is to my mind discordant and distasteful.

These remarks relate only to the adverts and not the actual product of which I know little. You see these adverts don't influence me at all, at all. Barman give me a pint of Persil.

Glasgow Herald 6 September 1981

Traffic In Gore And Violence At Peak Periods

IF future historians or archaeologists were to use television archives as a guide to our times then the picture would be of a society where 40% of the population are in law enforcement and State security agencies, another 40% being drug addicts or pedlars, rapists, kidnappers, pimps, pickpockets, racketeers or various kinds of social or psychiatric misfits with criminal tendencies.

The rest, a small minority being monogomous, hard working, uninspiring bores, considered unsuitable or unworthy material for television scriptwriters. "No wonder they had economic difficulties," will be their conclusion.

Here is a sample from this week's programmes. *The Professionals*, *The Sweeney*, *The Deceivers*, described in the *Radio Times* as dealing with "cons and swindlers, a look at the misdirected talents of the criminal mind".

The Cover is "A ruthless offshoot of the Secret Service", according to the *TV Times*. Then a new series *Hill Street Blues*. Another "realistic" look at an inner city police precinct. Are there no outer city police precincts in America?

The Treachery Game has a title which is self explanatory.

Note that nearly all are in prime viewing time. There are differences. Indeed, the same series might vary its approach from week to week. Given the subject matter of these programmes violence is almost inescapable. However, it is the treatment of violence that matters.

In this week's *Sweeney* which is an excellently directed, well-acted, highly-professional product, a youth has an affair with the wife of an imprisoned underworld boss. It ended with the youngster falling into his mother's arms, beaten to a pulp by the paid musclemen of the cuckolded husband.

The point, if there was one, eluded me. It seemed an exercise in gratuitous violence.

The central characters in these programmes, like Messrs Doyle and Bodie in *The Professionals* have remarkable, one might even say miraculous, physical resilience and strength.

These civil servants or public sector employees have a lifestyle which clearly leans heavily towards booze and all-night carousals. Though, on the morn after the night before they can still pursue criminals or enemies of the state for miles, clamber over roofs and walls, and still have enough puff left to apprehend and give chastisement to all the assorted baddies.

I did two Burns suppers last week and was out the game for days. It's not fair.

I agree with those who can see no artistic justification for the "soft porn" that occasionally masquerades as television drama. But it is the often hysterical reaction to sex and sexuality in contrast to the deafening silence about the glorification of violence, which bugs me.

After all the former tends to the creation of human life, the latter to its destruction. Robert Burns expressed the relative values most succinctly

> "The dieties I adore.
> A social peace in plenty . . .
> I'm better pleas'd to make one more
> Than be the death of 20."

Censorship is no solution. It merely opens the door to those bigots who would ban anything and everything that doesn't conform to their prejudices. It may sound trite but is nonetheless true, the only solution or sanction is to switch off or over.

If enough do it they soon get the message. Things, even particularly unpleasant things, should not be repressed. Violence should be portrayed on television. It is how, and in what way. Violence has no moral authority. This was highlighted in two films, the first being *Shaft*.

Again it was a quite brilliantly produced film. It seemed to glory in the gore. Despite its gloss I found it unacceptable. Then *My Darling Clementine*, was about the Earps, led by Wyatt, and helped out by Doc Holliday doing battle with the Clantons, culminating in yet another version of the famous gun battle at the OK Corral.

The 1860s must have been as violent as any time in American history. John Ford's brilliant direction caught the period and evoked a mood that showed the violence without glorification and with a poignant sadness. It was quite beautiful. Though I don't expect the Clantons, who once again bit the dust, to share this view.

Glasgow Herald 31 January 1981

Does The Lens Put Us Truly In The Picture?

ALL of us were overjoyed as the ordeal of the American hostages ended. Their seizure was a criminal act which, if adopted as a tactic by other regimes, would make impossible civilised diplomatic relations between countries and peoples.

To trade people's lives for money is outrageous by any standards except those of the kidnapper. Yet my unease at the television treatment was considerable. The coverage was so extensive as to amount to a media overkill. Camera crews were everywhere: Teheran, Algiers, West Germany and Washington.

Dancers must have been tripping over them at the various inaugural receptions for the new American president. They popped up again in Plains, Georgia, to follow the involvement of the new ex-American president in the negotiations for their release. They materialised yet again in the assorted homes of the hostages, "recording" for our benefit the reactions of mums, dads, wives and fiancees.

The veracity of such television is highly questionable. A television's camera in someone's living room doesn't only record a situation—it changes it. You do not see a mother's reaction to her son's liberation, you see a mother's reaction in the presence of a camera to her son's liberation. Which is something different.

Another thought insidiously persists. How would the media have treated the same story if it had been 50 Sri Lankans held to ransom by, let us say, some Central African dictatorship? It is certain that the coverage would have been only a fraction of that given to those held by the Ayatollah.

The media seem to have acquired an exchange rule that determines people's entitlement to coverage. One white Anglo-Saxon equals 60 Arabs, 90 Africans, etc. Or that the citizens of the two big military giants rate higher priority than others. It reminds me of Claude Cockburn's story about the sub-editor at *The Times* who could write headlines such as "Earthquake in Chile—not many killed".

Glasgow Herald 24 January 1981

Ring Of Truth In The Corridors Of Power

SATIRE is a much-abused word, often used to describe plays, reviews, television programmes and other "intellectual" activities that are essentially and sometimes even crudely caricaturist.

Now there is nothing wrong with caricature as most cartoonists will assuredly assert. To exaggerate, even grossly, a distinctive feature of an individual or a situation to highlight a fundamental characteristic is a quite legitimate exercise.

It is not, however, satire which is the art by which a basic absurdity or contradiction in an individual, a group, or an outlook is exposed by subtly using their own language, behaviour, and arguments and deftly turning them into a form of self-indictment.

To give a comparative illustration. *Not the Nine O'Clock News* was caricature. *Yes Minister* is satire. The actors in this outstanding series, Paul Edington as Hacker, the not-so-bright and rather spineless Minister, and Nigel Hawthorne as Sir Humphrey, the Permanent Secretary who makes Macchiavelli look like a simpleton are now getting the accolades their acting so richly deserves.

The writers must also get their due. Anthony Jay and Jonathan Lynn are producing brilliant scripts with a satirical quality seldom ever seen on television. People speak of life imitating art. Real life and true art are so inter-related as to be inseparable. *Yes Minister* rings true for a very good reason.

It is true. In general the fundamental relationship between a Government Minister and the highest ranking civil servant in the Ministry is as described in this series. Governments come and go while the country is run by these full-time professionals in the higher echelons of the State.

It is all held together by the old boys' network. School pals, the alma mater, the Eton Boating Song, the Varsity rugger match, Henley, the MCC, Wimbledon, a few select London clubs, are only some of the strands that are woven into the fabric of their "world".

When at Oxford or Cambridge a career in the Civil Service is mooted it is not as a Post Office counter clerk or hospital porter but a position in someone like Sir Humphrey's department. After all he was at school with Pater. Plays bridge with Uncle Reggie. And is married to Mother's second cousin. Their system produces some brilliant men.

It also produced and nurtured Burgess and Mclean, Philby, and Blunt. A self-perpetuating bureaucracy which, like all others, resists any change likely to undermine its authority.

Yes Minister is doing more to educate our people about the realities of our system of Government than all the political theorists and lecturers put together.

Glasgow Herald 21 May 1981

"Dallas"—The Next Time They Should Shoot To Kill

SOME months ago, *Dallas* was glorious and glossy televisual hokum. An ingredient as necessary in its own way as roughage to the average diet, and fulfilling a somewhat similar function.

A world where things like halitosis and sweaty socks didn't exist, where inflation and illness were peripheral nuisances. All concerned rightly played it for real. Such unreal material, unless treated seriously, collapses into farce.

One now suspects that everyone involved is jaded. It simply isn't possible to write, ad infinitum, weekly self-contained stories, portraying the development of real people, in real situations, in the real world. This is beyond the creative imagination of almost anyone.

Soap opera scriptwriters have therefore no alternative but to devise plastic, stereotyped characters to use as hooks on which to hang each week's plot. This, however, is no excuse for turning the Ewing beings into clones.

For example JR is now played with three expressions. The Leer—lascivious or triumphant dependent on whether he is about to do, or has just done, something or someone. The Grimace—a pop-eyed look of simmering male-volence. The Smarm—trying unsuccessfully to conceal malicious intent. JR's villainy is now comic, like the evil squire of silent melodrama.

It might have been better for all concerned if Sue Ellen's sister had been a better shot.

The highlight this week was little Lucy's wedding. She is the most enticing of the Southfork womenfolk. Her head and backside are beautifully proportioned for a seven foot Amazon. Maybe it's this departure from precisely proportioned physical perfectibility so boringly evident in the others that makes her appealing.

Besides, she proves we haven't cornered the market in wee bachles.

It is difficult to accept that Gary—the alcoholic son of Jock and Ellie, who escaped from JR by running away to a place called Knots Landing, which sounds like some place in Southern Africa where Zulus overran an army outpost, but is actually a nice, upper middle-class ghetto in Southern California—could be Lucy's father.

He towered over the wee yin as they walked down the aisle arm-in-arm to the groom and presiding clergyman, who sported that currently fashionable born-again look. Some academics insist that the wedding ritual retains strong elements of paganism, and point to the number of jokes and anecdotes from different cultures about its arousal effects as proof of their thesis.

157

Here this Freudian angle was grossly overplayed. As proceedings approached their climax, Sue Ellen, convinced that JR was up to his old tricks (as he was with the bridegroom's sister), turned to find her lover from college days.

Wet lips glistening, her smouldering eyes met his in tryst of good, or maybe even bad, things to come. Meanwhile Pamela, sick to the back teeth with Bobby's entrepreneurial endeavours and consequential neglect of wifely needs, gave the glad-eye to Alex, a publisher who, as our American cousins would put it, has the hots for her.

It then spread like an epidemic. An attractive lady, previously married to a truck-driving, bricklaying, rather eccentric young lawyer with a name like Petrochemical, was smitten.

She could barely control herself while making a play for Ray Krebbs, the illegitimate son of Jock.

It must have been the heat. I'll tell you something, it doesn't happen at weddings in Clydebank, Govan or even Bearsden. The only person apparently unaffected by this aphrodisiacal tidal wave was the big man himself. Burnished face, crowned with a carefully coiffured thatch of grey, Jock hung about like the father of the Midnight Cowboy.

I was watching in the company of former devotees. Their interest quickly dissolved into laughter as cliche followed cliche. The writing is on the wall for this series and by the standards of last week's episode, that's where it belongs.

Glasgow Herald 7 February 1981

Pamela's Wide Eyes Have It

FOR about the first time in two years, I watched *Dallas*. Nothing has changed. The women are all long legs, succulent lips with uniform teeth flashing in the sun.

It raises the question—are there no wee bachles in Texas? After a while you start to yearn for Hilda Ogden.

The actors lived down to their reputations.

Pamela has left Bobby and not before time. He is trying to become tough like JR, which is like Danny La Rue playing Al Capone.

Have you noticed Pamela's eyes? When she's angry, they get larger. When she's surprised, they get larger. When she feels lovey-dovey, they get larger.

By the end of the programme she looks like a humanoid owl.

JR is the same old JR. A combination of Dick Dastardly and the bad squire from the old silent melodramas.

But after observing Norman Tebbit and Mrs Thatcher at work, it's a pleasure to watch someone as civilised as JR.

Daily Record 7 March 1983

Oh, I'm Getting Dizzy Over "Dynasty"!

I watched *Dynasty*, son of *Dallas*, for the first time last Saturday.

It had all the same features including the fabulously oil-rich family headed by a Big Daddy father-figure.

In fact Blake Carrington could easily be Jock Ewing slightly touched up by plastic surgery.

Maybe Jock got fed up with Miss Ellie's simpering and Sue Ellen's whimpering, changed his name, and scarpered into the loving arms of a big blonde in Denver by the name of Krystle.

As the titular boss of another family, Blake (or Jock) keeps fit by whizzing round a house so big that it makes Southfork look like a single-end.

Blake's son Stephen is married to someone called Sammy Jo, who's a girl. Stephen, we learn, is homosexual, though any bloke married to a Sammy Jo might easily have a problem.

Stephen's mother isn't Krystle, but a broad called Alexis, who is really Joan Collins pretending to be an actress.

She is seen having pizza and champagne for breakfast. Her boyfriend, whose name I didn't catch, is sharing the meal, turns away and holds his chest as if pained by a coronary spasm.

Considering the eating habits, it could just as easily have been heartburn.

Meanwhile a psychiatrist-cum-surgeon by the name of Toscanni keeps popping in and out of the action.

He describes himself as one-third shrink, one-third cutter-up and one-third Italian . . . which sounded more like a Mafia hit-man than a Neapolitan member of the medical profession.

Blake's baby grandson comes home from hospital where, with any sense, he would have stayed.

Claudia, a mentally-deranged woman, was everywhere. I could sympathise. Mental derangement could easily be induced by this series.

Daily Record 13 June 1983

To Boldly Go To The Mindless World Of Mr Spock

STAR TREK is essential viewing in the Reid household by the decree of my youngest daughter.

This week, from behind my newspaper, I distinctly heard laughter. Now, to my ears there is nothing that quite compares with the uninhibited, unforced natural sound of a child laughing. The cause was soon made clear: somebody had stolen Mr Spock's brain.

Yes, there he was, none the worse, except for a certain vacuity about the eyes and retarded mobility familiar to anyone who has been within the confines of the Press Bar near closing time on a Friday night.

159

A suggestion that he might be stoned out of his mind by a heavy bevvy, or words to that effect, was quickly rebuffed. A lady with a mini-skirt had apparently materialised inside the "Enterprise" and knocked the whole crew flat by pressing a button on her bracelet and had then pinched Old Pointed Ears's grey matter.

Captain Kirk was clearly upset. He depends a lot on Spock's brains. In fact if the lassie had stolen his no one would have noticed. The starship is full of tokens. There are the token negroes, the token Chinaman, the token women, the latter all leggy and wearing hotpants or leotards.

There is a token Russian who is identifiable by his execrable accent. There is even a token Scotsman, called by brilliant stroke of originality, Scotty. Just to make sure that you do not miss the point he always has to say lines like: "Kaptin, over here, surr."

All ends up well. Kirk and Dr McCoy and a few others beam down to this planet and are immediately attacked by big hairy men that look like a group of folk singers whose van has broken down on the way back from a gig.

However, a few wee touches of the laser guns and the hairy ones are oot the game. Anyway, it is discovered that the women, who all live underground and possess these nasty bracelets, are the real culprits.

Kirk and his gang eventually find the secret of how to carry out a brave retransplant by placing McCoy under what looked like a hairdryer. Through this he absorbs the necessary information and then is able to operate and put all the nerve ends together by some process that looked like soldering. When he is finished, Spock jumps up without even a hair out of place. Not kidding, I have lost more blood shaving.

The best line of the week was from one of the surface-bound hirsute males who described the delightful looking female with the pain-inducing bracelets as one of those who "give us pain and delight". How profound and true.

There are millions of sci-fi fans. They deserve something better than this.

Glasgow Herald 7 March 1981

Diabolical Night With The Glamorous Grandmothers

"HEY missus, hey mister, see me, ah'm sentimental." This in all truth, I can say. But my sentimentality has limits. These were considerably breached by *Nationwide.*

It featured the finals of the "Glamorous Grandmothers Competition" which was embarrassingly diabolical. Setting aside the question of whether women should be paraded and evaluated like human cattle, the criteria of judgment should surely change as between different age groups and categories. Not so.

The winner could have been a contestant in any other "beauty" contest. If this particular granny had a "hielan hame" her "brae" would be like Sauchiehall Street on a Saturday afternoon full of aspiring sugar granddaddys.

The alternative to growing old gracefully is not to strive pathetically and even desperately to some youthful image. Women are all too often brainwashed into conforming to a stereotyped concept of feminine beauty.

It is all tosh. A Barbra Streisand wouldn't have reached the quarter-finals of this competition. Her hooter is somewhat bigger than the standard variety.

Women are the best opposite sex that men have got. Uniformity of body or mind is neither desirable or possible. If I may paraphrase Shakespeare: "Time cannot wither, nor custom stale, their infinite variety." Thank God!

These 20 grandmothers were, I think, fine-looking women. The element of doubt creeps in only because some seemed to have sprayed their faces with cellulose paint that formed a glossy façade behind which their real selves lurked.

As they walked with the traditional mincing steps, presumably considered sexy, to meet their male inquisitor, I felt a surge of sympathy for them and anger for those, including the BBC, who were submitting them to this indignity.

The crass and blatant determination to squeeze every last drop of slush out of the proceedings resulted in a finale of unbelievable banality. The grandchildren in little piping voices sang "Grandma, we love you".

The camera closed in on a wee chap who looked like Harry Secombe as a child. His painful scowl was perfectly understandable in the circumstances. I knew exactly how he felt.

Glasgow Herald 28 March 1981

On Glasgow's Glories

LEGEND OF BUTCH AND SOMEDANCE

NOT for nothing was he known as the "Somedance Kid". In the Govan of those days "Hops" had nothing to do with a plant that flavours beer but was a much more potent brew known as a dance.

These dances took place in the town hall and were organised almost on a rota system by a wide assortment of local clubs and institutions from the Knights of St Columba to the Freemasons. From ladies' badminton groups to the local association of turf accountants called, I so believe, because their most regular patrons always complained of "turf" luck.

The "Somedance Kid" frequented all the dances with complete and absolute indifference to the aims and objects of the sponsoring body. He loved them all and would enthuse, "somedance, eh?" His pal was an apprentice butcher by the name of Cassidy known to one and all as "Butch".

Butch Cassidy and the Somedance Kid were Govan's answer to Cesar Romero and George Raft. They could dance a tango which made all the other men green with envy and caused some concern at dances organised by the local Rangers Supporters Club.

Immediately one set foot on the floor the back became as stiff as an ironing board, as straight as Sauchiehall Street.

They danced only with a select coterie of females who also attended every dance. You could tell them a mile away, for they never looked into the face or eyes of their partners. Instead their heads were held back and inclined to the left or right at an angle of approximately 45 degrees. They also had a fixed glacial smile that has become so fashionable since the advent of Mrs T.

As someone who, in his youth, thought that a dance was like a trade union branch meeting—in other words a chance to stand up and state your case—I didn't particularly fancy perambulating round the floor with these ladies. You couldn't even leer at them. However, I digress, Butch and Somedance were sensations long before Peter West ever cast a jaundiced eye over a sequinned dress.

I can see them yet jerking and twisting around the floor. Little abrupt stops and starts that probably slipped a few feminine discs. Their heads would suddenly and for no accountable reason swivel quickly one way, then the other.

Then the lumber regions of their partners weren't helped when the Somedance and Butch would rudely bend them over a left arm and leg at the end of some particular piece of intricate footwork. "Oops" and "ahhs" followed their terpsichorean progress with sometimes a more articulate form of vocal encouragement such as, "Gaun yersel Butch" or "Smashin' Somedance".

I don't know what happened to them. Rumour has it that they came to a sticky end somewhere in South America while trying to get their hands on a few quid or whatever the name of the local lucre was. They were probably trying to raise the entrance fee to the local Cantina so as to have a go at the Paso Doble.

My theory is that the advent of the new fashion in dancing where the sexes do not touch drove them both from Govan.

The last time we met "Somedance" put it most succinctly. "Ye canny even get near them noo, never mind stretching them ower yer knee." Too true "Somedance". They are also too big.

A welder in Fairfields says it's all Germaine Greer's fault. Not me, I blame Robert Redford. He wasn't a patch on the real "Somedance" and he couldn't even spell the name properly.

Glasgow Herald 10 January 1983

THE DAY SCOOPDOOP WAS ON TO SOMETHING BIG

THERE was amoaning and awailing from what the Anglo-Saxons call children and we call weans. The Scots word is better. I would rather be a wean than a child. What about you?

Anyway there they were, amoaning and awailing and making one helluva noise. Anxious mothers poked heads out of windows to inquire the cause of these lamentations. The weans were all crying: "Santa's dead. He's been gored to death by his reindeers."

The mothers angrily asked: "Who told you that?" The weans pointed to one of their own kind. An angelic-looking youngster—me. It was true, I had started the rumour. For badness, said my mother, for devilment, said me. Anyway, I got a battering. Ever since then I've had no time for squealers, stoolpigeons, or tell tale tits.

You must have wondered what happens to tell tale tits when they grow up. In the strictest confidence I can tell you, they become investigative journalists or gossip columnists. When these guys talk of five shopping days to Xmas they mean something different from the rest of us. You see, they would shop their granny for a good story.

For example, take Scoopdoop McGlone. He used to be the media terror of

163

all the miscreants in Govan. Nobody, apart from bookmakers, escaped his eagle eye. His daddy, you will understand, was "Happy Harry" the punter's pal. You must have seen him at the Ayr racing. He was the bookie that wore running shoes.

Scoopdoop, as his friends called him, that meant his mum and I, was an intrepid investigator. One day he burst into a well-known watering hole just off Govan Road where I was, already comfortably ensconced, and excitedly croaked: "Jimmy, I'm on to something big." Now, Scoopdoop was an inveterate woman-iser. I thought that this was probably his quaint way of telling me he was winching an Amazon.

Height, of course, like everything else, is relative. Scoopdoop, you should also understand, was rather wee. Toatie, in fact. He even referred to Gordon Richards as the big yin and looked like a much smaller version of Ronnie Corbett.

He pushed his hat (we used to call this kind of hat a split pea) to the back of his head, just like Alan Ladd did in the current movie hit, and continued: "I'm on to something big and I need your help."

As it so happened I was then reading all the American private eye stories by Dashiell Hammett, Raymond Chandler, and sundry other detective novelists, or should it be novel detectivists? So I was therefore youthfully vulnerable to such a proposition. More than ready to fantasise as Govan's answer to Sam Spade.

"OK, OK," I said, "level with me. Give me the whole story right from the start." To the barman I drawled "Same again Sam, and a Scotch on the rocks for my friend." Sam said: "Look son, my name's Erchie and if you want a hauf fur yer pal why don't you say so."

Cold eyed I looked at him, flashed my trade union card, and said: "Less lip and give with the drinks."

Scoopdoop had difficulty drinking his drink on account of his shaking. He was shaking like the lead singer with the Ink Spots. "Look," I said, "let's have it from the top."

Scoopdoop looked over his shoulder and dropped his voice by about two octaves as if he were Mrs Thatcher, and said intently: "I know who shot Cock Robin."

Cock Robin was the nick-name given to the local flyman who ran a pitch and toss school. Recently someone had peppered his bottom with pellets from an airgun as he strolled down Harmony Row. His mob were searching high and low for the poor silly sap who had done this foul deed.

"Cool down. Don't get excited. Tell me everything." Scoopdoop went to: "As you know, Cock Robin isn't taking this sitting down. His pride and some other things have been hurt. To put it bluntly, he's bealin'. There is a contract out, to find and deal with whoever done it."

This was bad news. Out there in the mean streets, where the flickering lights danced in the reflections on the puddles, the last thing the people needed was an outbreak of gang warfare. What would happen if Bampot Gasket, who earned this soubriquet through his total incompetence as a motor mechanic and ran a rival pitch and toss school, or one of his gang, had lacerated Cock Robin's bottom?

The ensuing mayhem could be such that the Scottish Development Agency might decide not to do anything for Govan, thus guaranteeing an immediate upsurge in the local economy and the provision of more jobs. That sort of thing could break up homes.

To Scoopdoop I said: "Give it to me straight." He licked his lips nervously and muttered: "It was the Bampot."

Later, as I walked the lonely streets I got to thinking, life is really strange. Scoopdoop had the biggest story of his life and couldn't use it.

And I, a hard-bitten sonofabitch, was going to do something for all the ordinary little guys who needed law-abiding streets on which their women could walk without fear.

I went into the snooker hall where Bampot hung out, sidled up to one of his gorillas and said: "Look Buster, take me to your boss or I'll bust yer lip." Before he could respond a voice rang out, "Haw Jimmy, how's it gaun?" It was Bampot. The same baby-faced sadist that won the dux medal at our school.

"Bampot," I said, "let's have a little parley." I told him the score and advised him to leave the town pronto for his own sake and for the sake of all the little ordinary men and their little ordinary wives and their little ordinary children, all living in little ordinary houses, etc. He got the picture. "Right," he said, "I'll get my teddy bear and then it's on my bike and offsky to the Big Smoke." Well you all know what happened. Life is funny. Ain't it strange how the cookie crumbles?

Bampot is now a well-known quizmaster down south with something called "Labour Exchange Challenge" and Cock Robin is skint and spends his time with racing pigeons. Needless to say, he always gets beat.

This only goes to show that in a free-market economy, mobility of labour is the way to get ahead. I give this advice to the unemployed in the new year by paraphrasing the immortal words of Mr Norman Tebbit, "Get on your bikes and you too can be a Bampot".

Glasgow Herald 20 December 1982

GOING FOR A SONG

"HEV you ever been lonelee, Hev you ever been blue, Hev you ever been tired, Since you've been on the buroo?" The singer was the Sammy Cahn of Partick and he was giving it laldy at the party.

Everyone was encouraged to shout out a subject and the maestro would make up a brand new lyric to a well-known tune right there and then. It was clever stuff for people were trying to catch him out. One young lady suggested that the love life of an eccentric sheep might cause him difficulty. At once he started singing "I get a kick out of ewes".

A gent who had been to a football game and was suffering from the gastronomic delights he had consumed at half time grumbled "Mouldy pies". It was more a complaint than anything else but quick as a flash our wordsmith extraordinaire was away. "Oh manky flies steeped in these mouldy pies up tae yer thighs." The melody was Spanish Eyes and he even contrived to look like Engelbert Humperdinck.

It was about then I realised we were in the company of a unique talent. He then for my benefit proceeded to pay vocal tribute to those associated with this paper in a revamped version of "Hark the Herald angels sing".

He then gave us a Scottish medley starting with "Anderston Cross I wish you were whisky, Anderston Cross Och aye, Anderston Cross I wish you were whisky and I would dri-hink you dry" and ending with a song called "The hypochondriac's lament", his words to a well-known Gaelic air. It went something like this—"Wherever I wander my ailments come too, I'm full of bronchitis and asthma and flu, My arches have fallen, my bottom it sags, so when off on a journey I put these things in my bags."

Then came the chorus: "Oh Calamine lotion and syrup of figs and milk of magnesia and liquorice sticks, I've plenty of pills too, inhalants as well and see all the doctors they can all go to hell." At this juncture I thought to myself, if this bloke doesn't watch he might end up on the BBC's Hogmanay programme.

During a respite from his creative endeavours I got talking to him. He was obviously aware of his special talents: "My genius," he modestly admitted, "sets me apart from other men, like a Protestant in Croy." I tried to find out how or where he had developed this amazing facility with words. "I'm a natural," he said. He insists that his formal education is sparse and no he didn't do crosswords. In fact he didn't approve of them. His act was good clean family stuff.

As we left he was singing: "The loveliness of Harris seems somehow sadly gay. The glory that was Troon is of another day. As I sit here alone, forgotten in Kilchattan, My thoughts go home to my city by the Clyde—I left my heart in dear old Glasgow, I left my liver in the Horseshoe Bar. To be in fabled Garngad," and then there was a reference to his Dad but somebody had closed the door and his voice was no longer wafting down the stairs.

As I said to my wife at the time that man could make a fortune writing Country and Western songs if he was prepared to lower his standards.

Glasgow Herald 13 December 1982

WAN SINGER

THE Clydeside school of singing requires a very special technique. My uncles were expert practitioners.

At New Year parties, they would excel.

The object seemed to be to hold on to a note as long as possible and to end each phrase or even word with an emphatic "ah".

It went something like this: "Ra pale-ah moooon-ah was shiningngngng-ah."

Each rendition lasted about half-an-hour and the matronly admirers would demand silence and give encouragement by screeching: "Wan singer, wan song!" and "Gaun yersel, Erchie!"

On Saturday I was watching *The Main Attraction* on BBC-1 and there, unmistakably, was Elaine Page, fresh from asking Argentina not to cry, belting it out as an obvious convert to our Clydeside school of vocal projection.

I forget the song for it was quite forgettable. What stuck in my mind was her technique. She sang about "Set you Freeee-ah, from A to B-ah".

My wife said something like: "Jimmy, do you want a cup of tea?" and I found myself retorting: "A bit of hush for the singer. Gaun yersel, Elaine."

Daily Record 1 August 1983

MORGAN . . . A SUITABLE CASE

THE author of a newly-published novel was described last week by a reviewer in one of our so-called quality newspapers as "a surrealistic psychodramatist".

Now there's a mouthful. I don't know what it means, but it sounds impressive.

Edinburgh during the Festival and London anytime of the year are full of guys and dolls who can make with this kind of language.

From time to time, they pop up on the telly talking about the inner meaning of a book, play or film. If something bad happens to a woman, it has nothing to do with the fact that, sometimes in life, something bad can happen to a woman.

Oh, no—it is the author or director subconsciously seeking revenge on his mother because she refused to let him suck his thumb when he was a wee nipper.

This is a thriving business where people tell us about books we have just read or plays we have just seen.

Over the years, they have explained things to us like the social significance of the Beatles.

In our ignorance we might have thought that their songs were tuneful, well -constructed and had lyrics which occasionally made a comment on our times and that people therefore liked them. How wrong we were.

The songs of Lennon and McCartney, we are told, can be understood only if seen as the anguished cry of a generation deeply hurt by uncaring father-figures such as Harold Wilson and Max Bygraves.

What I want to know is why these intellectuals have ignored the inner mental implication of Scotland's popular culture.

For example, Scottish comedians, in the mould of Hector Nicol and Mr Abie are literally teeming with deep and subtle inner meanings. As Hector Nicol might say, "I'm as mental as anyone".

I have made a study of two of Scotland's legendary comic figures, Tommy Morgan and Sammy Murray. Who knows, if I play my cards right I might end up being interviewed by Melvyn Bragg.

Tommy Morgan's role in the downfall of Hitler has been greatly undervalued.

In the blackest hours of the war, Churchill's speeches were said to have rallied the nation. But what about Tommy Morgan's famous song of defiance against Hitler:

> "He'll sink a few more sma' boats I suppose,
> But he'll never sink the Duchess of Montrose.
> He may bomb and bomb and bomb us,
> But we'll never turn a hair,
> For there'll always be a Rothesay at the Ferr."

I have it on the highest authority that when Hitler heard of this song, he virtually gave up hope of ever conquering the Scots and instead invaded Russia as a soft option.

Tommy also enriched our language with sayings such as "Clairty, Clairty" . . . "Where's the scruberrr" and "The wee weasel was ferr wabbit". They don't write like that nowadays.

Sammy Murray was another genius who knocked them out regularly at the old Queen's Theatre in Glasgow.

Sammy's most famous song was "Awra King's hoarses, awra King's men, marching doon the Gallowgate and marching back agenn".

The 'Kings' referred to had nothing to do with the monarch, it was another Glasgow theatre famed for its pantomime horses. You will thus notice the subtle double meaning of the lyric.

At that time, there was also on "boards", as they say in showbiz, a lady who went by the name of Suicide Sal. Was her act a very cleverly-concealed argument for euthanasia? Now there's a thought.

Daily Record 7 March 1983

THESE ARE THE GIRLS I'M NOT ASKING FOR

WE were leaving to go to dinner with a family friend when one of our daughters said: "Tell Ruth I was asking for her."

When you come to think of it, such messages are daft. You can ask after a person's health or financial circumstances or sex life—or even its absence—but what's the point of a big, meaningless "asking for"?

Some years ago, one friend was always asking me to tell another that she was asking for him. So I would say: "Joe, Aggie is asking for you."

Joe would always nod absent-mindedly, so one day I decided to insert a negative into the message.

"Joe," I said, "Aggie is *not* asking for you."

Joe was obviously startled. "What do you mean she's not asking for me?"

I paused for effect and then said quietly but with great emphasis: "Aggie is very definitely not asking for you."

He was worried, and later that day he phoned Aggie.

"Look," he said, "what's all this about you not asking for me? What have I done that offends you so much that you are not quite definitely not asking for me?"

Aggie was mortified, because she fancied him strongly.

"Joe, I'm always asking for you. In fact, only yesterday I told Jimmy to tell you that I was asking for you."

So Reid was exposed—and not for the first time—as a bit of a manure-stirrer. It was all in a good cause.

Joe was so relieved to know that Aggie had, in fact, asked for him that he asked her for a date. The following year they were married.

I told this story to a pal who, for some strange reason, rather fancies Jane Fonda and Raquel Welch.

He started going about saying to people: "If you bump into Jane or Raquel, will you please tell them. I'm not asking for them."

He was convinced that once they heard he was not asking for them they would immediately fly over to demand of him an explanation. His charm and charisma, he reckoned, would then do the rest.

It sounded screwball to me, yet reports are coming in that he was recently sighted walking down Govan Road with a long-limbed North American beauty who looked remarkably like Miss Fonda.

Well, you never know—so here goes . . .

Will someone please tell Hannah Gordon, Bo Derek, Claudia Cardinale, Sophia Loren and the girl who was the lead trumpet in Ivy Benson's Band that I'm not asking for them, most definitely.

I only hope they don't all come at the same time.

Daily Record 11 July 1983

SMALL ROOM TALK

LAST week, I wrote about the significance in the Govan of my childhood of having a lavatory in the house.

A lady who claims to be an academic has written to tell me that the working class on Clydeside always used the word toilet and never lavatory.

Well, to be blunt, missus, we actually spoke of the lavvy and rarely put in the tory whether in reference to toilets or elections.

Could I suggest sewage centre as a more contemporary, all-embracing term?
Then, on reflection, that is a term which would be much more appropriate to those groups of intellectuals who study the behaviour and language of ordinary working people as if they were a separate and inferior species.

Daily Record 16 June 1983

THANKS FOR THE MEMORY

YOU might think nostalgia is lost in this modern age. It's not. I saw nostalgia last week alive and kicking in Govan.

At the corner of Kintra Street and Summertown Road, women were hanging over window-sills and talking to each other and some other neighbours in the street below.

Yet, according to those professional observers who study our changing lifestyles, the practice of "hinging oot windies" belonged to years gone by.

Isn't it great. The experts are wrong once again . . . hingies are here to stay.

Daily Record 27 June 1983

PUBS AIN'T WHAT THEY USED TO BE

IN the "good old days", men were men and pubs were pubs and never the twain should part, or so it seemed.

Pubs were places where nothing was allowed to interfere with the serious business of drinking.

The furnishings were plain, wooden tables and chairs; the colour scheme a vivacious dark brown, mottled with cigarette smoke and alcoholic fumes.

In many respects, those pubs looked like the saloons in cowboy movies—except, of course, for the saloon gals.

Round the bar was a brass rail raised about 10 inches off the floor. You could lean with an arm on the bar and one foot resting on the brass rail.

This posture could be kept for hours . . . and frequently was.

Small men used the rail for another purpose. They would hop on it to gain temporary elevation from which to order a round of drinks.

A wee round face would suddenly pop up and mouth to the barman: "Three haufs and three hauf pints"—and then sink once again into the surrounding sea of taller mortals.

The public bars were generally big, commodious places. Singing or music of any kind, or anything that could remotely be called entertainment, was banned —as were women.

These pubs were havens for male chauvinist pigs. I can remember a barman asking a customer who had just explained how he spent most of his time at work or in the pub: "I suppose the wife hardly ever sees you."

"No true," said the barfly, "she's got ma photie."

In those days, few agonised about their alcoholic lifestyles. If you asked a heavy drinker or a right bevvy merchant if he had a drink problem, the answer might be:

"Aye, I've a problem alright—ah cannae get enough of the stuff."

Then into this scene came well-intentioned liberal reformers like me.

Let's civilise our drinking habits was our plea. Bring music and games into our pubs. Equality means that women should have the same opportunity as men to acquire cirrhosis of the liver.

We won. Lounge bars got bigger and bigger, with fitted carpets, space-invader machines, plastic tables and plastic music.

Not surprisingly, this drove many a man to sobriety. Others chose to drink in the discomfort of home rather than in the cacophony of the modern pub.

These reminiscences were inspired by an advert currently being shown on television.

Two young lads are seen going into an old-fashioned pub where the clientele are quietly brooding, sipping their beverages, and apparently enjoying themselves.

There is a blissful hush and no infernal machines shatter the peace.

The two young fools rush off to another pub which is a den of din and dolly birds.

Now, what I want to know is this—can anyone please tell me the name and address of that FIRST pub?

Daily Record 4 July 1983

"HEY, MISTER, CAN YOU CHANGE HALF A SQUID?"

PITY the man with soul so dead who never to himself has said: "Oh, how I could go a Chateaubriand or a good plate of tatties and mince." When it comes to eating, I am like the French. Maybe a good meal isn't a joy forever but the memory lingers on to tickle your fancy. It should be treated as a cultural event. A convivial ceremony where the company and the food should be savoured.

This was not the Scottish tradition. The tendency is to blame the Calvinist streak which we are told decrees that everything is OK, as long as you don't enjoy it, including sex. When it comes to food many of us apparently hate experimentation. You often see Scots examining menus for the familiar dishes. Our esprit de grub stakes seems to be mixed grill or a steak well done with chips or French fries if you are from Kelvinside.

Some years ago I was in one of the best restaurants in London with a workmate. Our host was either a journalist on an expense account or a national trade union official. In other words somebody with plenty of money to spend. The menu was enormous in size and opened out like a melodeon. It was in French which is double Dutch to me but I insisted that the waiter explain each item and ordered something I had never before tasted.

My mate, a beloved colleague in every other way, ordered sausage, eggs and chips with tomato sauce. This wasn't even on the menu. Now there is nothing wrong with sausage, eggs and chips except that you can get it every morning at home or in any transport cafe, so why not, I remonstrated, try something entirely different? His reply was quite simple: "I know that I like sausage, eggs and chips and I don't know that about the rest."

The logic in a certain sense was impeccable. To some, eating is like stoking a boiler. Shovel it in and be done with it. We even talk of people "making a meal" of something as if it was a term of abuse. To such people "the Galloping Gourmet" was a middle-distance runner from some third world nation called Gourma.

It is the same with the drink. Some guys have never in their lives drunk anything except haufs and hauf pints and talk disparagingly of Conservatives. Until fairly recently our pubs were functionally designed so that nothing enjoyable would ever be allowed to interfere with the serious business of drinking. There are a few such places left. They are called "Men's Pubs". Refreshment dens for the Men Sahibs.

"But the times they are a changing" which is about the only coherent sentence I ever picked up from Bob Dylan. Package holidays, a certain Cypriot gentleman active in the catering trade and more enlightened licensing laws have done the trick. It is great nowadays to see punters sitting in eating places in the West End that look like a glass house from the Botanic Gardens and discussing with their wives whether the mussels are in season. I didn't even know they had a season.

Recently in Spain I saw a Scottish football fan stab his finger at something on the menu and ask what it was. "Squid," he was told. "Right, yer on" was his reply. It was a large plateful, approximately half a portion. He tasted a bit, obviously didn't like it and asked the head waiter: "Hey, mister, can you change half a squid." Aye there is no doubt that our language has lost something through decimalisation.

Our housewives, too, are also now experimenting in the kitchen and I hope that this remark doesn't offend my feminist readers. Some blokes are going home at night to such things as marinated mince which goes down well in Whiteinch with a bottle of Chateaux neuf de Tesco. A new favourite emerging is Wiener Schnitzel and square sausage vindyloo. A friend of mine reckons that the word vindyloo relates to its purgative qualities, and is shouted as a warning.

We are now cosmopolitan. In Glasgow there are Greek, Italian, Chinese,

172

Indian and Pakistan restaurants. It's hard to imagine a Scottish restaurant or takeaway in Milan or Athens or Karachi. Come to think of it, Scottish restaurants are not all that popular in Scotland.

Some years ago long before he became President of France, Francois Mitterand came to Scotland heading a delegation from the Nievre region. For some reason or other I was invited with a few other Scots to meet them at a dinner in a Glasgow hotel. Everything on the menu was Scottish except the wine.

We had Arbroath smokey paté, Scotch salmon, Angus beef and so on. One of the French Deputies was overwhelmed and said to me: "I didn't realise how wonderful was your Scottish cuisine." I didn't let on that it was news to me as well and sort of insinuated that this was our daily fare.

However, it did go to show that we have the raw materials. All we need is a little Gallic imagination and voila, Caledonian Cuisine could be all the rage. Mind you, over the years I have been in a few canteens and cafes where it was already all the rage. Here is an exchange of views overheard in an Italian restaurant in the East End of Glasgow a few years back. "Haw, missus, whit kinda pie is this?" The large and rather imposing proprietress replies: "That, sir, is my Pizza." Silence for a moment and then the riposte: "You know something, missus, your Pete's a bampot and so is your other son."

There is a music in the language of the people. This applies to people everywhere and at anytime. Shakespeare wrote in the idiomatic English of his time and he wasn't a bad scribbler. Robert Burns was at his best when he wrote in the language of his own Ayrshire folk. To grasp this innate music and harness it, to give expression to your thoughts must surely be at the heart of poetry.

Glinka, the composer, once observed: "The people compose the music, we arrange the notes." Yet we have had poets who wanted to invent a new language. Who constantly seek inspiration from their own navels. For them, there is no me and you and the bloke across the street. It is the great singular ONE.

They talk like this. "One has to come to terms with One's own personality and to find One's place in the great dichotomy that is life. One has to recognise that this inner tension is the very essence of One's artistic creativity." You will hear the kind of garbage at the next Edinburgh Festival when some literary phoney is being interviewed on television.

I prefer the Tom Leonards and the Tom McGraths. The language bequeathed to us and which is by no means static can encompass any thoughts that man is ever likely to think. And if you want to see beauty or find inspiration have a look at the stack of good people that are around. Above all have disdain for the pompous.

People who can make us laugh are worth their weight in gold. Here is something that made me laugh. It's a poem by Jimmy Copeland. I hope it does the same for you.

173

"Teresa huz took up the Judo,
She's been at it for two or three weeks,
Ye wid laugh at her Japanese jaikit,
And her wide perra Japanese breeks.

She comes breengin hame efter each lesson.
Wi' a new wey tae flatten a man,
For the heid filla says she's improvin',
That's him she keeps callin'-Black Dan.

An' she wants me tae be her opponent.
She gets mad when ah don't take her on.
She says—See you, ya wee bachle,
Ah could melt ye wi just the wan haun.

So last night we went tae wir scratcher.
Ah wiz reachin' tae pit oot the light,
Here, she stood up in bed like a mad yin,
An' said—Come oan Boabbie, let's fight.

Well, ah got her doon efter a struggle,
An' ah'll tell ye—the victory was sweet,
She agreed it wiz better than Judo,
But she called me a durrty wee cheat."

Glasgow Herald 28 June 1982

NOT A LOT OF PEOPLE KNOW THIS, BUT...

IT'S amazing how, over the years, you accumulate a vast store of irrelevant and totally unimportant information.

A doctor in the RAF once told me that Ethelred the Unready had different coloured eyes. So have I.

So it's smashing when someone talking to you suddenly notices and says: "Jimmy, your eyes are different colours."

To which, with practised nonchalance, I reply: "So had Ethelred the Unready."

The impact is immediate. Admiration surges forth because you know something so staggeringly inconsequential.

Try it. Try explaining to people something important like Einstein's Theory of Relativity and they hoot at you with derision.

Tell them that Napoleon was sorely afflicted with haemorrhoids and they look at you with new-found respect.

Mind you, sometimes an apparently stupid irrelevancy can be important.

I remember listening one evening to a couple of learned historians arguing in the staff club at Glasgow University how Napoleon's particular problem could have affected the outcome to the Battle of Waterloo.

As the battle raged, old Bonaparte was laid low with his affliction, completely incapable of sitting astride his horse with his hand up his juke (inside his coat, to the non-Glaswegian), or shouting out instructions to his army.

The soldiers, minus his inspired generalship, got flummoxed and—according to one of the historians—were defeated.

Makes you think, doesn't it?

Many years ago, I picked up the useless piece of information that claret was the national drink of Scotland. It's true.

When people were poking fun at Roy Jenkins because of his fondness for this noble drink, I kept a diplomatic silence.

Claret-loving is not only a weakness of the effete English middle-classes that Roy, despite being Welsh, is taken by some to epitomise.

Claret-swilling is historically a favourite Scottish pastime. This was confirmed by a recently-published book called *Knee Deep in Claret*, the story of wine and Scotland.

There is no doubt about it, we are descended from a long line of "winos".

This probably explains why in the more cultured parts of Scotland such as Govan, Partick and Greenock, they used to sell draught "Rid Biddy". Which was probably spiced-up claret.

One pub used to have white "Rid Biddy" for the discerning punter who wanted the right wine to go with his recently-purchased poke of clabby doos (or mussels).

A pal of mine from Clydebank used to say: "On a Friday night, give me a big plate of tatties and mince *au vin* and a bottle of Chateauneuf de Lanny, and I will call no man Master."

For some inexplicable reason, he suddenly started drinking vodka and beer chasers, and from then on became morose and chilly and never looked forward.

In company, he used to intone in a doom-laden voice things like: "Many are cold but few are frozen for so it is written."

In fact, he became a right pain in that place where Napoleon was so terribly afflicted.

There is no doubt about it, drink moves people in mysterious ways.

Daily Record 14 November 1983

On Sports and Sportsmen

IT'S ALL SPORT... FROM THE LOCARNO TO LUCERNE

IS chess a sport even if it is the world championships in Lucerne? Admittedly this is not a question that has been troubling my mind recently, or at any time when you come right down to it. We weren't exactly chess conscious in Govan. A pawn to us was a communal wardrobe that housed your good suit from Monday till Friday.

So there I was, sitting at the *Herald* sports desk during my weekly visit, sipping coffee. At least that's the term used by the machine which dispensed the fluid. Something surely challengeable under the Trades Description Act. The Sports Editor, returning from the Editorial Conference, breenged back to his chair and said to his assembled colleagues: "It has now been decreed that chess is a sport and henceforth shall be reported on our already pressurised pages."

To be honest that is not a verbatim report of what he said. It's the gist. You see he seemed a bit miffed about something. This suspicion was apparently confirmed by the fact that my carton of coffee bounced three feet in the air as he gently rapped the table to emphasise his words.

So chess is now a sport and that's official. Doesn't matter what the Olympic Committee or any other bunch of Johnny Come Latelies might think—the Editorial Conference of a nearly 200-year-old paper has spoken and that is that.

Now, as you know, I have been known to challenge decisions from on high. It's a kind of principle. The trouble was, that I had always considered chess to be a sport. None the less a man's got to do what a man's got to do, and so I asked for the reasoning by which this decision was reached. "Because it's competitive," was the reply.

This explanation of a perfectly reasonable conclusion struck me as being somewhat inadequate. If my memory serves me right, sex is competitive. At least it was when I went to the Locarno. If it had been considered a sport and included in the Olympics then I also knew a few potential gold medal winners, according to the stories as relayed to the apprentices during the tea break on a Monday morning.

Politics is certainly competitive. Polling day is like a cup final, with rival supporters sporting the team colours. If politics was a sport it would explain where ice hockey got the idea for the "sin bin". Many aspects of life not hitherto considered sporting are intensely competive. War, commerce, religion, academic life, and the finals of Miss World are a few random specimens.

I suppose, like all other things in life, sport cannot be delineated in precise terms. It overlaps, as does everything, into all adjacent categories. Where does sport end and entertainment start?

Some years ago the Reid family were watching skating on the telly. It was the Winter Olympics. Now you should know that our household (note the collective pronoun) is the nearest thing to a matriarchy outside the General Council of the TUC. The males are in a minority of one—me.

A young British participant had just won the gold medal to the approval of all the Reids bar one. Guess who. Right first time, me again. My argument was that the silver medallist had displayed more athleticism and had been marked down by the judges because he lacked a certain grace. Grace, I argued was in the eye of the beholder and was largely a subjective judgment. The girls thought these remarks were stupid and unpatriotic. Anyway the winner was lovely. I had to make my own supper that night.

Since then I have kept quiet about a lot of "sports" that seemed to me not to be sports at all. Well it's no fun making your own supper. But the controversy about chess as a sport opened the floodgates and liberated these pent-up opinions. It was simply a coincidence that I also happened to be going on a diet.

So here goes. Any human activity that involves an aesthetic judgment in deciding the merit of a performance is not a sport. It should come under the jurisdiction of the Arts Council and not the Sports Council. For example, the floor exercises in gymnastics are more akin to ballet and choreography than any sport. At its worst you can see little women stuffed with anti-puberty pills flouncing around on a mat to the sound of music like undersized, second-rate ballerinas. At its best it wouldn't be out of place on the stage at Covent Garden or the Bolshoi. In either case it should not be viewed in the context of a sport. Otherwise ballroom dancing and painting have a claim to a place in the Olympics. How would you rate the respective merits of Picasso, Matisse, Salvador Dali, and Andy Warhol? Who is qualified to judge?

The first time I saw Zatopek run, his head started to roll and loll from side to side after only two laps. My pal understandably concluded that the poor sod was knackered. He eventually won by about two laps and went on to achieve something that is unlikely ever to be equalled—he won the 5000 and 10,000 metres and the marathon at the Helsinki Olympics.

If part of the scoring system had been the award of points for artistic impression then Old Emil would have been away down among the also rans. The more you think about it the more nonsensical it becomes. Imagine a high-jump competition and wee Willie McGlumphy from Yoker wachles up and clears three metres with ease but with a new indescribably ugly technique that, like the Fosbury Flop, is destined to become part of athletic history, known for evermore as the "McGlumphy Wachle". The judges, holding up their cards, give Willie 10 out of 10 for performance. After all he did smash the world record. However, for artistic impression Willie gets only an average of four out of 10 and is thus beaten by a graceful geezer who had difficulty clearing two metres.

One suspects that McGlumphy's pals would be inclined to assail the judges with the multi-purpose tools of the field events like the javelin and the hammer, and who could blame the lads. To them Wee Willie's Wachle is beautiful—a style forged, fashioned, and perfected over the years in jumping the wall after clocking in at his place of employment.

At chess you win only if you checkmate your opponent or force him to concede. The way you flourish your queen is of no importance. Pele when he sold the goalie that glorious dummy at the Mexico World Cup and then missed the open goal was not given some consolation points for artistic improvisation.

I know that many great sportsmen and sportswomen also bring to their performance or game a superb beauty. Just as Nureyev brings a superb athleticism to his dancing. Sport, art, and culture should and do relate and impinge. There must still be some point of delineation, even if only to keep the commentators of Come Dancing out of Grandstand or Scotsport.

Sport can be decided only by a performance that is measurable, be it in goals, tries, runs, points, or in beating an opponent within a definable area and a prescribed ranged of activity or by time or distance. Aesthetic judgments have no place in according victory or defeat in sport. That is for a festival of the arts, like the Govan Fair.

Glasgow Herald 18 November 1982

KNOCKING DOWN THE CHAMPS

I call it the Benny Lynch syndrome—the tendency for some Scots to luxuriate in the failure of sporting heroes. A champion who does not follow success with ignominious defeat, which need not necessarily be sporting is somehow a cheat in their eyes.

Poor Benny provided them with all the ingredients for their jaundiced titillation. He zoomed to the top, became flyweight champion of the world, but then his reckless, self-destructive life-style plunged him down just as fast into the morass of the down-and-outs.

Thus a sporting legend was born—a legend that spawned a million anecdotes. I have personally met about 5000 Glaswegians who claimed to have been pals of Benny and bought him a large whisky when he had been down on his uppers, as they say, and badly in need of a drink. "Benny Lynch," they avow, "was the greatest." Whether this would still be their opinion if he had been abstemious, had built up a business empire, and was alive, a happy and contented old gentleman, is another question.

Jim Watt, one suspects, could win a place in their particular hall of sporting fame only if he suddenly became an alcoholic, frittered away his money and business, ended up skint, and drank himself to an early grave.

You see the name of this game is to claw down champions. When your mind cannot rise beyond your own navel then others seem to be on a high horse from which they must be dragged.

A well known footballer goes into a pub with some friends and has a pint of lager. The eyes of the brethren are on him. The incident is related with relish to others. "I saw Joe Bloggs of Rangers/Celtic in the boozer last night downing a dozen pints."

By the time this is relayed through the gossip's kiss of death, which is a form of mouth to mouth vilification, the player is "reliably" reported to have consumed 18 whiskies, 12 beer chasers, and a motley assortment of liqueurs.

These reflections are prompted by the malicious delight some people are taking in Sebastian Coe's defeat at the European games in Athens. I actually heard a guy gloating to his companion that this "pretty, pretty glamour boy had got his come uppance". You got the feeling that he had never forgiven nature for having constructed him along lines diametrically different from Robert Redford.

For my money Seb Coe and Steve Ovett are the finest middle-distance runners in the world today. This season both have been plagued by injury and are obviously below peak fitness.

Coe, who runs as if he was a human hovercraft, gliding effortlessly over the ground, is aesthetically a delight to watch. I hope that both he and Ovett can overcome their current difficulties and once again bring delight to those millions who derive no perverse pleasure from seeing a great athlete beaten.

On the same theme, I am also worried about Jock Wallace. A few more defeats for Motherwell and the knives will be out for big Jock. The sharpness of the attacks on Wallace will be commensurate with the ecstasy which greeted his advent to the top job at Fir Park. In fact the main cheer leaders then will probably be the first volunteers for any proposed lynch party. His training methods will be ridiculed by those who only a few weeks ago were applauding his he-man approach to the game.

Some years ago I saw Jock Wallace with unbridled enthusiasm seek to demonstrate to a small company how Ferenc Puskas had swivelled and scored that priceless goal for Hungary against England. Mind you it helped that he was demonstrating without a ball. What sticks in the mind, however is the man's abundant love for the game.

So, if for no other reason, I hope that Motherwell quickly get some good results. Otherwise the knives will once again be wielded by those who delight in cutting others down "to size", as they would put it.

Glasgow Herald 16 September 1982

WHAT PRICE THE SPORTING LIFE?

SPORT is harmless for spectators. For sportsmen it can be very damaging. Eventually, all sport will carry a Government Health Warning.

Sport advertising will be banned and games might even be taxed to make them prohibitive to the innocent young.

Take squash, where two men batter a ball off a concrete wall with the aid of an undersized tennis racquet in what can literally become a fight to the death.

Players are regularly carted from the court on stretchers. Whether squash should be forbidden for men of 35 and over is a question rampant in medical circles.

You might well ask what men of 35 are doing battering a wee ball off a wall—but that's another matter.

Running is also a health hazard. It can cause a lot of harm including stress fractures, a form of metal fatigue for the human body.

Let's face it—if God had wanted men to run at great speed or over long distances he would have given us four legs like the cheetah or humps like the camel.

You might have heard of athlete's foot, well doctors are now concerned about athletes' heads.

This is a form of punch drunkenness induced by the brain stoating about in the cranium as the athlete pounds jarringly round the track.

For the long distance runner this is useful. It creates the mental vacuity which enables him to run round the same old boring track, time and time again.

Team games are just as bad. The bevvy might make you temporarily legless but rugby can be much worse. You can be left permanently lugless with your ears chewed off in a scrum.

Football is another sport that's bad for you. You can always tell an ex-professional, he hirples or shuffles around on legs much the worse for wear.

Some sports promoters are trying to hoodwink us with talk of low-energy games such as snooker. "Look," they say, "there is no great physical effort involved." Don't be fooled.

Already there are signs of something known as "snooker backside",—much worse than tennis elbow.

In years to come, today's young snooker players will be walking around like half-shut penknives with the upper body at right angles to the lower parts and with Dennis Taylor spectacles perched on their noses to help them see where they're going.

The issue for our society is simple and yet complex.

It raises two questions. Should a civilised community allow people to harm themselves in these unnatural activities collectively known as sport?

On the other hand, would a ban not be an infringement of individual rights?

Anyway, how could such a ban be enforced? Joggers would start jogging at night in lonely dark, out-of-the-way places.

Sport would go underground. Athletes in dirty raincoats desperate for a fix, a secret throw at a javelin or a sleekit high jump would be easy prey for the sports pushers.

Sports shops would mushroom under the innocent guise of tobacconists. The only long-term solution is to educate the young about the chronic dangers of sport. Show them the benefits of growing up to be a nice, healthy slob.

People like myself should go round schools telling youngsters about the blessing of sloth and laziness.

Sometimes we have to be cruel to be kind. We will have to show our kids grown-up pictures of footballers' legs or of a boxer's face or rugby players' brains—though these would have to be magnified many times to be made discernible to the human eye.

The Department of Health should make films showing young girls refusing to dance with sportsmen.

If need be we should really frighten our children with warnings of how what might start as a prank or teenage bravado, could end with them playing golf and being condemned to spending the rest of their lives as inmates (or members as they call it) of an institution known as a "golf club".

We owe it to our children—they must be told the truth. Every time I look at an old athlete I can't help thinking—there but for the grace of God go I.

A SOBERING THOUGHT.

Daily Record 28 November 1983

ON FOOTBALL

Going, Going, Gone Are The Days Of Loyalty

SOME football managers must have hides like the rhinoceros. They extol the virtues of commitment and loyalty, to players and public alike, while everyone knows that at the drop of a hat or a few quid they would pack their bags and shoot the craw to another club faster than Cameron Sharp runs 100 metres.

Of course there are clubs who deserve all the disloyalty they get. Those who will virtually bribe a manager to break his contract with some other club so as to bring his dubious talents to their set-up. Until fairly recently this was so rife that the trafficking in managers resembled Spaghetti Junction in the peak hours.

It was like an auction where contracts meant nothing and a gentlemen's agreement, as the late Mr Goldwyn once observed, was not worth the paper it wasn't written on.

These days would appear to be over. Repentance of an unprincipled past has nothing to do with it. You see, to entice another by dangling greenbacks before his cash register eyes has one inbuilt snag—it requires money. That's why the poor are seldom accused of bribery. This also probably explains why we now seem to be moving into the era of cut-price managers.

Hibernian sacked Bertie Auld, reportedly because he and his two lieutenants were costing £50,000 annually and their successors only £25,000.

Is a cut-price war imminent? Usually these take place when a commodity is plentiful, when supply exceeds demand and when potential purchasers can no longer afford to pay the old price.

Well, many senior professional footballers were freed last season by clubs in serious financial difficulties. There are few, if any, jobs available outside the game. Most would jump at the chance of becoming a manager without much haggling as to wages and conditions.

We might even see auctions along the following lines: "Do I hear £7500? Yes, from the gentleman in the trilby hat over there. Anyone bid £7000? Yes, £7000 from the gentleman in the torn jacket in the left-hand corner. £7000 once, twice, going, going, gone. The manager's job at Auchenshuggle United goes to you, sir, at a salary of £7000 per year. You do understand, sir, that this contract also requires that you exercise and train the chairman's greyhounds. Just give your name and address to that gentleman standing over there with the four greyhounds. Yes, that's him in the loud checked suit with the one-armed bandit strapped to his back. Yes, come to think of it he does look a bit like George Melly."

Glasgow Herald 9 September 1982

Managers More Than Mere Planners Of The Game

HOW important are managers? If a team does badly the manager invariably gets his books. If it does well he receives accolades and is hailed as a tactical genius.

To put this question into perspective let us imagine the following: I have 11 footballers immeasurably superior in all departments of the game to those available to Bob Paisley. I would back with hard money, which means my own, that my lot would beat Bob's mob nine times out of 10. If my players were slightly better than Bob's then his lot would beat my squad by a similar margin. This is somewhere near the measure of managerial skills in terms of the deployment of available talent.

There is, of course, another dimension, and that is in the recognition of potential talent. This is not simply a question of a good scouting system. It involves the ability of a manager to perceive the best role for a particular player. Brian Clough's utilisation of John Robertson is a classic example of this kind of perception.

There are some managers whose talents can become a catalyst for progressive change in the affairs of a club and whose impact leaves football irrevocably changed. Jock Stein is such a man. I believe we have not yet fully grasped the impact he has had on Scottish football.

Apart from his successes with Dunfermline and Hibernian, he transformed Celtic into a club of international renown.

Another interesting aspect is that when he was brought to Celtic to coach the reserve team he was brought into the first team as a stop-gap centre half because of injuries. During a period of about two years he captained Celtic to League and Scottish Cup triumphs—by far their most successful period until he returned as manager.

People keep telling me he wasn't a great player. I think he was better than he gets credit for, but, more to the point, as a player he brought leadership and cohesion to a team.

What quality does Stein have? Let us discard words like charisma, so beloved by would-be intellectuals, and come right down to brass tacks. Stein is a leader. He has a brilliant tactical grasp of the game, but so have others. In addition he could inspire confidence or to lapse into jargon, motivate players.

I wonder how long Jimmy Johnstone would have lasted in this game without the firm handling of Stein. Imagine if Jock had got a hold of George Best at an early age. Things might have been so different for the most gifted player these isles have ever produced. Stein was strong, and that is putting it mildly, with those who needed that kind of handling. Yet with others he could be encouraging, mindful of their sensibilities.

When Jackie Charlton took up his first management job at Middlesborough he brought his team up to Scotland for a pre-season tour. He told me then it was to sit at the feet of the best manager in the game, Jock Stein. That is the esteem in which this man is held in other countries and by outstanding professionals.

He helped more than any other single person to bring Scottish football tactics into the second half of the twentieth century.

The most hopeful sign in our game today is to be found in the squad of young managers who are in the Stein mould. They are not vague figures. They do not hide. They know a bit about the game, and they try to be leaders. They cannot all be winners, but directors should be giving them more support. They deserve it.

Glasgow Herald 20 January 1983

Methinks Maclean Doth Brood Too Much

SOME time ago Dundee United won 6-1 and the manager fined the players. On Saturday they won 3-0 and the same manager once again "done his nut" and imposed another fine.

At Tannadice when this boyo declares: "It's a fine day, today", the last thing people think about is the weather. It's more likely to be another short pay for his subordinates. If Fred Winter ran his stables along these lines, then John Francome, his champion steeplechase jockey, would be in the poor house.

A pro rata application of this peculiar incentive scheme to a defeat must surely involve the rack and other instruments of medieval punishment. You might not have noticed, but Dave Narey's legs are a bit on the long side, as if somebody's been pulling them.

All of this begs certain questions. From whence or whom does Jim Maclean of that ilk, to the manager born, get his imperious mien? From what is derived his bland assumption of absolute power?

Could he be, as he apparently believes, a genuine 22-carat guru sent to lead the lost tribes of Scottish soccerdom from the wilderness unto the promised land flowing with fans and money and highly profitable lotteries and undemanding sponsorships and players who unquestioningly do as they are told at all times?

Is it true, as is whispered in the market places all along the road and the miles to Dundee, that many moons ago he was found as a tiny handful in swaddling clothes floating on the Tay in a wicker basket by the daughter of a local pharoah, otherwise known as chairman of the board at Tannadice? Gee whizz, what a scouting system.

Mind you, if he made a habit of docking my wages, I could very easily come to the conclusion that he did, indeed, descend from a long line of wicker baskets.

His style, though, is more Elizabethan than Old Testament. For example, in Shakespeare's "Cymbeline" someone addresses the Queen's son thus: "You are most hot and furious when you win." Yes sir, that sounds like our man.

He also has about him a faint whiff of Hamlet. He broods on his vision of soccer perfection and its awesome standards of human application. To Maclean life must seem a poor substitute for football. His zeal for the game is not in question—it IS the question. Zealotry does not help one to keep that sense of fun without which we lose our sense of proportion.

The most glorious memories of football are always of those who played with panache and flair and a certain abandonment. Baxter, Wee Jinky, Best, Pele, Cruyff, Puskas, di Stefano are recalled with relish by the fans, for in addition to their manifest skills they exuded an exuberance and a sense of fun.

Football is decidedly not a matter of life and death. It is still, however, too important to be taken seriously, a fate which should be reserved only for trivia.

Jim Maclean should take himself and football a little less seriously. He has built Dundee United into one of the best sides in the country. Maybe if he relaxed a bit and stopped treating his players like children he might manage to go that stage further and build a great team. Given the much smaller resources available to him, that would be an achievement of greater significance than anything thus far recorded by Celtic, Rangers, and Aberdeen.

Just try to imagine Johann Cruyff accepting a fine for playing in a team which had won 6-1. The mind boggles.

Glasgow Herald 25 November 1982

Fergie's March From Govan To Gothenburg

"I showed little emotion which surprised people. We had a game that night and I decided to return to Aberdeen. My faither would have wanted it that way.

"In the car on the road back the floodgates opened and I cried."

Alex Ferguson was telling me about his dad's funeral.

The old man had worked for many years in Fairfields, now known as Govan Shipbuilders. He died not long after retiring from the yard.

At Pittodrie, the eyes of veteran trainer Teddy Scott, followed Fergie as he hurried along the corridor.

"He helps people. Players, the staff, old players, pensioners, the lot. Aye, we are all better off because of him," he said.

The words were spoken in a rich Aberdeenshire accent. The affection and respect were obvious.

This didn't surprise me. I know Alex Ferguson. I know the Alex Fergusons of this world.

They came up the hard way and weren't hardened. They are tough, but then that's something different.

In Govan, we knew the difference.

The Fergusons lived in Govan Road, just round the corner from Neptune Street, otherwise known as the "Irish Channel".

The Reids' stately home was a few hundred yards away in a block known as the "slum clearance".

In Glasgow at that time, any slum with an inside lavatory was officially designated as a non-slum. It was a tough area. A cat with a tail was immediately recognised as a tourist.

Sure, it coarsened some. Demoralised others into accepting defeat without fight.

Yet the majority refused to be brutalised or beaten. They fought back in their own different ways.

We agreed that the great divide wasn't between good and bad. This was too airy-fairy for the reality of life in Govan. Good for whom—bad for whom?

To be or not to be a LIBERTY TAKER, that was the question. This was the ultimate distinction.

A liberty taker took advantage of those who were weaker than himself.

A real man would not do such a thing.

This, as I understand it, was the thrust of Alex's argument. I wasn't arguing but agreeing.

This conclusion was reached late at night—actually it was early in the morning—in the Fergusons' lovely home in the suburbs of Aberdeen.

There we were, two Govanites and Alex's wife, Cathy, who hails from the Gorbals.

We were in a generous mood and bestowed Govan citizenship on Cathy so that she might not feel too resentful.

Alex Ferguson is no liberty taker and no defeatist.

These qualities are now imbued in the team he manages. The team which has scaled the heights and tomorrow will play the famed Real Madrid in the European Cup-winners' Cup Final.

"I want to win," he tells you, "but it is important how we win."

Aberdeen have gone through the season without one player being disciplined by the SFA.

He is immeasurably proud for, in his eyes, a good end cannot justify bad means.

To traipse around Pittodrie just now is an amazing experience. You talk to Alex and he heaps praise on his assistant, Archie Knox, the backroom boys and the players.

You talk to Archie and his admiration for Fergie is a tangible presence.

Teddy Scott has been with Aberdeen for 30 years and says without equivocation that "the boss is the finest manager I've known". And "Fergie and Archie are the best management team".

There seems to be absolutely no friction with the board of directors, which is so unusual as to be almost bizarre.

They all like each other. Mind you, it helps being a family affair.

The chairman is Mr Dick Donald. The vice-chairman is Chris Anderson, and the rank and file is director Ian Donald, the chairman's son.

Yes, that's right, only three directors. Somehow you can't imagine a bureaucratic bottleneck in that boardroom.

The players, who are collectively one of the finest squads in Europe, are refreshingly free of arrogance.

Unlike some bigheads who in similar circumstances would be strutting around like prima donnas, demanding a fee for publicly breaking wind, never mind breaking sweat.

Yet fulsome and justified praise for everyone doesn't alter the fact that the focal point is that heartwarming honesty of Alex Ferguson.

An honesty which is more than not telling lies.

Alex's playing career spanned many clubs . . .

Queen's Park, St Johnstone, Dunfermline, Rangers, Falkirk and Ayr United.

His reminiscenses are peppered with praise for fellow players. Characteristically, his few criticisms are for those who didn't make themselves available when a colleague was in trouble.

In 1960, Alex was an apprentice toolmaker in the Remington Rand, Hillington. The apprentices in Scotland were on strike for higher wages.

Comparitively speaking, the Remington apprentices were well paid and Alex was also a semi-professional footballer.

Yet he led the Remington apprentices out on strike. "Why?" I asked.

186

"Ye cannae jist be concerned about yourself. Lots of other lads were desperately hard up," was his reply.

He became president of the Players' Union in Scotland from 1969 to 1972. I spoke to their AGM in that period as the Rector of Glasgow University, with Fergie in the chair.

He remarked on the coincidence and the fate that had brought us together after all those years.

Tomorrow night I'll be with him in spirit, for this Aberdeen team can tell Scotland something important about itself.

From the East and West, the North and the South, elements have merged into a potent force. Maybe it's more than football.

You see, at Pittodrie there are no tribal cries of sectarian divisiveness. No graffiti urging naughty things on a long-dead king or a prominent theologian.

Maybe the Northern Lights can show us the way in things other than football.

See's ma bunnet. Gie's ma rid and white scarf. Get that seat in front of the telly.

For tomorrow night, at least, Glasgow belongs to Aberdeen, particularly that place that is forever Govan.

When it comes to that, so does the whole of Scotland.

AwrabesttaeraDons.

Daily Record 10 May 1983

Why Football Is Dying On Its Feet

EVERYONE is talking, or so it seems from the noise, about how to revive Scottish football. If they mean in its present form and structure then they're wasting breath. Rigor Mortis doesn't respond even to the kiss of life. The only reason why the death knell hasn't yet sounded is because the bellringers haven't noticed its demise.

Any organism that refuses to change, or is unable to change and adapt itself to emerging circumstances, invariably dies. This is, or almost is, a law of nature.

In the post-war years, affluence and technology brought new lifestyles. The working class, always the source of football's finances, became, as compared to the 'thirties, much more affluent. Package holidays abroad and other things brought a degree of sophistication. To take the wife or the girlfriend out for a meal and to order a bottle of wine was no longer a bourgeois prerogative. The punters, and not before time, were getting in on the act.

Pubs changed. The big bar with sawdust on the floor designed for the serious business of drink by male chauvinist pigs was now on the way out. Big lounges with fitted carpets and no spitoons were in. A Pimm was a drink and not a Cabinet Minister. Television brought into our living rooms, particularly on a Saturday afternoon, sports that many hadn't even heard of, let alone seen.

Cricket was discovered to be an interesting physical game of chess and not a pastime for pansies.

Rugby was discovered to be a good game that had unfortunately got a bad name from the types who claim to be supporters. And then there was the racing. No longer was it a furtive dive up a close to put on an illegal bet with an illegal bookmaker. Now you could go into a legitimate betting shop (in the opinion of most punters it's now only the owners who are illegitimate), put on your bet, and then see your horses run, in the comfort of your own home.

Meanwhile, over these years of profound social change the organisers of football responded in the time-honoured fashion of the ostrich. It wasn't so much that their heads were in the sands of the past, it was the inevitable consequence of that posture. It presented their backsides to the future. Now we've heard of people leading with their chin, but this was ridiculous. As was to be expected the future kicked them in that exposed place.

In an age of improved standards of comfort and of much greater choice and diversity in leisure pursuits, football stood still. Workers with much higher expectations were expected to stand on the terracing unprotected from the elements. As most of the decent guys defected to the telly the lumpens, the demoralised proletarians, became more dominant. When you are anaesthetised with cheap wine you tend to be oblivious of the rain battering on your head, or the bloke behind in a similar condition urinating down your trouser leg.

Few of the people responsible are now about in the game. The current directors of football clubs inherited this situation. Belatedly they have tried to improve facilities. The Rangers stadium, for example, is quite magnificent. Other clubs, however, simply haven't the money to update the facilities. In the early 'fifties it might have been so different. People were still going in droves to the game. One can only now ponder as to where the money did go. It was certainly not to the players, who were tied to a ridiculously low maximum wage.

I honestly think it is too late. The great majority of clubs will collapse into a level of activity dictated by the funds available. Some years ago Rangers, Celtic, Aberdeen and a team from Edinburgh and Dundee should have applied for membership of the English league, making it in effect a British set-up. Only in that way could they have generated the income sufficient to give them a chance of competing in the 1990's with the best in Europe.

Today it is very doubtful if the English clubs would have them. It's unlikely that Rangers or Celtic would add anything to the gates at Tottenham or Manchester and a travelling support might not even be welcomed. Then there would be the expense of coming up here for the return game.

About two months ago I went to see Clydebank play. The Steedman brothers, who run the club, must be better magicians than Paul Daniels. There were plenty of seats and cover for the spectators. The ground was clean and spruce. There were also fewer than 1000. Much fewer. I found myself doing calculations about the gate money and wages, rates, expenses, and quickly gave it up.

Football as a game will survive. It is, after all, the greatest spectator sport in the world. However, the structure of the game in Scotland is so out of phase with reality as to be an irrelevancy. This crisis once again illustrates the folly of resisting change when it is opportune. Inevitably this leads to a breakdown and eventual collapse.

When Harold Macmillan, the wise old fox of British Conservatism, spoke those many years ago about the "wind of change in Africa", his words should have been heeded by the Europeans in that vast continent, such as Mr Ian Smith.

These words were also apposite to the structure and impending crisis of Scottish football, but were ignored in soccer's corridors of power. Alas, it is now probably too late for both.

Glasgow Herald 8 February 1982

Half A League And We Might Move Forward

ON the eve of a new football season people are supposed to look forward with anticipation. Instead I want to look back to the things that were but will not be again. To the massive crowds that turned out—dare I use the word—religiously every Saturday. To the time when the game spawned an entire culture and its own hard machismo humour that could sometimes be tinged with bizarre and even surrealist flourishes.

The Saturday football widow watching her spouse as he bedecks himself in the Rangers colours, a familiar weekly ritual, says almost with a sigh: "See you—you luv the Rangers mair than you luv me". Surveying his sartorial elegance in the mirror, her beloved replies: "Listen Hen, Ah luv the Celtic mair than Ah luv you".

Or the two wee Celtic supporters in the aftermath of a notable victory who accost a well known football scribe. One declares: "Hey mister, see me, Ah'd die for the Celtic". His mate thinks for a moment in search of a way to convey his even greater sense of commitment and adds: "See me mister, Ah'd die for the reserve team".

Alas, alas that's all in the past. Where once, as this folklore would have it, they would have laid down their lives, now they won't even lay down a quid at the turnstiles.

The fans have gone and will not return, at least in the numbers of yore. Some people in football seem incapable of grasping this point. They are like Spam manufacturers clinging to the productive capacity of the early '40s in expectation of a revival of sales to the level of war-time, when it was about the only food that was freely available.

The structures of Scottish football relate to the social conditions of the 1920s. The way clubs are run and controlled, where they are located, the whole league set-up, are products of a social environment that no longer exists. They take little or no account of the social impact of television, of the tremendously enhanced options available to a much more sophisticated working class. Football all but ignores the new status of women, who refuse to be permanently confined to the kitchen sink. The provision of facilities for female spectators at most grounds is still a joke.

Take this as an example. Population centres, particularly in our urban areas, have changed dramatically in the last 35 years. The brewers' pubs, the big retail stores, and other enterprises have moved to new strategically located catchment areas. Our football clubs have stayed put. So today it is by no means unusual to see a football stadium standing like a pathetic incredible hulk stranded among the flotsam of a derelict area, handy for the old "winos" and few besides. Conversely, many new and growing communities have no football team at all.

Think of the wasteful multiplicity of football stadia. In Dundee on the same street, within a few hundred yards of each other, there are two football grounds open for serious business for approximately two and a half hours every fortnight. Imagine trying to explain such a gross under utilisation of a capital asset to the likes of Lord Sieff, the boss of Marks and Spencer, or the convener of a municipal sports centre. It is ludicrous economics.

Football clubs, like all other organisms, must either adapt to new conditions or perish. A number of them, welded to illusions of grandeur born of all their yesterdays, seem not to realise this basic truth. My worry is that the perishers drag a lot of good clubs down with them.

Cosmetic exercises are worse than useless when major surgery is required. The status quo is blatantly untenable. Yet the dead weight of those clubs who fear that the necessary changes will mean their relagation to a lower grade of football block the way. It is a vicious circle.

The tendency is to confuse the future of football in Scotland with the destiny of some clubs. This is nonsense. The game as a game is unassailable in Scotland, as in the world, as the No 1 spectator sport. The game will go on; some clubs will not, at least with their present status.

We need to slash the number of league clubs by about half through a process of mergers and some becoming amateur or junior.

Some of the surviving clubs should over a period of time be relocated into areas and communities more likely to provide a secure long term base.

The Government, local government, and the Sports Council should be approached to see of it's possible to convert grounds into multi-purpose sports centres at the disposal of the communities that the clubs purport to serve. This would help to integrate the clubs into the social fabric of the community.

The commercial sponsorship of the game in Scotland is still at the peanut stage. Professionally handled, it could bring a considerable infusion of cash. Some clubs, from a very narrow base, are doing a remarkably good job in the business-promotional side and show what the potential could be in a properly structured set-up.

190

Despite everything, many good things are happening in Scottish football. A group of young managers are beginning to flex their muscles, and good luck to them. There are quite a few young players on the verge of greatness—let us hope the clubs allow them to develop and express themselves creatively. Ironically, the crisis in the game south of the border makes it less likely they will be enticed away.

If only we get the changes to bring our organisation of the game into the '80s our best years as a footballing nation could lie ahead, and not in the dim and distant past.

Glasgow Herald 12 August 1982

Today's Wizards Better Than The Auld Yins

IT'S funny how man's athletic performances have improved without question with the passage of time only in those sports where performance can be measured precisely. Apparently we have declined in those games or disciplines where no such yardstick can apply. What a coincidence!

This is how it is according to the Auld Yins. These venerable sages reject our modern footballers, rugby players, and cricketers as a load of rubbish as compared with the sporting giants of their youth. One has the suspicion that if there were no such thing as a stop watch they would also be arguing with similar conviction that Seb Coe and Steve Ovett couldn't live with the blistering finishing speed of Sydney Wooderson or Gordon Pirie.

I suppose the truth is that any performance can be objectively evaluated only if related to the times and circumstances in which it was achieved. The Wembley Wizards transported to the eighties intact with the level of fitness and tactical awareness of their times would probably be thrashed by the Scottish team that played this year in Spain.

To say this is not meant to invalidate their greatness. A Hugh Gallacher alive and kicking today would still be a star in the English first division. His skills would simply find expression for good or ill in the context of today's standards.

If we were really to take stock I would argue that our contemporary teams must have the edge over those from the past for at least one reason. Today all players are trying to play football. That wasn't always so. In my childhood defenders were not supposed to play but had the specialist responsibility of stopping others from playing. In my mind's eye I can still see Don Emery of Aberdeen, Tiger Shaw of Rangers, and Bobby Hogg of Celtic.

To a man they were built like Hercules the bear without the fur coat or sophistication. Legs like oak trees beyond the sapling stage. In those days defenders didn't kick the ball—they booted it. A range of less than 100 yards denoted a pansy or someone guilty of trying to play football. A heinous crime for a full back. Nearly as bad as abandoning the short back-and-sides hair style.

Some defenders, who shall be nameless, could actually kick an opponent

191

further than 100 yards. Barry Sheene would be thinking twice about making a comeback if he was a winger that had to face these guys every week.

There were a few who tried to be constructive but they were considered eccentric. Willie Woodburn, who could run faster going backwards than the average centre going forward, was a case in point. He was a great ball-playing defender who was ahead of his time, as were Neil Franklin of England, Johnny Carey of Manchester United, and Malky McDonald of Celtic.

These fellows would be in their element today, when a full back whose merits are exclusively defensive is now the exception, and rightly considered a dead loss. Danny McGrain typifies the new approach. He is as good going forward as most midfield stars. Mind you, he still shoots for goal like an old-time full back.

Bob Paisley in his last season as the Liverpool manager tells us that his team will play with defenders all of whom will be expected to go forward as the flow of the game dictates. We saw glimpses of this on Saturday at Wembley in the Charity Shield game against Tottenham. On one occasion Hansen, the Scottish centre back, burst through into the opposition penalty area and just failed to score.

The trouble is that some players and managers seem to think that playing from deep in your own half means a series of short square passes that count for nothing in territorial terms. Worse still, it also means that by the time you reach halfway the opposing team is back in a strong defensive position.

I am personally fed up watching players pussyfooting about in their own half. Gordon Strachan has emerged as a world-class player in the last year because he has stopped footering around and has become a more adventurous attacking player, running at defences, passing forward, inviting the return, and, in general, making life difficult for the opposition. That is what football is all about. As Bob Paisley keeps saying, it's a simple uncomplicated game.

Glasgow Herald 26 August 1982

Rangers Must Evolve To Ensure Survival

POOR old Rangers—they are not really poor, but you know what I mean—are getting haw maw from a' the airts and pairts. "Where are the Tims on yer books?" is the cry. Surprise, surprise, there isn't one. As a wee blue-nosed friend of mine opined: "I bet they hivnae got a Seventh Day Adventist either?"

That might be so, but it must be well nigh impossible to run a football team in Scotland without playing a Catholic unless you really try. Just try it. Try and organise a team in any street or workplace and recruit solely on footballing skills. If there are no Catholics then you must work in a Faculty for Wee Frees.

In a soccer sense, Tims can be useful. They all kick with the left foot— honest, it's true, everybody in Glasgow knows that. Ah yes, God does indeed work in mysterious ways. Did he make Catholics left-footers or left-footers Catholics? This raises fascinating theological questions.

What is the religious significance of being two-footed? And what about my big pal from Govan who could only head the ball and was hopeless with both feet—was he, or is he, a Satanist?

Feet apart, in a multi-religious society such as ours, a team consisting only of one denomination is only possible if the club is exclusive to that denomination.

This is the Rangers tradition. It isn't in the rules or constitution. If it was, then change would be easy. You would simply amend or delete the offending paragraph.

Change is always more difficult when you are dealing with the complexities of human minds, the prejudices, relationships, friendships, and contacts that evolve into a lifestyle and then a tradition. The Rangers tradition unchanged cannot produce a Catholic player, for it evolved on the basis of Protestant exclusiveness. Now to some extent, all of us are prisoners of our own history. The people at Ibrox are no exception. To simply malign them for so being is neither fair nor helpful.

I happen to believe that Rae Simpson and his board want to play a Catholic, which isn't surprising for they are stigmatised throughout Britain for failing to do so.

It is never easy to break the chains of the past. Sometimes, however, it is absolutely vital. The most significant thing about the past is that it is past. From the earliest times an inability to adapt to changing circumstances has proven fatal. History is replete with the remains of those things that could not change. From dinosaurs to Czars.

For business, social, and footballing reasons the need for change at Ibrox is compelling and should have taken place years ago. It didn't and, as we know, long overdue change is generally more painful. In any event, the present Ibrox board has been left to carry the can.

Rangers are the most highly-capitalised club in Scottish football, with assets that make them a major public company. To survive as a large-scale business entity the club must appeal to a much wider section of the community than it has been able to attract in recent years.

This is not only a matter of having a good football team. Rangers were always supported—whether playing well or not—by a large number of what might be termed respectable working-class and middle-class Protestants. Rangers haven't changed, but they have. For a whole number of reasons many of them are no longer happy to associate with what they now consider to be the socially divisive and dangerous consequences of manifest bigotry.

A large magnificent modern stadium cannot be filled by the dwindling numbers who want a fortnightly emotional re-enactment of the Battle of the Boyne.

Nobody can hold Rangers completely responsible for the language and behaviour of their fans. Just as we cannot put all the blame on Celtic for the hooligans who chant pro-IRA slogans at Parkhead and thus endorse atrocities in Northern Ireland.

There is one difference. In the eyes of many people who are not Catholics the continuing failure to play a Catholic amounts to a (dare I use the word?) blessing of those whose behaviour over the years has brought disgrace to this proud club.

There is another problem. It is now questionable whether Rangers can sustain a serious and long-term challenge to Celtic while excluding from the team such a chunk of the potential and available talent.

Let us take Glasgow as an example. In the city Catholics constitute about 35% of the population. Given that, historically, Catholic schools have tended to concentrate on football and not other sports like rugby, you could calculate that at least 40% of the top footballers coming through at any one time will be Catholics.

If we assume that the scouting systems are about equal but that Rangers ignore 40% of the potential and Celtic take in 100%, then in such circumstances Celtic will win on most, if not all, occasions.

That is the mathematics of the situation. Much more important is the social argument. Rangers as a club have strong historical Protestant connections. They should be proud of all that's best in these traditions.

Celtic make no secret of their Catholic origins. We are now living in an age of ecumenicalism. The Pope on his visit to Scotland this year was received by the Moderator of the Church of Scotland.

Just as important was that young people like my niece and her friends from Jordanhill Training College were at Bellahouston Park. They received coffee and sandwiches from Catholics who were obviously delighted to extend a welcome to this or any other bunch of "Proddies".

You see, at long last the great majority are now realising that Protestants and Catholics also happen to be fellow Christians.

The Rangers board should grasp the nettle. Go out and buy a very good Catholic player. Don't worry about the bigots. They are far outnumbered by the many good and decent Protestants and non-Protestants, and Jews, and Catholics, and peoples of other persuasions who want to live in peace and tolerance and will warm to your courage.

It is never easy to break with the past. But the future is beckoning.

Glasgow Herald 16 December 1982

Old Firm Chanting Still Full Of Hate

I HAD not been at a Rangers-Celtic game for 16 years. The sheer unadulterated hate had been too much. I have seen both teams playing others but together they created an atmosphere that was unclean. All the nonsense about the greatest club game in the world cut no ice with me. To go for so called enjoyment seemed somehow obscene, and those whose work took them there had a strong case for dirty money.

But friends and journalist colleagues kept telling me that things had improved; that physical violence at Old Firm games was now rare; and on New Year's Day I ventured forth to see and hear for myself.

My first reaction is to agree that actual physical violence has decreased. The banning of booze and the preponderance of seated accommodation has obviously helped. But the verbal violence is undiminished. The chanting is still full of limitless hate and cruelty, directed at players, their wives, a long since dead king who apparently favoured white horses, and a clergyman who resides in Rome. The Rangers manager was simultaneously being urged to retire and to stay on his present occupation for a long, long, time.

All of it was predictable, and providing you took a philosophical viewpoint, humorously acceptable.

I did, however, take exception to the Celtic fans chanting slogans in support of the IRA. In Northern Ireland innocent men, women, and children are being indiscriminately slaughtered and maimed, yet at a sporting occasion in Glasgow louts, safe from the fire, sing the praises of those who perpetrate those foul deeds. This has nothing to do with whether or not you believe in a united Ireland. It has everything to do with murder as a means of achieving your objectives. Once you accept that you are a gangster, however you dress up your actions.

I think the Celtic board should tell these people that they can either support Celtic or murder, but not both, and that, in future, any such songs or chants will lead to immediate eviction from the ground.

As to the game itself, I thought Rangers deserved a point. John Greig's tactics were successful. His team are not as talented as Celtic but they kept right on top of Burns, MacLeod and McStay and stopped them from settling into their usual pattern. Only Burns, a supremely talented footballer, escaped from the midfield stranglehold.

The Nicholas goal that won the game was a flash of genius which no one could predict or contain. The sheer power in his shot is uncanny. He doesn't seem to draw his leg back far enough to impact real power. Like a champion boxer who can knock an opponent cold with a short, crisp punch Nicholas seems to inject drive into his shooting with little apparent effort. His accuracy is staggering. Even when he misses it's a near thing.

But my man of the match was young Kennedy playing centre for Rangers. He has ability, runs well off the ball, and is good on the ground and in the air. It took world-class saves from Pat Bonner to thwart this obviously goal-hungry youngster. He is also extremely physical. Any more zeal and he will fall foul of the referees.

I didn't see Rangers' defeat by Motherwell, but it must surely rank as the worst result of the season for the Ibrox side. As someone who refuses to kick a man when he is down let me say a few words in defence of John Greig.

It is accepted by everyone that Greig is one of the nicest men in football and even in defeat exudes a certain dignity. To leave it there is to damn with faint praise. He is being made the scapegoat for factors not of his making or within his control.

First of all, to make a player manager of a team in which he played the day before was a great mistake. Workmates are inclined to be incredulous of a former colleague who suddenly becomes boss. Indeed, only in the last year has Greig had what could be termed his own team.

Unfortunately, this has coincided with Aberdeen, Dundee United, and Celtic reaching a degree of excellence not seen in Scottish club football for many years. These teams are among the best in Britain and if Celtic were stronger in defence they would be among the best in Europe.

Greig has brought some good players to Ibrox, but the clamour for immediate success is not giving them or him time to establish a more composed rhythm and pattern of play.

On New Year's Day there was too much frenzy. I know it's hard, but Rangers fans should try getting behind their team for a change when things are going wrong. It might help.

There are, of course, other problems which I referred to some weeks ago. Rangers should go out and sign talent unrestricted by any stupid taboos. Otherwise it's goodbye to any hope of success.

Glasgow Herald 6 January 1983

But Me No Butts; Adhere To The Law

WALK up to someone in a public place, in front of many witnesses and some policemen, butt him in the face and see what happens. Within seconds you will have been huckled away by the coppers and charged with assault. You will then be tried in a court of law and if it is proven beyond all reasonable doubt that you did indeed butt someone in the face, you will then be convicted and punished.

The punishment will vary. It could be a fine or a term of imprisonment, or both. That is the law of the land, and very sensible too.

If people were allowed to "work the heid" on one another with impunity then social intercourse would be so fraught with danger that only those with thick skulls would feel free to walk the streets.

At Pittodrie on Saturday professional footballers were butting each other like stags in the mating season. I hate to spoil their fun but (or should I say no butts about it) they are supposed to be involved in a football season.

My questions are not to the clubs, the SFA, or the referee, but to the Chief Constable of the Grampian Region. How come no footballers were arrested on Saturday for conduct that would certainly have led to an arrest if it had occurred elsewhere?

Does the law of the land cease to apply once men walk on to a football pitch?

Clubs moan at the cost of policing their grounds during a game, so presumably quite a number of the chief constable's men were at Pittodrie. Are we to understand that all of them failed to see acts of physical assault that in no way could be construed as a late or misjudged tackle—actions that in any decent working-class community are associated with the dregs of society?

If they didn't see, then the chief constable should send them all to have their eyes tested. If they saw and chose to ignore these actions, then I want to know on whose authority are they empowered to ignore such flagrant breaking of the law?

If a young man can break the law on a football pitch, then how can the police justify arresting him for a similiar offence in Sauchiehall Street, Princes Street, or Union Street?

You would be as well giving the louts legal immunities, as we do with foreign diplomats.

What have the law officers in Scotland got to say on this matter? Is a football pitch a no-go area for the police? I thought these only existed in parts of Belfast and Londonderry and that our Government was determined that even in these places the law of the land would prevail.

No doubt the clubs and the SFA will do something to try to repair the damage done to the name and repute of football. No doubt the players' union, which rightly fights for players' rights, will also tell them of their responsibilities to the game and to society at large.

Once in a place where I worked, a lavatory attendant, who happened to be a Pakistani, was quite savagely attacked by another worker. The management and the union representatives, including myself, agreed that if the assailant could be found and identified then by common consent he would be handed over to the police and, if found guilty, would subsequently be fired. There is no way responsible people would allow their industry to be fouled by such behaviour.

Trade unions, managements, industries, professions, sports, and all aspects of human relations require some kind of dignity. Without dignity a person, or a profession, becomes squalid. What we saw on Saturday was against the law. It was also squalid.

Postscript: Overheard in a Partick bistro—"See that big yin that plays for the Jags, a butter wid melt in his mooth."

Glasgow Herald 27 January 1983

Change Is The Name Of This Game

NEXT season the Scottish Premier League will include Aberdeen, Dundee United, Dundee, St Johnstone, Hearts and Hibernian.

All from the East Coast.

Tagging along will be Celtic, Rangers, St Mirren and Motherwell. From the West.

Dundee United have won the Premier League and Aberdeen have captured the footballing hearts of Europe with their Gothenburg conquest.

Is this dominance of the East one of those coincidences, transient in character, that happen from time to time?

I don't think so. Change is a precondition for survival. This is as true for football clubs, political parties and nations as it was for the dinosaur.

An inability to adapt to changing circumstances means you're for the broth pot.

The gap in attendance between Rangers and Celtic as compared to Aberdeen and certainly Dundee United has narrowed considerably.

Something else is happening. Although gate money is still important, more and more the economics of football are being determined by activities outwith the field of play.

Sponsorship now looms large as the financial saviour. Here is where Rangers and Celtic will run into difficulties.

Celtic currently have one of Europe's great potential talents. A young man called Charlie Nicholas.

His contract is about to expire and clubs all over Britain and Europe are queuing up to make offers, one of which he will find difficult to refuse.

It is just possible that some big company could sponsor Nicholas in such a way as to make it worth his while to stay at Parkhead and in Scotland.

There is, however, a snag. Company sponsorship is intended to create goodwill. A company that sponsors Celtic or Rangers would create a certain goodwill.

It would also engender a great enmity.

Just imagine you're a managing director of a big company. Would you sponsor either of these two clubs?

For sound business reasons, it would be much safer to sponsor the likes of Aberdeen.

The irony is that the bigotry which made these two clubs "great" might eventually cut them right down to size.

Daily Record 16 June 1983

ON ATHLETICS

Running And Laughing All The Way To The Bank

ELEVEN years ago on a visit to London I was being entertained in the reception room of a television studio by a man who was one of the legendary figures of post-war British athletics. The talk was of a current runner whose undoubted abilities were marred by inconsistency. My companion said: "He is running in the wrong events. He would be a natural for the steeplechase and would in my view, be a serious contender for the gold medal at the next Olympics."

"Why does he not take your advice?" I asked. "Well, there isn't the same money in steeplechasing. A world-class middle-distance runner can receive £400 to £500 appearance money at the big international meetings." Only the figure surprised me. In today's inflated currency this would mean at least £1000.

In retrospect, my surprise was naive. For years we had seen star athletes traipsing around the world, without any visible means of support, and living the life of Reilly. In material terms, their lifestyles were only a few degrees inferior to that of the Aga Khan.

This thought flitted through my mind in recent months as I read of the difficulties the British athletics authorities have in persuading some stars to participate in their major events. The explanation is always the same. The programme for the individual athlete has been carefully worked out by his coaches. The delicate balance of his body's chemistry would be upset if he went down the road to race at the Crystal Palace next Friday. But his metabolism would be improved no end by running in Timbuktoo the following day.

I suggest that our athletics chiefs should see the guy who holds the purse strings in the multi-national company that is sponsoring the meeting. Ask him to offer the reluctant runners a few extra quid. It's amazing what this might do for their metabolism apart from improving the delicate balance of their bank account.

Have you ever wondered why so many stars of the track seem fond of racing in that clockwork country called Switzerland? My own theory is that they do this in order to stash away their "expenses" in those vaults for which the Swiss banks are famed.

Ach well, what does it matter? The last real pristine pure hand-knitted amateur was Wilson of the *Wizard*. My only real complaint is the hypocrisy. Pay the guys the money but do it openly. You might as well for nobody nowadays is kidded.

Glasgow Herald 19 August 1982

Fingus—A Real Amateur

THE Commonwealth Games which open in Brisbane today week are known as the Friendly Games. The friendliness is already bursting out all over. "Whingeing Poms," cried an Australian official as the Scottish team complained about the accommodation and threatened a walkout, run out, or hop, step and jump out depending on your discipline as Ron Pickering or David Coleman would put it.

The converted office block set aside for the Scots apparently didn't provide the comforts to which our athletes, most of whom, according to press reports, are unemployed, skint, and living on handouts from relatives, have become accustomed.

Anyway, just for your benefit, I managed to get, for a substantial cash payment, an exclusive interview on the eve of his departure for Brisbane with Fingus McPhail, our best medal prospect. Fingus, known to friend and foe alike as "Fish" Fingus on account of the scales he carries to weigh his prizes, was in an expansive mood. As he put it, "I am a real amateur and will not compete for money. Gold and silver trinkets or tokens of my athletic prowess are much more appropriate as well as being a bloody good hedge against inflation."

Fingus, as you all know, weighs in at 18 stone and is our best all-rounder. He is being tipped to win 11 gold medals if his supply of pills doesn't run out.

He explained to me the hardships of life at the top in the athletic world of today. "Jimmy," he said, as he swung his Porsche in a graceful arc into Great Western Road. "Jimmy, Jimmy," he went on, for he has this habit of having three shots at your name which is presumably a hangover from his training in field events such as the hammer. "I have been on the dole now for 12 years and it hasn't been easy."

As he is still only 22, one could appreciate the difficulties. "I live close to penury in a penthouse flat overlooking a man-made lake in the foothills of the Campsies. Running up and down the stairs can be very good for building up stamina," he added. "How often do you do that?" I asked. "Everytime that swine of a maintenance electrician goes on strike and puts the lift out of commission," Fingus said with that killer instinct look we last saw when he miscued his javelin throw and impaled it in the buttocks of his arch rival in the decathlon. You must remember it. The Russian was just attempting the high jump and it was reckoned cleared the bar by four metres.

Fingus then catalogued for me the sacrifices he made to hone his body to its present shape. "I did it all for Scatland, my beloved Scatland. What a wunnerful people," he proclaimed in a voice ringing with insincerity. He had also lapsed into the Americanese picked up on his monthly visits to his pharmacist coach in Palm Springs, California.

When asked how an unemployed down-and-out could afford the air fares he looked at me with incredulity and said, "You mean you don't know that I am an expert hang glider?" After my admission that I didn't, Fingus continued. "I just take a running jump off Dumbarton Rock and don't come down till I am over Palm Springs."

All right, so Fingus is a fictional figure, but only just. What is not a fiction is the widespread use of drugs. Young women in gymnastics with the bodies of little girls, pumped full of pills to delay or stop the onset of puberty. Field athletes of both sexes with bodies of grotesque unnatural proportions. Hormone injections and experimentations that have already destroyed the natural sexuality of these human guinea pigs. Blood transfusions and infusions and all the other shenanigans that are becoming part and parcel of modern international athletics.

It is loathsome. No longer will there be contests between human beings but between freaks and clone-like creatures.

Think of this. At the recent European Games some gold medal winners were on drugs as part of their training schedules. How many we will never know. It is coming to the stage where an athlete who will not as a matter of principle take drugs has a diminishing chance of success against the "Junkies".

Glasgow Herald 23 September 1982

ON RUGBY

A Thug Is A Thug

WERE there no police at the rugby-game-cum-gang-war between Heriot's FP and Edinburgh Academicals last Saturday? The violence was so bad that the referee had to stop the game. If representatives of the law were present I would like to know why no one was arrested.

There is an arrogance in some sports that assumes criminal activity within the game is a matter for them to sort out. This is an impertinence. A thug who acts like a thug should be treated as a thug and be subject to the full sanction of the law whether his thuggery takes place in a disco or on a playing field.

Sports authorities have no responsibility for enforcing the law; that belongs to the law enforcement agencies. I am assuming, of course, that footballers and rugby players are not above the law or the agencies of the law. If that is so then I again ask! If there were policemen at Goldenacre last Saturday, why have no charges been preferred against those responsible for the mayhem and fisticuffs? Maybe the chief constable of the area concerned will let us know.

Glasgow Herald 9 December 1982

I'm Feeling No Pain In Defeat

ON Saturday I ventured forth to pastures new, to Murrayfield to have a swatch at the rugby scene.

Scotland were favourites to beat Wales and, as everyone knows, this is invariably fatal for Scottish prospects.

And so again it proved on Saturday.

The Welsh won, deservedly so, for Scotland didn't really play until the last 10 minutes.

Mind you, there is little pain in being defeated by the Welsh. It seems to hurt much more when we lose to England.

I was captivated by what can only be described as the Murrayfield ritual. We arrived at the car-park about two hours before the kick-off.

Hundreds of cars were already there. The car boots were open and revealed the goodies. A boundless variety of drinky-poos.

201

Whisky, gin, brandy, vodka, beer, a wild assortment of wine, including "champers".

Not only the spiritual needs were tended, food was also available.

It was like Hogmanay in the afternoon without the worry of what would happen to your carpet.

I even volunteered to sing but apparently that is taboo.

As the witching hour grew near, when the referee would blow his whistle to indicate that hostilities might commence, people started making their way to the stadium.

There were more women than you would see at a football game. It was a family affair.

Everyone, or so it seemed, wanted to use the toilets before going to their seats. They queued in an orderly fashion.

In the men's loo, everyone was surprisingly talkative. Now this is unusual, for some reason men tend to be morose while toileting.

They look straight ahead in a posture that could be described as anti-social.

These rugger types were different. Very voluble indeed.

One fellow was particularly extrovert and spoke all the while to the assembled throng.

His excitement was such that he inclined to emphasise a point by swinging his body round.

This is a dangerous practice and can easily dampen enthusiasm.

The game itself was an anti-climax and further confirmed my belief that the rules badly need amendment.

At present the referee and his constant whistling for technical offences that few can comprehend, are undermining rugby's appeal as a spectator sport.

However, the actual game was secondary. It was the atmosphere that held me enthralled.

There was no swearing though rugby has its own four letter words.

"Ruck" someone behind me shouted, and for a moment I thought I was back at Ibrox.

I was also intrigued by one of the Scottish players called Tomes, who lumbered about like an animated mountain.

He also sported a head band which gave him the appearance of an oversized Red Indian who had lost his way as he tried to get home from the battle of Little Big Horn.

This image was heightened as he seemed to be attempting to scalp some Welshmen without the aid of a tomahawk.

You were somehow glad he was on our side.

After the game we all made our way back to the cars. The boots were again opened, drinks and socialising resumed.

Actually its a pity the game had to interfere with the jollification.

The atmosphere, the relaxed gaiety was most sane and civilised.

Roll on, Twickenham. Oops, sorry, "Twickers," old chap, "Twickers".
Aye, and the same to you, Jimmy.

Daily Record 21 February 1983

ON CRICKET

How Dare You Contradict Me?

LIFE is full of contradictions and I have my quota. No I haven't. Yes I have.
No. Yes. Well okay, I have no contradictions. That isn't true either. Let me
re-phrase it; I have as yet an indeterminate number of contradictions. Phew—
to proceed. One of these contradictions is a beezer.

The fortunes of the English national football team are of no concern to me as
long as they are beaten. Yet I have many good English friends in English soccer.
My dislike (it's actually a bit stronger than that, but I can't tell the truth all the
time) even persisted through the reign of Ron Greenwood, surely one of the
finest gentlemen ever to have trod the turf. At the more ignominious performances by our Southern cousins I can be seen writhing on the floor feigning
cramp to conceal my shameful convulsive laughter.

When it comes to cricket it's an entirely different story. I espouse the
Sassenach cause with fervour. During my apprentice years I would get an early
pass out from the foreman to dash home to catch the last two hours of the Test
on Thursdays, Fridays, and Mondays. It cost badly needed cash, but who cared
when you could watch Graveney, Cowdrey, Peter May, Laker, and Lock and
other heroes on the telly. A six-year sojourn in London with access to a lot of
good cricket confirmed my affection for the game in general and the English
team in particular.

You will thus understand that recent events in Australia are not to my liking.
The collapse of the English batting at Brisbane was intolerable. Defeat and its
acceptance are part and parcel of any game. What makes failure unacceptable is
when it is brought about by a lack of commitment and not ability.

Big Bob Willis should tell some of his "stars", including the marvellously
talented David Gower, that unless they show a bit of bottle when the chips are
really down then there can be no place for them in the English team. Now for
the third Test. Let's have a rehearsal. "England, England." Aye there's no
doubt about it, the world is full of contradictions.

Glasgow Herald 9 December 1982

ON BOXING

Splutter! Splutter!

A SPLUTTER is an incoherent noise, or to speak hastily and with some confusion.

Spluttering is often accompanied by splattering where those nearest can get splashed with the spitting sounds of the splutterer.

Well, I wouldn't like to have been near the ringside last Wednesday when Harry Carpenter gave his television commentary on the world flyweight championship fight between Charlie Magri and the unfancied Filipino Frank Cedeno.

Harry spluttered through round after round and kept telling us Cedeno couldn't punch.

Unfortunately for Magri, Harry hadn't told Cedeno that he couldn't punch.

Blissfully unaware that he couldn't punch, he was blithely punching Charlie into oblivion.

Harry spluttered many gems. For example, he told us that the fight was a "simple equation: who can stand the heat?"

Harry, you old splutterer, that isn't an equation. An equation is an expression of equality and has nothing to do with who can stand the heat and it certainly had nothing to do with this fight.

Magri was in no way equal to his opponent. The no-punch Filipino fairly blootered wee Charlie.

However it was the next fight that had ME spluttering.

Frank Bruno is a superbly muscled young black giant from London. By comparison, his opponent Bill Sharkey looked like an overweight, out-of-condition, hard-drinking midget.

In a school playground, the kids would have stopped this fight right away as an obvious mismatch.

Bruno somehow or other got low enough to deliver an upper-cut somewhere in the region of the midget's face.

The midget flopped to the canvas and wisely didn't rise until after the count of ten.

This was supposed to be a boxing match. To me it looked a woeful mismatch.

I am no great fan of boxing. After watching this bout, I am even less a fan.

The only people I have any sympathy for in the fight game are the boxers. And, sadly, most of them end up skint.

Daily Record 3 June 1983

ON TENNIS

By Gad, This Isn't Cricket

IT was bedlam and sounded as if all the inmates of St Trinian's had plunked school and descended on the Centre Court at Wimbledon to see Bjorn Borg and Jimmy Connors play in the semi-final. There were also plummy middle-class adult voices adding a decibel or two to the general clamour.

As the sounds subsided to silence, just before the serve, a solitary voice piped out time and time again: "C'moan Jimmy." I would know those unmistakable dulcet tones anywhere. It's wee Shuggie, a plater's helper from Govan, who used to think that Methodists were meth-drinkers who had signed the pledge, until his big pal pointed out, it was a school of acting founded by some geezer called Stan S. Slavsky.

What was Shuggie doing at Wimbledon? Mind you, he has been a poor lost soul with nowhere to go since the Albion Dog Track closed.

Dan Maskell didn't like the noise and thought that the umpire should have stamped it out. All very well for him in the sanctuary of the commentary box to pontificate so. But what about the poor umpire perched on the top of a pair of ladders like a marooned house-painter—a sitting duck for any well-aimed projectile. The police, Dan told us, were moving in, to try and stem the excitement.

People were fainting and being helped out by St John's ambulance men. All that was needed to make wee Shuggie feel right a home, like as if he was at an "Auld Firm" game, was for somebody to urinate down his trouser leg, that is if he wasn't wearing the kilt.

Despite everything, Borg and Connors produced the best game of tennis I have ever seen. For sheer sustained skill and athleticism it will take some beating.

John McEnroe, in the other semi-final, got himself into more trouble. His young face distorts with rage as he fulminates against the whole world which, he is apparently convinced, is conspiring against him.

It is difficult not to feel sorry for the lad. He clearly needs a rest from the pressures of these big-money competitions and he desperately needs help.

One thing is clear—you can't accuse the BBC of getting its priorities wrong. The coverage of the Borg/Connors game ran on until the finish. National news and everything else was delayed. Suddenly a news flash by David Vine interrupted the proceedings. John McEnroe, we are told had sworn at newsmen.

What! Was the security council of the United Nations being convened to consider the situation? And the journalists, the poor journalists, how were they recovering from the shock of actually hearing four-letter words?

It transpired that two journalists got so excited they started punching one another. By gad, this isn't cricket, nor was it. I had to wait until midnight to see highlights of the Second Test at Lord's between England and Australia.

Glasgow Herald July 1982

ON HORSES AND DOGS

Look, No Script

HE is an unfrocked driving instructor whose unfrocking is a story in itself. He had got embroiled in the celebratory feast of a pupil who had just passed his test. Unfortunately his next pupil was the daughter of a Chief Inspector in the Strathclyde Constabulary. The young lady objected to his being drunk in charge of a vehicle, particularly one that she was in. She also didn't share his view that with each new intake of whisky he had become more and more irresistible to those among us who happen to be female.

Some people think he was a bit lucky to get off on the more serious charge. The defence lawyer argued that he was as intoxicated as a newt and couldn't do anything to anyone let alone a strapping young lass, a squash champion with a Black Dan at karate in a car that had stalled in the middle of the High Street.

As they say, "It's an ill wind . . .", for our miscreant has found a new career, one could almost say a vocation, as a counter hand in a betting shop who doubles as a philosopher.

Between races, as the business sags a little, he philosophises to the assembled throng.

He speaks to no one in particular and thus to everyone. His pearls of wisdom droppeth like the very dew . . . "Politics is the opium of the God-fearing." Instinctively you feel that his voice sounds like that heard by Moses when he went for a walk up that mountain. Its effect was startling. Immediately there was a hush among the punters. The Chinese looked to him as if he was a contemporary Confucious.

"Politics," he continued, "is used by clergymen as a diversion from the realities of religion." He surveyed the silent throng and spoke thus: "If God had wanted us to be politicians he would have given us another face."

He then turned away, which was the signal that his pronouncements were over for the time being and that idle chatter could recommence.

I discovered him a few weeks back. It happened like this. I hadn't yet made my weekly contribution to the material well-being of the bookmaking fraternity. This omission was nagging at my conscience and so I went into the nearest betting shop to see if they would be so kind as to take my money. The counter clerk, our philosopher no less, was happy to oblige and gave me a receipt to add to my collection. You only hand them back if you win. Suddenly the sage looked over my shoulder and proclaimed in a loud ringing voice: "People who live in glass houses deserve all they get."

I thought it was a game and shouted back: "People who throw glass houses shoudn't get stoned." There was a gasp from the regulars at this impertinence. The sage narrowed his eyes and hissed: "Peripatetic punters gather no money and quite right, too," and disappeared into the back shop.

I decided to hang around to see what would happen and sure enough he reappeared in a few minutes, conspicuously cleared his throat as an indication that another pronouncement was imminent . . . "Better to remain quiet and be thought a fool than to speak and let everyone know that you have a brilliant percipient mind that can grasp the essence of life and crisply express it in words of simple and great beauty", then did an about-turn and again disappeared into the back.

His followers were by this time confused and alarmed. "What did he mean?" they asked one another. A discussion ensued and the feeling was that the sage was contemplating retirement. It was also felt that my cheeky intervention had given him a strong dose of the sulks and was the cause of all the trouble.

So I decided to try to retrieve the situation by an act of appeasement or even abasement, and on his return loudly proclaimed: "No man is a peninsula, least of all he who would try to smart-mouth a sage", and walked out.

I have been back occasionally just to listen to the Master. Last week he came away with a couple of brammers. "He who is without hope is a hopeless case and should at the first opportunity get blootered." And then there was this gem: "The meek have every reason to be meek and shall inherit that which is their birthright—nothing."

Have we discovered Norman Tebbit's scriptwriter?

Glasgow Herald 16 August 1982

When A Street Bookie Ranked With A Doctor On The Social Scale

THE most beautiful sign that I've ever seen was "Alf Crum of Mablethorpe". Emblazoned on plates above the bookie's head such names as this enliven the racing scene. It's only at a race track that you see the wee bookies anymore. Wee only in relation to the corporate size of the big, computerised, bookmaking companies.

When I was a kid the street bookie was an integral part of our community culture. Part of the everyday scene. A back court was his place of business and when it rained he moved to the black close.

The bookie was a component part of our life; an asset or facility like the local family dairy or butcher. His suits must have been specially made for him with voluminous pockets all over the place. At paying out time you could see him stretching into a pocket that seemed to run all the way down to his toes and you could imagine the money breeding in there.

Alas, many of these characters have gone to that big starting price paradise in the sky. Others have just gone. Packed their bags and departed the scene, victims of technology and "progress".

Such bookies are an endangered species. If they were birds, of the feathered kind, people like Sir Peter Scott would provide them with sanctuaries. As humans they are left to fend on their own.

Tony Queen is one of the last of this tribe; a street bookie of the old school still in business in an off-street betting shop.

He is a good representative of the genius. A character whose rasping voice purveys commonsense as if it were common. He has all the main characteristics of his fellow bookies of the times. As bookmaking was not respectable, bookies were all of working class origin. Usually from families poor even by the standards of those days. Tony was born in Maitland Street, Cowcaddens and was a bright lad who did very well at school. Given different domestic circumstances he would have gone to college and might have ended up as a solicitor's clerk.

He must think of these missed opportunities as he ruminates at his holiday villa in the Balearic Isles.

The good bookies of Tony's era had a business integrity that the watchdogs of the Stock Exchange might envy. This was essential. Operating illegally as they did made it vital that a man's word was his bond. If it wasn't then this soon became known and his flow of business which was based on trust soon dried up. In other words those lacking in integrity were in the wrong business.

During the last war Tony was conscripted into the Army as an enlisted man, was soon commissioned and was an acting captain when demobilised in 1946. With £400 demob money he decided to become a bookie.

He wasn't a complete rookie as a bookie. His father, a moulder to trade, worked during the depression for a bookmaker. Nonetheless young Mr Queen set out with some qualms to lift lines up a close at the corner of Ruchill Street and Shuna Street in Maryhill.

How do you let people know that you were lifting lines? You couldn't advertise in the local press or hang a poster round your neck saying "Support you local bookie and here I am". The police would have taken a dim view. Tony tells of a woman stopping and asking: "Ur ye loast son or ur ye looking for somebody?"

This I think leads to another point. Street bookies could only operate with the co-operation of the local people. They had to become part of that community and the successful ones did to a quite remarkable extent.

In the Govan of my childhood Geordie Stephens, a local bookie, was one of the most respected of men. He ranked in social status with the GPs. In terms of popular esteem he was probably top of the pops, Stephens was a gentleman.

He helped decent families who were in trouble, quietly and discreetly. He was actually a steadying influence in the community.

In areas such as Govan, once you were accepted then that was that. There was nothing mealy-mouthed about it. You were one of them. And so it was in Maryhill.

Tony tells of women bringing out cups of tea in the winter and commiserating, "Ye must be cauld son." To those women all men who were not exactly geriatrics were addressed as "son".

It was of course a reciprocal process. The local kids, particularly from the really hard up families, got a few pence each week from the bookie. Today a man in the street with his wife and children might stop Tony Queen and remind him, "You used to give me thrupence a week pocket money."

This was typical of the relationships that existed. Yet in the mythology of those times the bookie is portrayed as a lout in a check suit with no culture and even less morality. In "Love On The Dole", a play and successful film about the pre-war depression, the bookie was the "heavy", the amoral swine who corrupted the chaste and respectable working class heroine.

Bookies were seen as the urban equivalent of the bad squire Sir Jasper of Victorian melodrama. In British films he was easily recognisable for he always wore a flashy camel hair coat and used more hair cream than Sammy Davis Jnr. He was shown as a slightly up-market spy and played by someone like Bonar Colleano. A trace of an American accent helped imply a gangster connection.

In Glasgow at any rate this just wasn't true. Nobody would trust the local gangster or tearaway with a bet. Invariably he was a bully and a bevvy merchant.

There were of course exceptions, but the street bookies of Glasgow were good citizens. They had no sense of public relations as a profession, which was no doubt due to the fact that they didn't think of themselves as a profession. They would do work for charity and make it a condition that their efforts went unsung.

About seven years ago Tony Queen asked me to speak at a "Beachcombers" dinner. It was a gathering of bookies and publicans that met regularly to raise money for the physically and mentally handicapped. I think they raised over £2000 that night alone. You haven't heard of these activities because a pre-condition was that there should be no publicity.

In 1961 betting shops were legalised and although we didn't know it at the time, this was the beginning of the end for the wee bookie. Tony opened a shop in Maryhill and then in different parts of the city. He eventually sold them to the Stakis organisation which subsequently sold them to the Tote.

In a certain sense this was inevitable. Gambling was always potentially very big business. The problem was that ordinary people without a credit account with an accredited bookmaker had no legal means of placing a bet except with an illegal street bookie. Once local betting shops were legalised the large-scale business organisation of bookmaking became possible. Like so many other aspects of modern development "progress" claimed as its first victims local colour and character.

People talk of the need for community policing and of getting the bobby back on the street. I would like to see the bookie back on the street as well. I know it isn't possible. Ach well, we still have nostalgia. Did I ever tell you of the time Big Al the Punters' Pal gave us all a fright when it was noticed that he was wearing spiked shoes? Well it was like this. Bill the Rat Catcher said . . .

Glasgow Herald 6 October 1982

Aintree Shouldn't Happen To A Dog

NEXT Saturday is the annual torture of horses known as the Aintree Grand National, surely the cruellest horse race in the world.

Many splendid beasts will come crashing down—some to their deaths.

There are those who will argue that the jockeys are also in danger—but then they choose to ride.

The horses have no such option.

Last year a young woman rode with the declared intention of being the first female jockey ever to complete the National course.

The TV commentator was most excited as the exhausted horse was driven past the finishing post.

You might be interested to know that the horse later died.

The Scottish Grand National at Ayr later this month is much more civilised—and so are the spectators.

Daily Record 4 April 1983

The Bookie's Where Every Line's A Winner

AS you will have gathered by now, in every sense of the word I'm a punter.

For example, my contributions to the Famine Relief Fund For The Children of Broken-Down Bookies are regular, but—it should be noted—never substantial.

Well—you've got to be daft to bet heavily in the hope of ever beating the bookie.

So my wagers are modest. Yet, if it weren't for such pittances, where would Ladbrokes be?

It would be Lads Broke, and Corals would be on the rocks, and Tony Queen on Social Security.

Some months ago I stumbled on a gem of a betting shop with a counter clerk who is also a bit of a philosopher.

Last week in one of those intervals scheduled to break the monotony of giving the bookie your money, he declared to all and sundry: "Verily I say unto you, those who live by the sword generally make a good living."

210

There was a silence while everyone tried to fathom the inner meaning of this latest profundity.

After the next race he was at it again.

"Just because you're a hypochondriac doesn't mean you aren't sick."

At this, there was a ripple of applause. A bloke turned to me and said: "Ah tell ye Jimmy, he's the greatest thing since Garry Owen."

"I didn't know Garry was a philosopher," was my muttered reply.

"Och aye," he said. "Read between the lines. The philosophy is there all right. You won't believe this, but he's a better philosopher than he is a tipster."

After backing his nap, Peaty Sandy, in the Grand National, I could well believe it.

Daily Record 11 April 1983

You're Always On A Loser At The Bookie's

THERE used to be two greyhound tracks in the Govan district of Glasgow—the White City and the Albion.

On a Saturday night after the final race at both venues, the bookmakers would be counting their winnings and the punters their losses as they streamed down Broomloan Road.

No doubt the punters were dreaming of what might have been, or of next week, when a wee boy waiting for his daddy asked his grandmother: "Grannie, is that the dugs comin' oot?"

The wise old lady replied: "Naw, son—that's the mugs. The dugs are still inside."

I was reminded of this story of human folly last week while queuing up in a betting shop to give my little financial contribution to the material well-being of my local bookmaker and his dependents.

There can be no doubt that anyone who frequents betting shops to be treated like a mug must, in all essentials, be a mug.

Think of it! You are taxed 10 pence in the pound on every winning bet unless you pay around 10 per cent of your stake in tax beforehand.

Place-betting is now calculated at one-fifth of the odds. The simple mathematics now make it impossible for the punter to win. He is on a thrashing to nothing.

The main beneficiaries are not the bookies, who have largely become tax collectors for the Government and the Betting Levy Board. Indeed, nobody admits to getting their mitts on the money.

Yet owners and breeders fork out fortunes for yearlings and see this as a profitable investment. The big trainers also do not seem to be short of a bob or two.

The top jockeys, despite their clapped-in jaws and the clapped-out appearance, always seem to have large farms, even larger houses, fly around in private planes, drive expensive cars and sip champagne.

One thing is certain—it's the five bob bets in the local betting shops by the old age pensioner and countless thousands of other small-time punters that sustain this conspicuous opulence at the other end of the market.

My complaint is that nobody seems concerned about protecting the betting shop punter against the ravages of a grossly unfair system.

Parliament moved quickly to protect those who play roulette when the casinos were legalised in this country.

Some were claiming a second zero for the bank. MPs argued that this gave the management an added advantage and therefore made this practice illegal to protect the punters in the casinos.

Such concern by our custodians of democracy for the devotees of roulette is in stark contrast to their contemptuous disregard for the punter who frequents the betting shop.

Over the years, there have been many committees of inquiry into different aspects of contemporary life.

Why not a committee to examine the law as it affects those who use betting shops?

At present, the small-time working-class punter is being robbed, and there's no other way of putting it. The odds were always against him.

Today the tax and the whole set-up guarantee that he cannot win and must always lose. This is no longer gambling . . . it's highway robbery.

Daily Record 1 August 1983

Why Jockeys Play Safe

ON Saturday, Lester Piggott rode a horse called Adonijah in a field of six. Piggott got himself, and of course the horse, boxed in.

A gap appeared and he didn't go through. When a bigger gap opened, Adonijah made late progress and showed that given an earlier clearer run, he would have won.

A few months ago I'm sure Piggott would have gone for the first opening.

But in the past few weeks Piggott, as well as Willie Carson and Steve Cauthen, have been given suspensions for what's been called reckless riding.

In other words they were penalised for doing what a jockey is supposed to do . . . try their utmost to win.

The mysteriously appointed Stewards and the Jockey Club, who run British racing, would be doing a better job for punters if they suspended some of the jockeys who sit on horses like stookies because they've been told NOT to win.

And it doesn't take any of the gangster stuff or drugs such as you see on telly and films to get horses NOT to win.

The trainer and the connections of the horse, as they are called, simply tell the jockey: "We don't want you to give him a hard race."

Which really means: "Look, buster, we are not trying today and if you're first past the post we'll have your guts for garters."

Punters are more important to racing than owners, trainers and the Jockey Club put together.

If they would only all stop punting for a month they would soon realise their power. The racing game would collapse.

Maybe, then, some punters union could negotiate a charter that, for the first time, would give them a fair deal.

Daily Record 29 August 1983

Punting About In Paper Boats

AS regular readers will know, there is a philosopher masquerading as a counter-clerk in a Glasgow betting shop. I paid his place of work a visit last week.

He came to the grille and coughed discreetly, which is his usual imitation that a profound pronouncement is imminent.

"If Jesus was a Jew, how come he has a Spanish name?" the sage asked. After a slight pause, he retired once more to his lair in the back shop.

The punters then excitedly debated the question. "Is Jesus really a Mexican name?" asked one.

"Sure it is," replied another. "Everybody ower there is called Jesus. It's like Jimmy over here."

Then one wee fella piped up:

"I once saw on television how this Scandinavian bloke built a paper boat and sailed it from the Nile right tae America.

"He was showing how it might have been done thousands of years before."

Big Charlie, an unemployed boilermaker, was having none of this. "Ye canny hiv a paper boat," he said with great vehemence.

"How no?" said his pal.

"It stands tae reason," said Charlie. "Ye canny weld paper. It would just burn."

The wee fella, whose original theory was being shot down in flames, protested: "So what?"

Big Charlie looked at him with something close to contempt and said: "How kin ye build a boat withoot welders?"

"Anyway they widnae know the road," said someone who hadn't yet spoken. "They wid need a really good pilot tae dae that trip."

"Here, wait a minute," said the wee fella, "that Pontius was a pilot."

And everyone started battering him with betting-slips.

Daily Record 3 October 1983

When Big Boab Had Our Racing Syndicate In A Flap

THE horses I back are safe.

Only a lunatic would consider pinching them and kidnappers would have to pay the owners to take them back.

Mind you, I once had a stake in a syndicate that owned a high-class racing animal.

It was a big greyhound dug called Boab. The original Big Boab.

On the track it was known as Flashmacann, on account of the biggest shareholder in the syndicate was a gentleman called Alfie McCann who hailed from "Wine Alley", a well-known middle-class suburb of Govan, in Glasgow.

Alfie was also the trainer, and Big Boab was going to make him rich and the rest of us affluent. At least, that was the theory.

So, in the with-it language of today, you could say "I had a piece of the action", though in this case "inaction" might have been more appropriate.

We were going to make our money at the "flapping" tracks. Unregistered greyhound racing venues where the rules, to put it mildly, were a trifle lax.

By shrewd and adept handling, Alfie would steer the dog to occasional brilliant—and, to the rest of the world—totally unexpected victories.

We would all be told when it would win and could bet plenty on Big Boab at big prices.

Alfie's methods had the simplicity of genius.

For a period, the dog would be kept housebound except for the rare sortie to the backyard for wee-wees or anything else that crossed Boab's mind.

Boab's diet was to be meticulously planned. Stodgy pies, rice puddings and as much as he wanted.

However, the great dietary secret was a doughball created—for you couldn't call it cooking—by Alfie's mother-in-law, a formidable lady in her own right.

After consuming two of these, Big Boab could barely get his belly off the floor, let alone run 500 yards. In such a pathetic condition, the dog was beaten time after time.

When his handicap was just right . . . when the start Boab was given by the other dogs was such that even a geriatric greyhound pulling a sledge might have a chance . . . then the syndicate would strike.

We would all take turns to walk Big Boab. He was fed on best liver and lean meat.

In his next race, we backed him with the most of our worldly possessions. He ran like a sea-lion in tight shoes.

Maybe it had been an off-night. We started all over again.

The same thing happened. Every night was an off-night.

A lot of lolly had been lost. Members of the syndicate met in a mean and revengeful mood.

214

They decided Big Boab was to be "put down" which was a hypocritical way of saying "kill the swine".

A few days later, I met Alfie trudging morosely along Govan Road. "Have you done away with Big Boab?" I asked.

"Naw," he replied, "I hidnae the heart."

"Instead, I took him out to the country and ran away frae him."

Daily Record 14 February 1983